IF YOU AIN'T

RANGER

YOU AIN'T.....

IF YOU AIN'T RANGER YOU AIN'T.....

CHRIS PITTARD

OLYMPIAD PUBLISHING
SAN ANTONIO, TEXAS

OLYMPIAD PUBLISHING COMPANY
1777 N.E. LOOP 410, SUITE 600
San Antonio, Texas 78217

ISBN: 978-0-578-47497-7

Cover Art and Inside Text Design: Jessica Tilles

Printed in the United States of America

ACKNOWLEDGEMENTS

I'd like to thank my two editors, Karen Pittard and Fred Williams for hanging in there on this very personal project; and I'd like to thank LTC (Ret) Gary Powell for his review of all the chapters on Ranger School for authenticity and accuracy. I'd also like to thank Melody Davis, Harold "H.J." Mathis, COL (Ret) Cornell McGhee, MG (Ret) Dana J.H. Pittard, and CPT (Ret) Del Powell for their comments and feedback as this went from a work-in-progress to a book. Thanks guys!

CONTENTS

WHAT IS RANGER SCHOOL?

RANGER SCHOOL HAS BEEN DESCRIBED AS *"THE 61-DAY TRIAL BY HELLFIRE THAT A MAN HAD TO PASS TO BECOME A TABBED RANGER. IT CULMINATES WITH A WEEK AND A HALF IN THE SWAMPS OF FLORIDA THAT SLASHED 16 POUNDS OFF THE AVERAGE RANGER TRAINEE, CAUSED HALLUCINATIONS, SKIN DISEASES AND EVEN HAIR LOSS DUE TO MALNUTRITION, STRESS AND 20-HOUR DAYS EXPOSED TO THE ELEMENTS, AND MADE SURE THAT NEARLY HALF OF ALL CANDIDATES NEVER STITCHED THE SACRED BLACK AND GOLD RANGER TAB ONTO THE LEFT SHOULDER OF THEIR UNIFORMS.*

I GOT MINE AND SO DID MY BROTHER. WE ENDURED ONE OF THE TOUGHEST MILITARY TRAINING SCHOOLS IN THE WORLD.

AND WE DID IT, MAGNIFICENTLY."

Kevin Tillman

PROLOGUE

In a darkened classroom, a flickering light streamed from the lens of an eight-millimeter projector to the white screen at the far end of the room illuminating the dust as it swirled in the air. Standing next to the projector was SFC Theodore Kittlested, the senior training NCO for JROTC at Eastwood High School, El Paso, Texas. Kittlested, an older white Army sergeant, faced us dressed in his normal khaki uniform, with his flat-top haircut and Army-issued horn-rimmed glasses, better known as "birth control glasses" because they were so ugly.

"The film today is about the United States Army Ranger School. Maybe the toughest training the Army has to offer. It's an eight and half-week course that's conducted over some of the roughest terrain imaginable in Georgia and Florida." Kittlested said.

"Rangers have served in the United States Army in Korea and Vietnam and can trace their heritage all the way back to the Revolutionary War," Kittlested continued, "Yep, you gotta be a real man to be an Army Ranger! Most of you will never be Army Rangers." He looked around the room and chuckled.

"Enjoy." And he started the movie.

On the screen emerged the faded color images of men dressed in jungle camouflage uniforms, wearing jungle-crushed soft caps with bills. They moved through the jungle in a kind of staggered single file, carrying M-16 rifles, with load-bearing equipment hung on their bodies; festooned with hand grenades, flashlights, ammo, canteens and knives. Their faces were painted in war-like camouflage patterns obscuring their features, giving them the look of serious warriors about to do serious damage to the enemy. The patrol leader made a sign with his fist—raising it so that everyone in the patrol could see him. Like a well-oiled machine, the patrol stopped and crouched on the ground facing outward searching for the enemy.

The deep voice of the narrator described the action on the screen as a typical patrol executed by students in Ranger School, the premier small-unit training course in the world, training our American soldiers to become United States Army Rangers. The narrator described the Ranger training as the toughest in the world. It involved three phases: the first phase at Fort Benning, Georgia; the second phase, mountain training, in northern Georgia; and the final phase, the jungle training conducted in the swamps of northern Florida.

The narrator stated, "Ranger School is designed to subject the students to simulated combat situations and prepare them to be the best soldiers in the world."

The next scenes were of Ranger students, jumping out of airplanes, climbing mountains, rappelling, and patrolling in the swamps of Florida. The more iconic images were of Ranger students trapping, killing and eventually cooking various wild game animals like reptiles and squirrels during their survival training. Finally, the last montage was of the Ranger students graduating and having the distinctive black and gold Ranger Tab pinned on their left shoulders.

"The attrition rate is high in Ranger School, and only the best succeed." The narrator said.

All the graduates looked pretty uniform with their hair cut to the scalp, great physical conditioning, and all appearing to be about six feet tall. They were daunting-looking men, the epitome of Army manhood.

Like the narrator said, "The best of the best." I didn't see any Black faces amongst the Ranger students, but that didn't strike me as unusual, not in 1969.

After the film ended, Kittlested turned on the lights, "Any of you think you can be Army Rangers?" A handful of tentative hands went up. "Well, if you want to be an Army Ranger you better start now. Get in shape and be the best cadet you can be, because like the man said, only the best survive!" He smiled again.

As a 12-year old, 4' 10", freshman in high school, in my first year of Junior Reserve Officer's Training Corps (JROTC), this was the image I had of Ranger School and United States Army Rangers. In the fall of 1969, at the height of the Vietnam War, I knew I wanted to be an Army Ranger. But, I also knew I didn't fit the image so how could I expect to become one of these larger-than-life warriors?

I had always been the weakest and the smallest kid in class, and never as physically imposing as these images of Army Rangers. But as I sat there, I was determined that someday I would become an Army Ranger.

In the back of my head, as always, that little voice of doubt said, *"You'll never be an Army Ranger, you're too small and weak; you'll never make it. You'll never be an Army Ranger…ever."*

On the contrary, one never knows what life has in store…

CHAPTER 1

The Beginning

It began with my father, a tall, dark-skinned, proud Army officer. In 1969, he was a lieutenant colonel in the Air Defense branch of the Army, assigned to the 11th Air Defense Group at Fort Bliss, Texas, the "Home of U.S. Army Air Defense Artillery." My younger brother, Dana, and I grew up playing army with play guns and doing our little patrols on our bikes around our various neighborhoods on the Army posts and Air Force bases where we lived. I was familiar with the concept of the Army, but of course, had never been personally exposed to the ins and outs until I joined JROTC.

In 1969, for the first time, I had the opportunity to take JROTC. When first matriculating at Eastwood High School in El Paso, Texas, I had never heard of ROTC in high school. I didn't want to take P.E. anymore, I'd had enough of being made fun of during the last five years in P.E.

And when I found out ROTC took the place of P.E. for the health requirement, and didn't involve running or jumping or playing sports, I knew I'd rather be in ROTC. Mom asked about this "ROTC" and the counselor explained it was an Army program like the one in college to help teach kids about the Army. The counselor further explained that I would be issued uniforms, had to buy Army-style shoes, and learn to march just like the regular Army. There were two non-commissioned officers in charge, SFC Kittlested and First Sergeant Patino, both retired from the Army. I asked if I had to run or play sports or any of that stuff that I hated about PE, and the counselor said "no." I liked the idea, and my mother was in favor, so I signed up for JROTC. I hoped that as a 12-year old freshman in high school I would be accepted as a member of JROTC. I looked forward to this school year for the first time in a long time. I was tired of being the youngest and weakest in my class which had been the case since the fourth grade. Before then I'd been a regular little kid, competing with my peers and having a good time at school.

✧   ✧   ✧

In the summer of 1962, at the tender age of five, the Army sent my father, then a Captain, to Korea to serve a one-year hardship tour of duty without his family. My parents decided for that first year we were to live with my grandmother in North Central Philadelphia, right there in the heart of Philly, in a primarily African-American neighborhood.

My mother, a Department of the Army civilian employee, had been reassigned to the Frankfurt Arsenal outside Philadelphia for the duration of our stay in Philly. While in Korea, the Army selected Dad for promotion to Major, and to attend the year-long U.S. Army Command and General Staff College at Fort Leavenworth, Kansas. C&GSC is a prestigious course for Army officers whose potential for greater rank had been recognized by the Army. When Dad was selected for C&GSC my parents decided that it was best for the family that we stay in Philadelphia. This meant Dad would be separated from the family for two years.

That fall, I started first grade at Whittier Elementary at the age of five. I don't know how my mother managed that feat, because I wasn't supposed to start first grade at that age since I wouldn't turn six until December. But somehow, she managed to get me in, and I started first grade younger than anyone else. At that time, as a light-skinned, green-eyed, little African-American boy, I was close to the same age and size as my peers, so I pretty much fit right in. The students reflected the demographics of the primarily African-American neighborhood, although the teachers were almost exclusively white, many of the administrators were Black.

One thing that set me apart from my more parochial classmates was my experience as an Army brat. Having lived in Texas and Okinawa, where I had learned Japanese as my first language, I had a different perspective of the world. They knew very little about the world beyond the boundaries of Fox Street, Lehigh, Broad Street, the Park in the Dell, and what they saw on television. Their entire universe consisted of Philly, and maybe parts of south New Jersey. I also stood apart when it came to grades and my scores on those standardized basic skills and intelligence quotient tests. Apparently, I did so well that the school began tracking my progress as I entered the second grade in 1963.

That fall of 1963, the school district subjected all the students to a battery of tests to gauge our IQ and assess our reading and math levels. That year, the district implemented an acceleration program for what may be categorized now as academically "talented and gifted" students to push them through the school system as quickly as they could absorb the material. Another classmate and I, an African-American boy, were selected for this inaugural program in our school. As a result, in spring 1964, as a seven-year old, the school dual-placed me in the second and third grades. In the morning I would attend second-grade classes, and in the afternoon I would attend third-grade classes. Sort of confusing, but at the time it seemed normal, and my teachers and classmates treated me like a rock star.

For me, that all changed when we went to our next assignment at Fort Totten, New York. Dad had returned from Fort Leavenworth in May 1964, and informed us our next assignment would be right up the road outside New York City. That was an exciting time because the World's Fair was being held in Queens and we wouldn't be too far from Queens living at Fort Totten.

Fort Totten was a small Air Defense Army post on Long Island, which served as an important link in the North American Air Defense system and as headquarters for the First Army. The Army had promoted Dad to Major by that time, and he was the highest ranking Black officer on post, a nice distinction for us, and one we would get used to over the next seveal years.

❖　❖　❖

Fort Totten, a very picturesque little post, was nestled under the Throgg's Neck Bridge that spanned the East River. Don't ask me who or what "Throgg" was or why it was named "Throgg's Neck" but it certainly made for interesting conversation. Fort Totten sat on Willet's Point, on the end of a peninsula surrounded by the East River and the Little Neck Bay which opened into the Long Island Sound; a very pretty and quaint post, reflective of the Civil War era of architecture, with red-brick buildings and tile roofs, where water sports and clambakes were the norm in the summer. We stayed in a quaint red-brick and white-wood quad-type apartment building, that housed four families. Although we were the only Blacks in the building, Dad was the highest ranking officer, so we had a good relationship with the other families and enjoyed playing outside with all the kids.

Dad got me involved in little league baseball that first summer in 1964. Because of my age I played "T-Ball" where the ball is placed on a batting tee, something like a golf tee, but much higher at waist level. This gave us younger kids a chance to hit the ball and learn the fundamentals of hitting without the stress of trying to hit balls being pitched at us by other little kids. We still learned the basics of baseball, how to run the bases, field ground balls, and catch fly balls. The important aspect about little league was playing with kids my own age. The young boys that played were somewhat diverse, mostly white, but also some African-American boys as well. This was significantly different than what I faced my first day at school.

CHAPTER 2

P.S. 169

The first day of school, my mother drove me to P.S. 169, the elementary school military kids from Fort Totten attended. The school was located in the town of Bayside on Long Island. Mom took me to the school to register me and to get me oriented to my new school, my fourth-grade class, and my new teacher. I would ride the school bus with the other military kids for the rest of the year, but on that day, Mom thought it best for me to be introduced to the principal because of my unique situation. I had successfully completed the requirements of both the second and third grade at Whittier, and she wanted to make sure there was no misunderstanding in that regard.

We drove up to the new school and parked in the visitor's parking lot. As I got out of our 1963 pastel green Chrysler Newport, I saw a three-story structure painted a light green with plenty of windows facing towards the street. This was a far cry from the six-story brown-bricked behemoth that was Whittier Elementary School, surrounded by a concrete desert punctuated by huge fissures erupting from the ground in Central Philly. Instead, this was a very suburban-looking building in Long Island, surrounded by grassy plains and white kids streaming in from buses and other private cars. I listened to the sound of school children happily chattering on the first day of school and wondered if any of them were my new classmates. As I stood there staring, Mom came around from the driver's side and grabbed my hand and led me toward the entrance.

As we strode through the double glass doors we saw signs directing us to our left to the main office. Mom led the way through the single wooden door with the single pane of glass and the sign, "Main Office, Principal's Office." Once we stepped into the room a large white woman, her mousy brown hair in a typical beehive, wearing a floral printed dress and tortoise-shell glasses, sauntered over to the wooden swinging gate and long counter that divided us from the rest of the office.

"May I help you?" She said in a high-pitched voice. An odd voice coming out of such a large woman.

"Yes, I'd like to register my son, Christan, in the fourth grade, and I would also like to meet with the principal." Mom replied in a somewhat condescending tone. She did not suffer morons easily or the little people who tried to assert false authority, and especially when they were all wrapped up in a supercilious white woman like the one facing us now.

I'm pretty sure she got that from my grandmother, Utensie Hillian, an imposing, dark-skinned, strong-willed woman, who had a long legacy of not taking any guff from white people. I'd heard all the stories about my grandmother while living in Philly. Her daughter, with her fiery red hair and personality to match, was the same way.

"I'm sorry ma'am but you'll have to fill out the proper forms before you can register your son, and quite frankly, he doesn't look old enough to be in the fourth grade." She smiled with that "you stupid Negro, don't you know the rules" smile.

Uh oh, I thought, *here it comes.* I'd seen Mom deal with these kinds of white people before…here we go.

"I am *NOT* going to talk with you. Now you go get someone who has some authority, either the assistant principal or the principal. I will *NOT* have you stand there and insult my son! Do you understand?" Mom was livid and everyone could hear the fury in her voice. I thought she would jump across that wooden divider and punch the poor woman. Yeah, now she was the "poor woman" because I'd been on the receiving end of that kind of tirade. But, yeah, she deserved it…take that!

"Yes, ma'am!" She raced out of the room to look for "someone in authority" as her white coworkers looked on from their desks behind the partition. I could see the fear in their eyes. They didn't seem inclined to challenge my mother when she was in lioness mode protecting her cub. Mom was a petite 5' 1", light-skinned, red-haired, Black woman, dressed in a wool navy-blue two-piece suit, white blouse, and matching heels, but I'm sure she looked a lot larger after she barked at their colleague.

I looked around the office as we waited. It looked like a typical elementary school office dotted with the desks of secretaries and their typewriters, and various papers tacked on the cork bulletin boards that covered the green-painted walls. There must have been a surplus of green paint. There weren't any people of color, unlike my last school which featured all kinds of Black people in the school's office. These were all white women, some young, others older, hunched over their typewriters trying to look busy as they studiously ignored us.

Within a few minutes, as Mom stood fuming next to me, an older balding white man walked purposefully out of one of the interior offices with the secretary, or whatever she was, in tow. He wore a gray three-piece suit, white button-down shirt, striped red tie, and rimless glasses framed his pale face and brown eyes.

He came through the divider, using the little swinging door, and stuck out his hand, "Hi, my name is Paul Schaumberg; I'm the principal here at P.S. 169. I understand you want to meet with me, Mrs...?"

"Pittard, Jackie Pittard, and yes, I would like to meet with you and get my son registered for school." Mom replied as she shook his hand, her ire somewhat tempered.

"Please come in. Carol, could you bring the proper forms into my office? Thank you." He indicated to the first woman we'd talked with. She nodded her assent and hurried to get the forms from one of the gray file cabinets that stood guard in the back of the room.

"Please come in," Mr. Schaumberg said, as he held open the swinging door, and led us back to his spacious office. When he closed the door behind us, he indicated the two burgundy leather chairs in front of his fairly large mahogany desk.

"Please, sit down."

Mom and I took our seats, and Mr. Schaumberg settled into his larger matching leather swivel chair behind his desk. "What can I do for you Mrs. Pittard?"

"Thank you for meeting with us. We appreciate you taking time out of your busy schedule on the first day of school." Mom's manner and tone had changed considerably.

"My son, Christan, completed both the second and third grade last year in a special program at Whittier Elementary School in Philadelphia. Here are his records." She handed a brown folder containing my school records to the principal.

He began to peruse my records and made some grunting noises as various documents caught his attention. "I've heard of programs like this, but we don't have them in this district. Both third and second grade, huh? Very impressive."

"Thank you," Mom said with some pride in her voice. "As you can see he scored in the top one percentile on the IQ test and at the fifth-grade level in math and reading comprehension on the basic skills test."

"Yes, very impressive," Mr. Schaumberg said as he turned to the test scores. Then apparently something else caught his attention. "These records must be wrong; they show your son is only seven years old. That can't be right."

"No, that's correct, sir. Chris is seven. He started the first grade at five and then went through the accelerated program." She smiled.

"But no one is seven in the fourth grade ma'am. That's too young!"

"That's why we needed to meet with you first, because you need to approve his starting the fourth grade at his age. We talked to the district office and that's what they told us." Mom informed him.

"I would like to call the district to confirm, if that is alright with you?" Schaumberg asked.

"That's fine; I spoke with a Ms. Ann Levy in the Superintendent's office." Mom pulled out a piece of paper from her purse and reviewed it.

"I'm familiar with Mrs. Levy; I'll give her a call." He excused himself from the office.

I was sort of sitting there quietly looking around his office as we waited. His office was paneled in redwood, covered by different plaques and awards for the school, and his college degrees.

"You okay Chris?" Mom turned to me with some concern in her voice.

"Yes," I answered, not sure what the big deal was. This all seemed normal to me, so I didn't know why the principal seemed so concerned with my age.

At that moment the principal returned to his office and again settled into his swivel chair. "I talked with Mrs. Levy and she indicated she already had a copy of your son's academic records and the district does not have a problem with him starting the fourth grade at seven. And since the district is fine with it, I will not stand in his way of advancing to the fourth grade, since he obviously earned it."

Quite a long speech, but it looked like I was going to start the fourth grade after all. Mom looked pleased; I guess she knew it was a done deal before we walked in that morning.

"I've taken the liberty of assigning Chris to Mrs. Laskey's fourth grade class, and I'd like to walk you up there once we're done here." Schaumberg looked pleased with himself.

"Thank you, that'll be fine." Mom said as she began to fill out the proper registration forms. Once she finished, she handed them back to the principal, and he added them to my academic folder.

"If you'll follow me." He stood up and again held open the door for us.

We trooped through the main office with the principal in the lead, and my mother leading me by the hand as we went to meet my new class.

❖   ❖   ❖

The principal, my mother and I, marched through the quiet hallways and climbed a wide staircase as we made our way up to the second floor to Mrs. Laskey's class. We stopped in front of a door that had "Laura Laskey" on a small brass plaque below the opaque glass embedded in the door. Mr. Schaumberg knocked on the door, poked his head in the class, and gestured for the teacher to join us in the hall.

I saw an attractive black-haired woman, wearing brightly colored clothes and costume jewelry around her neck come out of the classroom. She looked inquisitively at Mr. Schaumberg as she glanced in our direction and closed the door behind her.

"Mrs. Laskey, this is Mrs. Pittard and her son Chris. Chris will be joining your class for this school year. He is transferring in from Philadelphia where he participated in a special program completing the second and third grade in one year." Schaumberg explained.

Laskey's eyes got big with that explanation of my status. They got even bigger when Schaumberg continued, "And he's only seven years old."

"Seven?" Laskey exclaimed, "How is that possible?"

"I'll explain later," Schaumberg said. "Needless to say, the district has approved his entrance into the fourth grade, so he's all yours now."

Laskey looked down at me long and hard, and said, "That's fine; I hope he can do the work."

Oh boy, I thought, *here we go.*

Mom immediately jumped in, "He'll be fine, he scored in the top one percentile on the IQ tests and at a fifth grade level on the basic skills test." I could tell she was starting to get wound up.

"Okay, fine. We'll see." Laskey said, and the gauntlet was thrown.

"If you have any further questions let me know and we can talk." Schaumberg finished his part and ambled down the hall.

Mrs. Laskey opened the classroom door and Mom and I walked in to be introduced to the already assembled class. As I walked in I saw a class brightly decorated with drawings, maps of the world, books, and the names of all the students spelled out in big block letters strung out around the room where the walls met the ceiling. I also saw a classroom full of white faces sitting at their wooden desks with varying degrees of inquisitiveness. You could almost read their minds, *Why is this little black kid in our classroom?* They were about to find out.

"Class, if I could have your attention. This is a new student, Chris Pittard, who is joining us from Philadelphia." She paused, "and he is only seven years old!"

That little pronouncement elicited a gasp from some students, some unbelieving stares and startled whispering. As she introduced me to the class I knew I didn't look very imposing as a little, light-skinned, green-eyed Black kid. No longer the same age and size of my peers, or the same race, circumstances had thrust me into a hostile environment. It was almost as if I had landed in a space ship and asked them to "take me to your leader" like in some of my comic books.

Most of them had probably never come into close contact with an African-American; and it showed. Some of them even looked shocked and afraid. There was a real mix of emotions emanating from all these white faces staring back at me. And as I looked out at the class, I saw no friendly faces, no faces of color and everybody looked so much older and bigger than me. This was sort of frightening and I almost cried when Mom kissed me goodbye outside the classroom and assured me I would be fine. I wasn't so sure about that, but turned a brave face towards my new class.

Later that day, we went out for recess and I had a chance to see all the other fourth graders, and couldn't believe that not one of the Black kids from Fort Totten was in my grade. I realized I was the only Black kid in the entire fourth grade, and of course, the youngest. The fact that there were Black kids that played T-ball with me during the summer only meant that they were probably in the second grade, not the fourth, and I didn't know any of the Fort Totten kids in any of the other fourth grade classes. Coincidentally, there were no other Army kids in my class, so I was on my own.

The harassment began later that week. I didn't know it initially, but found out as the year went on that everyone else in the class was Jewish, including Mrs. Laskey. I found out during the first Jewish holiday when I was the only one left in my class. On those occasions, the school combined all the non-Jewish kids in the fourth grade into one classroom with one substitute teacher.

I looked forward to those days because my Jewish classmates weren't at school. My tormentors were exclusively boys, although they seemed to be egged on by the girls, like Debra, the cutest girl in class. Or they were trying to show off in front of the girls by making fun of the lone little Black kid in class. How brave of them.

One of my main tormentors was the boy all the girls "oohed" and "aahed" over, David, the biggest boy in class and the most athletic. He was tall, with what I'm sure the girls considered a handsome face, athletic build, and wavy brown hair. Another was Alan Greenberg, a tall, skinny, tortoiseshell glasses-wearing, limp-wristed, big-lipped kid, who wore his hair in a "bowl" cut. He probably appreciated a new person onto which everyone could heap their jokes and comments. I suspect he used to be that guy. In contrast, I was the smallest kid in the class, and apparently, in their minds, the easiest target.

The first day of torment began the first time I wore a short-sleeved button-down collared shirt. The shirt, a red and black plaid design, had the little loop on the back seam below the collar, so it could be hung up on a hook. A new shirt I proudly wore to school that day. Alan decided to be funny and make fun of my shirt by pulling off the loop. The first time happened at lunch.

As I stood in line in the cafeteria, he snuck up behind me, grabbed the loop with his index finger and violently pulled the loop up so it separated from the shirt. Of course, that also had the effect of ripping the shirt at the seam. Everyone laughed at me, but I wouldn't give them the satisfaction of crying. That happened when I got home. Mom wanted to know what happened to my new shirt, and after I told her, she decided to go see the principal. She called the school the next day and made an appointment to see Mr. Schaumberg before school started. I'm sure he was looking forward to that meeting.

When we walked in the main office this time, Carol, dressed this time in a pale, yellow dress, made it a point to greet us cordially. "I'll let Mr. Schaumberg know you're here," she said, and ran off to get him.

Rather than Schaumberg coming out to greet us, Carol escorted us back to his office. The door was open, and she led us in the now familiar office. Once we were in, Carol turned and left the office and closed the door behind her.

"How are you today Mrs. Pittard? And you Chris?" He said as he stood up to shake Mom's hand.

I wondered if he had nothing in his closet other than the same three-piece gray suit, because it seemed every time I had seen him in the past few days that's all he wore.

"Please sit down," he gestured towards the same two chairs. "What can I do for you today?"

Mom wasted no time, "My son is being picked on by his older, bigger classmates and it needs to stop." She said as she leaned towards him.

"What do you mean? What's going on?" He directed his questions at me.

I was mute, I really did not want to say anything, and wanted to get out of there. I felt like crying.

Mom prompted me, "You need to tell him what's been happening in class."

I was embarrassed to tell him, but at my mother's insistence, I began to tell my tales of woe.

"David and Alan make fun of my shirts and pull the loop off the back." I sniffled. I wore another new shirt, light green this time, and turned in the chair to show him the loop.

"Were you wearing the shirt when they did that?" He asked. *What a stupid question*, I thought; *of course I'm in the shirt.*

Mom answered, "Yes. Not only is he still in the shirt, but they are tearing his shirts by pulling the loops off the back. I think they're picking on one of his little friends too. Mitchell, right?" She looked at me for confirmation.

"Yes, him too." I answered.

"Okay, I'll take care of this," Schaumberg promised, "I'll make sure Mrs. Laskey is aware of what's going on and puts a stop to it."

Terrific, I thought, *that's just going to make it worse.* But you couldn't tell that to Mom, she was doing what she felt was right.

While we sat there, the principal called Mrs. Laskey and told her of the complaint and Mrs. Laskey promised to take care of the problem. *Yeah, right.*

As we left his office, Schaumberg said, "Anytime you have a problem please bring it to me and I'll take care of it. I want you to have a great academic experience at P.S. 169."

"Thank you." Mom said. I didn't say anything. I knew what was coming.

Once we left his office, Mom took me upstairs to my classroom. Mom's heels click-clacked angrily on the floor and stairs as we made our way to my classroom. She rapped on the door and Mrs. Laskey came out to speak with us. She was dressed in her typical colorful dress with matching accessories.

"You're aware of what those boys did to my son?" Mom asked. Mom, dressed more severely in her gray two-piece skirt suit, exuded anger and indignation.

"Yes. We don't tolerate bullying. I'll make sure it stops." Mrs. Laskey assured my mother. She looked down at me.

"Alright, thank you." Mom turned to me. "You'll be fine Chris. Let me know if anything else happens."

"I will." I said and turned to go in the classroom with Mrs. Laskey.

Obviously, I was late to class, and curiosity showed on everyone's face when I walked in the classroom with Mrs. Laskey. I wondered how she would handle the situation, maybe she would talk to those two boys by themselves after school or call their parents, or something else equally dire.

Instead, Mrs. Laskey allowed me to find my seat, and said, "Class we've had a complaint of students picking on other students and it has to stop. We do not tolerate bullying. Does everyone understand that?" And she looked directly at me.

"Yes, Mrs. Laskey," the class intoned. And all heads turned in my direction as they looked at me. I wanted to melt right through the floor.

And it just got worse, like I thought.

In fact, Mrs. Laskey seemed to get in on the fun as well. Whenever I showed any kind of educational insight or academic prowess she always played it down.

One day as we were studying geography, Mrs. Laskey put up a map of the Middle East that featured the country of Israel.

Laskey turned from the front of the classroom and asked the class, "What state most resembles Israel?"

I guess for a class made up entirely of Jewish kids, except me, a question like that made sense. I had my hand up first, which I'm sure didn't make sense to Laskey, but she called on me anyway.

"New Jersey," I answered.

She looked a little perturbed. And rather than applauding my answer, she said, "That was a nice educated guess Chris."

She refused to give me credit for my knowledge of geography, the shape of states, the shape of various countries, including Israel, and making the logical deduction. I had traveled all over the country, seen color maps of the country, and played with wooden puzzles using the shapes of the states as the pieces to make the USA whole. I knew the shape of all the states. I was smarter than these parochial, older, New York kids, and I think it angered her that I could answer a question about Israel before all the Jewish kids in the class who should have known the answer.

On another occasion, as we discussed current events, she asked, "What state has recently been subjected to an earthquake?"

Again, I raised my little hand before anyone else. Laskey looked around the class and decided the other morons didn't have an answer, so she reluctantly pointed at me. "Do you know the answer Chris?"

"Alaska." I answered.

Again, she downplayed the answer, "That was a good guess Chris."

Rather than acknowledging that I actually kept up on current events and knew the answer, she again ascribed my answer to guessing. I mean, how do you *guess* "Alaska" as the answer to any question in the fourth grade in New York City?

The next time I embarrassed her and her Jewish students was on a day when parents were invited to sit in on the class. Mom, this time dressed in a pink two-piece suit, sat in on that class and I really wanted to impress her and the other parents and embarrass these older kids. My version of payback for all the bullying.

Mrs. Laskey had greeted the parents as each came in the classroom. She stood before everyone in a pretty dark blue dress, almost denim, with red trim along the short sleeves and bottom of the dress as it bloomed out from her waist. She wore red earrings, necklace and bracelets. She was always well-coordinated, and today was no exception. She must have had a serious collection of costume jewelry.

"We welcome the parents who have taken time out of their busy day to visit our class on Parent's Day." She said.

"Your students have been spending their time learning about geography, history, math, vocabulary, music, and keeping up with current events." She continued.

"I'm quite proud of their accomplishments this school year, and hope you will be too. Do the parents have any questions?" She asked as she looked around. "If not, we'll get started with a question about current events."

Mrs. Laskey looked at us and asked, "What president of the United States signed the Civil Rights Act of 1964?"

My hand was first in the air. Mrs. Laskey ignored me, and asked another student, and she said, "President Kennedy."

Wrong answer dummy, hope you're parents weren't back there. My hand remained in the air.

"Close," Laskey said encouragingly, and continued to look around the room. I could see the sigh in her face, "Yes, Chris, do you know the answer?"

"Lyndon Baines Johnson," I proudly pronounced. The signing of the 1964 Civil Rights Act had been a big deal in my household, so yeah I remembered it because it had just happened a few months before. This was a classroom of idiots. He was our current president and they had no clue what he'd recently done.

Trying to give her other students an opportunity to redeem themselves, Laskey asked questions about the New York World's Fair. Before my slow-witted classmates could formulate answers my hand was in the air. I had been to the World's Fair at least three times that summer, and quite familiar with all the exhibits. Again, I had all the correct answers. She absolutely hated that, but my mother, in the back of the classroom, was all smiles. I definitely proved I belonged in the fourth grade and smarter than all my older classmates.

On another occasion, as a bonus word on a spelling test, which, by the way, I scored 100, Mrs. Laskey used the word "***supercalifragilisticexpialidocious***"—the word that formed the basis of that silly song of the same name from the movie *Mary Poppins*. I saw the movie and also saw the word in print, and was the only student in the class to get it right or even close to getting it right. Again, when she announced that I was the only one to get it right, she attributed it to another "lucky guess."

How do you "guess" *that* word? Here I was, the only Black kid in the class, the youngest, smallest kid in class, the only non-Jew in the class, and I was outperforming my older, white, Jewish classmates. She never gave me credit for being smarter than her Jewish students. This emboldened the more aggressive students to continue their torment of me.

Mom spoke to my second-grade teacher, Mrs. Faith Getson, who was also Jewish, on several occasions and told her how I was being treated in this new school. Mrs. Getson had previously recommended me for the acceleration program and felt I had great potential if properly nurtured. This was not a nurturing environment. Mrs. Getson called Mrs. Laskey, "that Jewish bitch," and advised my mother to get me out of there as soon as possible. I agreed with her sentiment and her description of "that Jewish bitch." No matter what Mrs. Getson might say or think, it was me in this hostile environment, and I had to figure out how to deal with it on my own.

One day, Alan came up to me during morning recess, with the other students watching. Mitch and I had just finished playing marbles, and I stood up to walk to the monkey bars, also known as a "Jungle Gym." Alan moved fairly close to me and looked back at his audience to make sure they were watching. He hesitantly reached out his pale white hand towards me as if he was afraid to touch me.

"Ewww," he squealed like a little girl, and pulled his hand back like he was afraid of getting some sort of disease or malaise; as if I were contagious or something, or as if my Blackness would somehow jump from me to him.

"Does it come off?" He shuddered as he moved closer and rubbed his hand on my arm.

I jerked back my arm, "Does what come off?"

"You know, that brown color," he replied chortling.

"No, does your whiteness come off?" I shot back. No laughing then as he moved back towards the other white classmates.

That didn't seem to deter my classmates from continuing their verbal abuse.

Over the next several weeks I was subjected to more and more racial comments. Every day we went outside for recess, and that was when they taunted me.

"What's wrong with your hair?" Debbie asked, pointing at my head.

"What do you mean?" I said, knowing what was coming next.

"You know, it's all like rough and curly, you know, like a sheep!" And all the girls laughed at me.

I held it in; I wouldn't let them see me cry. I started to tear up and turned my back and walked away as fast as I my little feet would take me. I got around the corner and ran for the bathroom. I barely made it before I started crying. I cried so hard I was sniffling. After a few minutes, I wiped my face and went back out to face them again. Somehow, it made it worse when the girls taunted me.

In a few days, it was David's turn.

I was on the monkey bars, swinging like everyone else. I was actually pretty good at swinging on the horizontal ladder and climbing the monkey bars. The bars were metal pipes constructed in cubical shapes that could be climbed on the inside and outside and towered ten feet in the air. They were also connected to the horizontal ladder which allowed me to swing and climb from one apparatus to the other. The horizontal ladder stood about six feet off the ground, about two feet wide and consisted of ten metal rungs horizontal to the ground. To use it, I had to step up on the two metal wedges that served as a platform on each pole that made up the end of the ladder, grasp the first rung, and swing to the next one until I got to the end connected to the monkey bars. I loved playing on the monkey bars. Of course, being Black, and on the monkey bars, gave the white kids plenty of ammunition.

"Hey, you look like a little monkey up there!" David laughed to the delight of whoever was in earshot.

Not very original. Of course, I did. Didn't everyone?

"You smell like Cheetah!" He laughed again and everyone yowled. He was attracting quite a crowd.

"You belong in a Tarzan movie like the rest of the natives!" He was really on a roll.

"Oh yeah, well you talk like Tarzan and look like Jane!" I yelled back down. "I bet you're scared to climb up here David!" And then I laughed, and continued to climb to the pinnacle of the monkey bars. I had never seen David climb, so I wondered if he was afraid of heights.

David looked around as his admiring classmates were waiting for him to accept my dare and climb up.

He looked up and yelled, "You little black midget, I'm going to get you!" And jumped on the lowest level of the monkey bars.

"Come on," I taunted, and sat on top of the monkey bars swinging my legs looking down at him. I was ready to climb down the inside if he came up the outside.

But as I suspected, he was afraid of heights, and about half way up, he stopped and yelled at me, "I'll get you when you come down." And jumped off the monkey bars to the admiring glances of the girls in the class.

When the recess bell rang, I waited until everyone filed into the building and swung down from monkey bars. I had embarrassed David, and I felt pretty good about that as I ran in to beat the class bell.

◇   ◇   ◇

This continued the rest of the school year. I no longer complained to my mother or the teacher, because that was futile, and I was too small to physically fight, but I did my best to fight back verbally. That was my only outlet for my anger and the only thing that kept me from crying all the time. Even with these little opportunities to let it out, I still kept it all in and became more introverted. Before I went to that school, I was very garrulous and outgoing, a real extrovert and life of the party; but this teasing day in and day out turned me into an introvert and created a hard-shell personality to help me ward off these kinds of verbal blows. I stopped eating in the cafeteria and began bringing my lunch to school. I sat in the auditorium either by myself or with one of my two friends in the class and ate my salami sandwiches with cheese and mustard or my PB&Js.

I actually did have a couple of friends in the class, Herbert, and Mitchell. Herbert was grateful, as the unathletic, fat boy with freckles, to have someone else be the butt of jokes and the object of torment. He was known as "Herbert sherbert;" but he was a pretty smart boy. He admired my "spunkiness" as he called it, and my intelligence. He, a nine-year old, taught me the game of chess at the age of seven; taught me strategy and how to outthink my opponent, much to the chagrin of several of my classmates. By the spring semester I challenged and beat my older classmates in chess—sort of my own version of *Revenge of the Nerds*.

My other friend Mitchell, was a little taller than me, wore glasses, was slight of build, and had curly brown hair. He befriended me to the point where I would spend weekends with him and his family, and attend Yankees games with him and his dad. Mitch took some abuse by being my friend—Alan and David would rip the loops off his shirts as well and call him names. Mitch and Herbert stuck by me through all of that and made that year somewhat bearable. But what those guys at school couldn't take from me was the ability to compete against kids my own age in a variety of sports.

⋄   ⋄   ⋄

My dad had previously taught me how to bowl, and that year I began my competitive career in bowling by joining my first league as a "Bantam" bowler and competing against kids my own age. In addition, I joined the Cub Scouts on Fort Totten that fourth grade year and had an opportunity to again socialize and compete with boys my own age. The Cub Scouts consisted of boys from all walks of life, and races. There were several Black kids in our troop.

From the moment I joined the Cub Scouts I felt like a little soldier. The Cub Scouts taught me about teamwork, earning merit badges, wearing a uniform and, in this case, some military drill and ceremonies from how to stand at attention, parade rest, facing movements and even marching in formation. The Cub Scouts was fun, and also helped me get through my fourth-grade year.

I only spent one year at P.S. 169. For whatever reason, the Army changed our school, and we attended a different school in Queens in the fall of 1965. Maybe Mom's complaints about my treatment at the hands of these Jewish kids weren't the only complaints from Army parents. The school seemed pretty prejudiced against anyone who wasn't Jewish.

CHAPTER 3

Exploring

The summer of '65 meant playing baseball with kids my own age and ability. Dad coached my little league team, and I increased my skills as a third baseman and shortstop. This year was different because we faced pitchers for the first time and it gave me the feeling that I was really playing baseball, like the big leaguers. I really enjoyed playing baseball and excelled at the game. In contrast to dealing with my classmates, it was a much different story when competing against my own age group…it almost seemed easy, and I usually did very well.

One of our favorite activities during the summer was to explore the "Old Post," the remnants of Fort Totten built during the Civil War or earlier. These old structures, covered in vines and overgrowth, attracted us like magnets, and the trails leading to the Old Post began right in front of our apartment complex. Whenever we could, my brother and I, and Tommy the kid who lived next door, headed out to the Old Post to explore and look for "stuff."

We loved exploring in the woods and pretending we were on missions, like the soldiers we saw on TV. We had little olive-drab backpacks with "U.S. Army" embroidered on the back flap and little straps that snapped on metal tabs on the back. The backpacks had shoulder straps as well that allowed us to wear them on our backs. Whenever we went out to explore the Old Post we packed our backpacks with what we imagined to be "essential supplies" for our "missions." We put in metal canteens with Kool Aid, bags of potato chips, and my beloved salami sandwiches or PB&Js in plastic baggies that folded over to keep them fresh. We wore our baseball caps, Keds tennis shoes, jeans, and white socks. That was pretty much our uniform. Mom allowed us to wear jeans on weekends or during the summer, just not for school. When we weren't playing baseball, we explored the ruins of the Old Post.

This morning was typical of mornings by the Bay, bright sunshine, with a few wisps of clouds in the sky. The air was warm with a breeze blowing from the water carrying with it a hint of places far away and the smell of the sea. We could hear the constant pounding of the waves against the rocks less than a hundred yards from our apartments and the tweeting of the sea birds that nested along the rocks close to the shore. This was going to be a fine day.

Dana and I dressed almost identically, in jeans, white tee-shirts, tennis shoes and socks. Mom insisted we wear jeans, not shorts, when going into the woods because of the mosquitoes, the bushes, and because you just never knew what could bite you or grab you out there. We were in the kitchen getting our supplies ready for the rest of the day.

"You boys going out today?" Mom asked.

"Yep," Dana answered, "to the Old Post."

"Are you walking or riding your bikes?" Mom further inquired, as she began to pull bread out of its plastic packaging to fix our PB&J sandwiches.

"Um, walking I think," I answered, looking for some bags of chips in the pantry. Mom always kept a supply of the individual bag of chips as snacks.

"Going by yourselves?" Mom paused, wondering if she needed to make more than two sandwiches.

"I think Tommy's going with us," Dana answered looking at me.

"Yeah," I said.

Tommy usually went with us. At seven years old, he was right between our ages and didn't have anyone else to hang out with. We would go over to his house on Thursdays to watch *Jonny Quest* because his family had a new color TV, and it was really cool to watch *Jonny Quest* in color. I didn't see him much at school because he was a few grades behind, but he was old enough to go exploring.

"Okay, then I'll make another sandwich for him," she said as she pulled two more slices of bread out the bag.

"Thanks Mom," I said as I picked out a few bags of Lays potato chips. "You want Kool Aid Dana?"

"Yeah, I'll get it," Dana said, as he got out the quart-sized canteens to fill them up with Kool Aid. The canteens were a dull metallic color used by soldiers to carry their water in combat. Unlike soldiers, we tended to put Kool Aid in our canteens.

"Make sure you rinse those things out before you fill them up," Mom warned.

"Okay." Dana said as he walked over to the sink. He began running the water to rinse out the canteens. Once finished he headed over to the fridge.

I had our backpacks open and ready to put in the sandwiches and canteens. I helped Dana fill the canteens from the Kool Aid pitcher in the refrigerator. I broke out some ice cubes from the tray in the freezer and forced them into the canteens to keep the Kool Aid cold during the day.

Just about that time Mom finished the sandwiches and wrapped them in their individual baggies. "Peanut butter and jelly okay boys?"

Yeah, like we had a choice.

"That's great Mom, thank you," I said. Maybe next time we could get salami, cheese and mustard sandwiches, like the ones I took to school. But today it was PB&J.

Mom placed one sandwich in each of our backpacks. "Here's one for Tommy, okay?" She pointed to the remaining sandwich.

"Okay, we'll give it to him." I said as we gathered up our backpacks ready to leave the apartment.

"Be careful," Mom said, "You know I worry."

"Bye Mom, we will," we chorused and rushed out the apartment.

We stopped at the door next to our apartment and Dana knocked a few times. Within seconds the door opened and Tommy stood at the door with his own backpack ready to go. Tommy was about my height, with reddish-brown hair, and a lot of freckles. He dressed similar to us except he had on PF Flyers instead of Keds. The PF Flyers were kind of cool, especially their commercials on TV.

"Mom wanted you to have this," I said and handed him the bagged sandwich.

"Okay, I'll put it with my stuff." He leaned over and put the sandwich in his already bulging backpack. Tommy's dad was the provost marshal for the post, giving Tommy access to all kinds of neat stuff we didn't have.

"Whatchu got in there today?" Dana asked as Tommy rooted around in his backpack looking for space for the sandwich.

"Um, I got a little knife my dad gave me, a flashlight, some binocs, matches, first aid kit, some water, and crackers with cheese." He recited as he found some room in his backpack for the sandwich and snapped it shut.

"Wow, that's pretty good stuff!" I said as Tommy hoisted his backpack over one shoulder. *I wish our dad gave us that kind of stuff*, I thought. *That would be pretty neat.*

"Yeah, Dad wants me to be prepared. Let's go," he said. Tommy was also a cub scout with us, and knew a little about going out to the woods.

We bounded down the steps of our apartment building and stood outside getting a feel for the day. It looked to be a beautiful day, warm and a little humid, a great day to do some serious exploring in the woods.

We walked across the street in front of our apartments and followed our favorite trail towards the Old Post. A beaten dirt path surrounded on both sides by some sort of green vegetation dotted with flowering weeds showed us the way to the Old Post. The ruins of the Old Post towered above us as we walked in single file along the trail. The old guy at eight, I led today with Tommy second and Dana bringing up the rear. He was youngest, so he was in the back.

"Where we goin' today?" Dana squeaked from the back. He had just turned six in March.

"What about those woods on the other side of the Old Post?" Tommy suggested. We hadn't done much exploring over there, at least in a while.

"Okay, through Old Post?" I asked trying to figure out the best route.

"Yeah," Dana said. Tommy nodded in acquiescence. We turned our faces towards the heart of the Old Post.

The abandoned fortifications of the Old Post rose before us as we got closer.

The closer we got, the more silent it became, and darker. The trees towered above us, providing cover from the sun, causing the temperature to drop the farther in we walked. The woods were filled with the sounds of songbirds tweeting, cicadas singing, bees buzzing about, and little animals, like rabbits and squirrels, running over the forest floor. Typically, we heard the boat traffic and water skiers on the Bay, but as we made our approach to the stone fortifications the woods became strangely silent. The crunching of our shoes on the leaves and small branches that littered the area surrounding the fortifications the only sounds. We weren't very stealthy. The trail had petered out in favor of the more open area leading to the fort.

There were gray stone steps that led to what appeared to be gun platforms and walkways that circled the ruins. We avoided going up the steps because we had been warned on countless times that their sturdiness was questionable and we shouldn't climb them. Although made of stone, they appeared to crumble with age. Instead, we ducked under them as we made our way farther into the Old Post. We picked our way through the overgrown vegetation and the inroads the woods had made on the outer portions of the Old Post. As we made our way under the outer areas we broke through into the interior of the stone structures. We huffed and puffed from the effort of climbing over all the fallen trees; and fought our way through the vines and undergrowth surrounding the Old Post.

When we broke through the foliage covering the outer wall we saw a larger flat area that looked like a town square in the middle of the fortifications. The sunlight broke through as individual rays streaming through the trees, bathing the square in a golden light, and putting the rest of the fortifications in deeper shadows. The larger towers that marked the side of the Old Post that faced the Bay on two sides were impressive in their massiveness. I imagined the brass guns in their positions overlooking the water, ready to repel enemy ships and blow them out the water. We just stood there in awe looking around at this throwback to another era; almost 100 hundred years ago. The towers and all the stone fortifications were covered in overgrown vegetation, vines and thick branches hugging the stone, some almost completely hidden from view.

Dana broke the silence, "Whoa, this is cool! Can we go up in the towers?"

"No, you know what Dad said about that…not to do it." I warned.

"Okay," Dana said with some disappointment, "Where do we go now?"

"The woods are off to the left," Tommy finally spoke up.

"You know where you're going?" I asked.

"Yeah, I've been back there before with my dad." Tommy answered.

"Okay, you lead then." I looked at Dana who shrugged his shoulders in agreement.

Tommy led the procession with Dana in the middle this time and me bringing up the rear. It was kind of spooky off in there and I didn't want anybody or anything sneaking up on us. I had an active imagination, and like Dorothy and her two friends, I was looking for "lions and tigers and bears, oh my!" I mean, you never know, right? So, I kept my head on a swivel and furtively glanced behind us every few steps as we moved deeper into the woods.

As we entered the woods on the other side of the Old Post, Dana and I looked around in amazement. We could again hear all the normal sounds of woodland activity, but we could no longer hear any sounds from the Bay; we were too far into the woods for that. We were in a different world; transported to a different place. Like over the town square, the sun shone down in rays of light between the branches of the trees, mottling the leaves with spots of light, creating shadows on the ground all around us. Being our first foray into any kind of significant woods, I found it exciting and scary at the same time.

"Look at that!" Tommy exclaimed almost as soon as we entered this forbidden kingdom. He was pointing excitedly at something on the ground.

"What, what?" I yelled, "What is it?" Our voices muted by the woods.

Dana and I rushed over to where he stood and saw a dead squirrel on the ground. The squirrel just lay there on its side, part of its underbelly missing and its intestines hung out, both bloody red and blue. Its eyes stared sightlessly at us as we looked down at its lifeless form, ants crawling over it.

"Eeeyew!" Dana said in mock disgust, "what is it?"

"Looks like a squirrel," Tommy said, "maybe eaten by a hawk or something."

"Oh yuck, really?" I squealed, but thought it interesting that the squirrel was partially eaten by a hawk or some other predator. This wasn't Rocky the Flying Squirrel on the ground; but one of the cute little squirrels we'd see jumping from tree to tree, and scampering up a tree when we chased them. Well, not any more, not this one.

We looked at the dead squirrel for a few moments, then pushed farther into the woods. Tommy led the way since he knew the woods.

"Where are we going?" Dana asked, after walking another few minutes.

"Ah, I thought maybe we could walk to the Bay on this side." Tommy answered. "It's pretty cool to see the Bay from this side."

"Okay," I said, as we pushed on farther, towards the Bay. After a few more minutes, Tommy put up his hand, and knelt on the ground.

"Hold up," he said, "I think there're some really big bullets over here."

Dana and I ran up to where he squatted on the ground. Half covered with dirt was a partly-opened old metal ammunition box. It was rectangular and covered with dirt. It might have been green at some point, but now looked a dirty brown with age and dirt. Down in the bottom, were a bunch of brass-colored things that looked a lot like real bullets.

"What are those?" Dana asked, peering into the box. None of us had touched the box yet. Maybe we thought it might blow up or something.

"Bullets." Tommy said again, "Really big ones. Maybe even .50 cal bullets." He pulled out his flashlight to get a better look at the contents inside the box.

"How do you know?" I challenged him. I'd never seen real bullets and didn't have a clue about them.

"My dad shows me his gun and I've helped him load the bullets into his gun. His gun holds .45 caliber bullets, and these are bigger than those, so I thought they might be .50 cal." Well that made sense, his dad was the provost marshal for the post, so he might know more about guns and bullets than me and Dana.

As we spoke, Tommy grabbed his flashlight out of his backpack and shined the light on the contents of the bottom of the can. They looked like really big bullets, gleaming in the light from his flashlight.

"What should we do with them?" I asked.

"Take 'em back with us and show my dad." Tommy said.

Hmm, okay, that sounded reasonable.

"Alright, let's go back now, that thing looks pretty heavy." Dana piped in.

"You guys got room in your backpacks for some extra stuff?" Tommy asked as he put aside his flashlight and dug into his backpack for something else.

Dana and I looked at each other, and I said, "Yeah, we can carry some of those bullets."

"Okay," Tommy said, and he pried the top of the ammunition can all the way open with the knife he had just pulled out of his backpack. "We don't have to take the whole box, we can carry a few of them to show my dad, then he can come get the rest if he wants." Tommy slid his hand into the battered ammunition box and pulled out a few rounds and put them in his backpack.

Following his lead, Dana and I reached down in the ammunition box, careful not to scratch our hands on the sharp sides, and grabbed a few of the bullets and put them in our backpacks. I closed my backpack with a flourish, but it seemed to get heavier with the bullets. Maybe it just seemed heavier with the knowledge that I might be carrying live ammunition that could actually kill somebody. That was kind of scary.

"We going back now?" Dana asked.

"Yeah, we're going back." I said, and turned around towards the trail we used to get into the area.

"I'll lead us out." Tommy volunteered, and we headed out with Tommy in the lead, Dana, then me.

The trip out was a lot faster than the trip in. We were no longer exploring, we had an important mission to perform and we tried to get back as quickly as possible. Within a few minutes, we cleared the Old Post and broke into the less dense foliage between the Old Post and our apartment. We didn't need Tommy to lead us from there, and we all broke into a run to see who could get back to the apartment first.

"Beat cha," Dana exclaimed as he got to the front door of the apartment first.

Whew! We gasped for air as we fought to get our breath; you would have thought the devil himself was behind us the way we ran back from the Old Post.

Tommy led the way to his apartment and went through the front door. It so happened his dad was at home. His dad was watching TV when we crashed into the apartment. He looked a little startled.

"Hey boys, what's up?' He asked. Tommy's dad, a medium-built man, with light brown hair, dark brown eyes, dressed casually in khaki pants and white tee shirt and tennis shoes, looked at us with interest.

"Hey Dad,"Tommy explained, "we found these bullets in the Old Fort."He opened his backpack and emptied out the contents on the floor and indicated we should do the same. As we emptied our backpacks, Tommy's dad knelt down to examine the contents of our backpacks.

"Well boys, this is real ammunition you discovered out in the woods," he said, "I'm very proud of you. Do you think you could find it again?"

"Yeah Dad,"Tommy volunteered, "no problem. What are they?"

"Fifty cal. Probably left over from World War Two." His dad said with a little twinkle in his eye. "We'll need to recover all that ammunition and see if there's anymore. Would you boys be willing to go back today?"

"Yes sir, I just need to tell my mom." I said.

"Tell you what, I'll go tell Jackie it's official business, how about that?" He grinned.

"Yes sir," Dana and I chorused, and that's exactly what he did. A few minutes later we walked back through the woods with Tommy's dad, the provost marshal, a military police captain, to recover a very valuable and dangerous cargo left over from WWII. Wow!

Tommy led the way, of course. It was his dad, and he had led the way the first time. When we got there, Tommy's dad pulled the whole ammunition box out of the ground and peered inside with his flashlight. There were about thirty more rounds in the old ammunition box. He carefully extracted each round and put them in a special metal container he had brought with him.

"This box lets me carry the bullets without them blowing up or discharging." He said. "The way you all carried them in your backpacks was a little dangerous and they could have blown up. You were very brave bringing them to me."

We puffed up our chests at that, along with a little bit of a shiver. *We could have blown ourselves up*, I thought, *wow!*

We stood guard, while he searched the area for any more rounds, but didn't find any. Once he finished his search, we turned again back towards our apartment and made our way home. Now that was an adventure!

That was our best adventure in the woods surrounding the Old Post. On other occasions we found dead animals, or the nests of various birds, but every day was something different. We pretended to be anybody we wanted to be and had great fun out in the woods. It was our first real experience exploring woods like that, and we had a great time. Those forays into the woods and the Old Post were the highlights of the summer.

✧ ✧ ✧

The other highlights of the summer surrounded the other important geographic landmark at Fort Totten—Little Neck Bay. The Bay lapped the shore to the right of our apartment complex, and we could see the water every day. A fence kept us from wandering down to the Bay under normal circumstances, but the post had a boat slip or dock where people kept their boats. You could see your neighbors out on the water fishing, skiing or just driving their boats on any given day. On one occasion, a neighbor invited us to go out on their boat just to experience the Bay, and that was great fun. We also had clambakes on the shores at the designated areas, where we consumed Little Neck clams with melted butter, lobsters, corn and potatoes. Talk about good eating!

Unfortunately, I couldn't go into the Bay because my efforts to learn to swim were not very successful. At the beginning of that summer, Mom thought it would be a good idea for me to learn to swim. I wasn't so sure, but warmed up to the idea because it meant that maybe I could get out on the Bay like everyone else.

On that first day at the post pool, I looked forward to getting in the water. I used to watch cartoons like *Popeye*, where it seemed so easy to swim underwater, and I just knew I could learn to swim in no time.

The first few days went well as they taught us how to put our faces in the water and hold our breath, as well as float across the pool with our faces in the water. I did well in the shallow end of the pool because I could always put my feet on the bottom of the pool if I began to panic. No problem. The first week of swimming lessons went well.

However, the following week, when it came time to go into the deep end of the pool, I really didn't want to go in. We were down at the far end of the pool with the diving board and the depth reading at "9 Ft." Pretty scary! And looking down into the depths of the pool was even scarier. I did not want to get in the water.

I guess because I showed some reluctance in getting in the water, the instructor, a young white guy, picked me up and threw me in the deep end, and I panicked. He had to jump in the water to get me out. At that point, I developed a fear of deep water, and I never went back.

I didn't complete the course and wasn't allowed to go to the pool by myself. Oh well, except for that, I had a good summer and I looked forward to a good fifth grade year.

Oh boy, was I wrong…again.

❖ ❖ ❖

Fifth grade at the new school in Queens started fine. I was still the youngest kid in the class, and still the only Black kid in my class and grade; but I was not the only non-Jewish kid in the class. This class seemed to accept me more than the last class. One of the disadvantages at that school, like the other school, it lacked a real playground with grass or a real sports facility for playing anything except basketball or handball. I learned to play handball and "wall ball" during this period in school, but didn't get the chance to learn basketball, at least not at that time. I got pretty good at handball and "wall ball" where my smaller size gave me an advantage. But of course, this would all change.

At this new school no one knew me, so I could make a fresh start. I would not allow myself to be subjected to the ridicule from the year before. In order to effectuate a change in the perception of me by my classmates, I decided to go by the name of Robert, my first name, rather than Chris, my middle name. The last class made fun of my name, "Chris piss" or "Pittard Retard," so, I changed my name to Robert. That lasted until my mother found out during the parent-teacher conference that I'd changed my name. Oh well, I tried to change the equation a little bit, and keep a little dignity. Mom was livid when she came home and confronted me about using my first name instead of my middle name. I'm not sure why the anger, but it manifested itself the next day in the most embarrassing way for me. I'm sure she intentionally wanted to embarrass me in front of my classmates so I wouldn't do it again.

My desk was near the front of the class. I could hear everything outside the door. That morning, I heard a couple of footsteps stop outside our classroom door. Then there was a knock on the door, and a school administrator walked in followed by my mother! *Uh oh.*

The teacher, Ms. Poole, stood and greeted Mom, "Hello Mrs. Pittard, how may I help you?"

Mom looked directly at me, and said, "I'm sorry to disturb your class Ms. Poole, but I wanted to make sure your class knows Christan's real name."

Since I was the only Black in the class and it was obvious Mom was my mother, all eyes turned towards me. You could see the question in my classmates' eyes, "Christan? Who's that?"

"I want you to get up here and tell the class your real name and apologize for not using your real name." Mom ordered.

There was nothing I could do. My face got hot with embarrassment. I had never been so humiliated in my life. This was really cruel. I stood up and trudged up to the front of the class and stood by Mom. I faced her, but she touched my shoulder and caused me to face the class. I turned and saw all these white faces looking at me with a combination of humor and empathy…many glad it wasn't them up there.

"My name is Chris, not Robert, and I'm sorry for using that name," I croaked. I could barely get the words out. I hung my head down and trudged back to my seat and plopped down. I wanted to cry. I wanted to sink through the floor. I just stared at the floor because I couldn't look at any of my classmates. How could my mother do this to me?

"Thank you." Mom said, and stalked back out the classroom with the school administrator in tow. She had put a stop to me using my own name. At that moment in my life I despised my mother.

My relationship with my classmates changed. No longer was I the cool little kid who could run pretty good and play hand ball and wall ball. Now, I was the little kid whose mother came to class, made him stand up in front of the class, and embarrass himself by apologizing for using his own name.

Kids can be cruel, and these kids were no exception. I again became the target of ridicule for my name, but also for the process in which everybody found out my name. I guess at that age, kids don't have much imagination when making fun of someone whose name is "Chris."

Getting up in front of the class with my mother really hurt and caused me to once again withdraw into my protective shell when, like a reluctant and nervous turtle testing the air, I had begun to stick my head out, but not anymore.

Luckily, within a few weeks of that incident, Dad informed us we would be moving to Richards-Gebauer Air Force Base, outside Kansas City, Missouri, near a little town called Belton. I was happy to be leaving this environment because I thought it couldn't get any worse. But, of course, it did.

Welcome to the home of the Missouri Compromise, and the last of the slave states.

Terrific.

CHAPTER 4

Missouri

We arrived at RGAFB in early October 1965, and were assigned senior officer's quarters. These were the best on-base housing quarters we'd ever had; primarily because of Dad's high rank among Army officers on this Air Force base. He also had the distinction as the highest ranking African-American officer of either service, Air Force or Army. Dad had been selected for promotion to Lieutenant Colonel before we left Fort Totten, so he was authorized the larger quarters. We lived in a single-story, four-bedroom house with a nice basement. The house had a carport instead of a garage, both painted in a nice lime green color, which matched our Chrysler Newport.

On one side of us lived a white family that hailed from the great state of Alabama, and proudly displayed their strong Southern heritage. They even named the dog Mississippi. Strangely enough, they became our best friends at RGAFB, and the mother, Barbara, became my Dad's staunchest supporter when he ran and served as PTA president of my brother's elementary school. They moved in about the same time we did and had three daughters. Cecilia and I in fifth grade; Carol in Dana's grade; and Linda was the baby. Cecilia, a blond girl with glasses, slightly buck-toothed, who "just loved horses," had a horsey sort of laugh, and stood several inches taller than me. Carol was slender and brunette, and Linda short and blond. All three girls were cute. Their parents may have had some concerns in that regard, but nothing ever happened between any of us. Well, not then anyway.

The school designated for the military kids to attend, Westover Elementary School, sat just outside the northern gate of the base. As a first grader, Dana went to that school; however, the fifth grade was full to capacity at Westover. As a result, the new arrivals in the fifth grade were required to ride the bus to a school off-base in the town of Belton.

A couple of days after we moved in, I boarded the bus to go to my first day at Cambridge Elementary School. My parents did not go with me that first day, maybe because the bus picked me up, or because there would be someone at the school to ensure I got to my new class. Whatever the reason, Cecilia and I boarded the bus by ourselves that first day. Cecelia and I stood outside our houses waiting for the bus. The morning had a slight chill as autumn had come to western Missouri. Cecilia and I dressed similarly in that we were trying to make a good impression. She had on a plaid skirt, white frilly blouse, oxford shoes and red sweater. My mother dressed me in my typical brown pants, brown hush puppy shoes, button down long-sleeved white shirt and brown cardigan sweater. Not much flash, but neatly dressed. I felt ready to face my new school and new classmates.

The bus, a typical yellow schools bus, painted with the words "Belton ISD" on the side, came to the base first and picked us up before proceeding into town to pick up the kids from Belton who attended Cambridge. I let Cecelia climb on first, but as soon as I hauled myself up the steps, I stopped at the first row of seats behind the bus driver and sat down. Cecelia stopped in the aisle and came back to the row where I sat. There were two seats on either side of the aisle. I sat next to the window and Cecilia sat next to me. I had developed this habit riding the bus in New York. Mom always told me never to ride in the back of the bus. At the time I didn't understand why, I just did it. Later in life I realized the significance of not riding in the back of bus, but then I was just a little kid obeying his mom. However, because I sat in front, every kid who got on the bus saw me or glared at me. Unbeknownst to me, and probably my parents, I was being bussed to a school that had only recently embraced the idea of integration, and not necessarily by everyone. All the other kids on the bus were white.

At one of the last stops before we got to the school, three white boys, who appeared to be brothers, got on the bus. They were very similar in their looks, about my age or older, freckled with sandy-brown, unruly hair. Their hand-me-down clothes, plaid wool shirts, threadbare dungarees, and shabby tennis shoes, looked like something out of *Li'l Abner* or *Barney Google and Snuffy Smith*, two of the Sunday comic strips depicting hillbilly humor and lifestyles that I read on a regular basis. As the biggest one got on the bus, he looked at me like I had horns growing out of my head and had just landed in a flying saucer.

His eyes widened in surprise, and he exclaimed, "We don't want no niggers on this bus and in our school!"

His brothers laughed, and I didn't say anything. I tried to process what he said and what it meant. I had never heard the term before. But apparently Cecilia had heard the word before because she stiffened in her seat and I could tell it made her uncomfortable, but she didn't say anything to the boys. Neither did the bus driver—a middle-aged, grey-haired, white man dressed comfortably in worn khaki pants, long-sleeved shirt and jacket. He had to have heard the term before, living and working as he did in semi-rural Missouri, but he didn't react either. Never turned around, only closed the door and continued the journey to Cambridge Elementary, my fourth elementary school in as many years.

The bus pulled up in front of a one-story building that spread over a much larger area than the schools I'd attended on the east coast. Standing at the curb was a larger white woman in a floral-patterned dress, bright yellow sweater, and sensible light-brown shoes. Her glasses reflected the bright sunlight and she held a piece of paper in her hand. When Cecelia and I descended from the bus she approached us and asked our names.

"Are you Cecilia Weatherly and Robert Pittard?"

"Yes." We chorused.

"I'm Mrs. Winters, the counselor, and I'm here to register you and take you to your new classrooms."

Cecilia and I looked at each other and said, "Okay."

We followed Mrs. Winters to the main office, reminiscent of the P.S. 169 office, and asked us to sit down as she got our records.

"You're both in the fifth grade, right?" She asked.

"Yes." We said.

"Okay, Cecilia, you'll be going to Mrs. Templeton's class. Sarah, one of our sixth graders, will escort you to your new class."

At that, Cecilia stood up as a freckled, redheaded white girl came over to take Cecilia to her new class.

"See you later." Cecilia said.

I just nodded, a little sad that my first friend here wouldn't be in my new class.

"Come with me." Mrs. Winters said, and led me out of the office to the hallway, my academic records in her hand.

We walked through the quiet hallways for a few minutes, passing several doors where I could hear the sounds of classes in session. The hallways seemed wider than those in my former schools. Plenty of art and posters on the walls, made for a very colorful display. After a few turns we stopped in front of a door with a window to see into the classroom. On the wall next to the door, a sign proclaimed Mrs. Beatrice Pritchard. I assumed my new teacher was Mrs. Pritchard.

Mrs. Winters knocked on the door and opened it as an older, gray-haired white woman, wearing wire-rimmed glasses, a light gray cotton dress with matching sweater, and sensible dark blue shoes, approached the door from the inside. The woman closed the door behind her as she stepped into the corridor. Mrs. Winters introduced me to the woman.

"Mrs. Pritchard, this is Robert Pittard, he will be joining your class this school year. He's one of the overflow students from the base." She explained.

Mrs. Pritchard smiled, "Welcome to Cambridge Robert. I'm Bea Pritchard, and I guess I'll be your teacher this year. Where are you from?"

She looked a little like Aunt Bea from the *Andy Griffith Show.*

Mrs. Winters jumped in, "He's in from New York. I have his school records for you." And handed my brown folder to Mrs. Pritchard.

Mrs. Pritchard opened the folder and immediately looked at me with disbelief. "You're not eight years old, are you Robert?"

"Yes ma'am." I responded. "And please call me Chris."

"Chris? Is that your middle name?" Asked Mrs. Pritchard.

"Yes ma'am."

"Okay, Chris it is." She smiled.

"So, how is it possible you're eight years old?" She looked at Mrs. Winters.

"I'll talk to you after school." Mrs. Winters promised.

Somewhat mollified, Mrs. Pritchard turned to me, "Okay, well welcome to my class Chris." And opened the door and indicated I should follow her inside.

"Goodbye Chris. I'll talk to you later Bea." Mrs. Winters said as she turned to walk back to her office.

When she first introduced me, she mentioned my age, and then said, "I still don't believe this, you can't really be only eight years old!" Even though Mrs. Winters had just told her there was an explanation.

"Yes, ma'am, I'm eight, but I'll be nine in December." I answered.

The class was incredulous, and you could hear the whispers and comments, shades of P.S. 169. Mrs. Pritchard pointed to a desk in the second row, right near the front of the class. When I sat down, I assumed the role of the smallest and youngest kid in class, and the only Black kid. Oh well, here we go again.

That entire day, after the teacher introduced me to my new fifth grade class, I thought of nothing else but the incident on the bus. I don't know why it bothered me so much, because I didn't know what a "nigger" was or what it meant. But that little white boy had used the word with such vitriol and hate that I knew it had to be something awful.

My teacher, a nice gray-haired older woman, had no clue how to deal with me. My mere presence somewhat discomfited her, and she seemed a little flustered with me sitting there watching her as I tried to absorb my new situation.

My new classmates didn't know what to make of me either. I'm pretty sure by the expressions on their faces they hadn't had much experience being around Black kids. Although none of them called me nigger, at least not to my face, it was still uncomfortable that first day in class. I happened to be the only Black kid in the class, in the grade, and as it turned out, in the entire school. Okay, this was another hostile environment I had been thrown into…here we go again.

My educational background was light-years ahead of the class and it showed within the first few minutes. They covered stuff I had done the year before, and maybe the year before that. By the end of the first day I felt completely bored with school and it showed in my total lack of attentiveness to whatever subject Mrs. Pritchard chose to discuss.

Although the school lacked the academic sophistication of my former New York and Philadelphia schools, it had the advantage of plenty of land surrounding the school and having softball fields and basketball courts. During recess, I watched as other kids used the basketball courts and played around on the softball fields. I looked forward to learning and playing both sports that year. However, as my first day at school ebbed, and the end drew closer, I dreaded the trip home. With good reason.

On the bus going home I again sat near the front with Cecilia. She was telling me about her first day at Cambridge when the same boys climbed on the bus.

The bigger one looked at me as if he didn't expect me to be there and said, "I thought I told you we don't want no niggers on this bus." And laughed with his brothers. Then they continued to the back of the bus. Again, the bus driver did not say anything or otherwise react to the comment.

Again, I didn't react either. When I got home, Mom asked me how my first day went, and I told her how the boys on the bus had called me "nigger" and I wanted to know what it meant. I could see Mom didn't want to tell me, but she also knew she needed to explain what it meant. She didn't pull any punches.

"You remember at your other school the Jewish kids treated you very badly and called you names, and that made you cry?" She said.

"Yes, I remember."

"Well," she said, "other white people have another bad name for Negroes, and that name is 'nigger'." She further explained, "When white people really want to hurt you, the worst thing they can call you is nigger."

I began to cry, "Why would they call us that?"

"Because they're ignorant, and many of them show their ignorance and hate by calling us niggers." She shook her head, but continued. "Do you remember those scenes on TV that showed Negroes being hit with fire hoses and having dogs set on them?"

"Yes," I said remembering those awful scenes of extreme racism and rage by angry white people.

"Well those are the type of white people that will call you nigger and teach their kids to call you nigger."

Tears flowed freely, "So, you mean that when they call me a 'nigger' it means they hate me?"

"No, not always, but it shows their ignorance and maybe their fear of Negroes."

"What can I do about it?" I asked.

Mom said to wait for Dad to come home and we'd discuss it. My father came home soon after and when he heard about the incidents on the bus he said, "I'm going to follow the bus tomorrow to make sure there aren't any more incidents!" His eyes showed an anger I'd not seen before.

"But what if they call me that name on the bus again? You'll be in the car behind us and won't be able to do anything!" I replied in anguish.

"We don't normally encourage you to fight, but in this case, you have our permission to hit anybody who calls you a 'nigger.'" Dad said, as he looked at Mom.

Mom looked at me and sadly nodded her assent.

"Really?" I asked surprised, because they never let me hit Dana. I had gotten into fights before at Whittier and in Texas, but they never approved.

"Yes, really," Dad said, "You know how to hit someone?" he asked.

"Yes." I answered.

"Don't start a fight, but if they call you that name I want you to finish the fight, understand?"

"Yep!" I responded. Now I felt excited and looked forward to the next day.

The next morning, I eagerly awaited the bus. Finally, my parents had given me the "green light" to do something about all this bullying I had endured for the past year and a half. I looked forward to the opportunity to knock the crap out of one of those white boys. It never occurred to me that all three might gang up on me, but I would still handle that if it happened. As we waited, Dad came out of the house and stood next to me. When the bus arrived, Cecilia and I got on, and sat right up front as before.

Dad, a very dark-skinned man, who stood 6' 2", was dressed in his full Army green uniform, green saucer hat with the gold oak leaves, all his ribbons, and more importantly his gold oak leaves of Major.

Dad, who cut a very imposing figure, followed us on the bus and told the white bus driver, "I'm going to follow the bus because my son told me you let some boys call him a 'nigger' yesterday, and you didn't do anything about it. I want you to put a stop to it. I've told my son he can hit anyone that calls him a nigger."

He gave the bus driver a hard look daring him to disagree, and stormed off the bus and strode back to our car. I was so proud of my dad at that moment.

The driver looked worried but didn't say anything as the bus pulled away from the house, and my father pulled in behind to follow the bus all the way to the school. He drove our mint-green Chrysler Newport, resembling a green prehistoric predator as it smoothly rolled behind the bus. I could see the car through the emergency doors at the back of the bus. I craned my neck every few minutes to make sure he was still back there, and drew some comfort from being able to see him following right behind us.

Previously, I had sat by the window on the inside of the seat; this time I sat on the aisle, so I had a better shot at hitting someone if I had to. When we got to their bus stop, the three boys got on the bus and just like the day before, the biggest one said with that nasally accent, "Hey nigger what're you doing on my bus?"

The white school bus driver turned around to say something, because he knew Dad followed close behind, and he knew he might get in trouble for not saying something to the white boy.

Before the bus driver could say anything, I stood up, balled up my right fist and hit that white boy with all the frustration, anger, and every other emotion that had built up over the past year and half from taking all that abuse from those Jewish kids at P.S. 169 to being called a nigger by these little rednecks. I hit that boy in the face and knocked him to the floor of the bus. His brothers stood there stunned.

"Don't call me that again!" I yelled at him. I didn't feel it until later, but, wow, that hurt my hand! But nothing felt better. I had finally defended myself and life wouldn't be the same again.

"Sit down," the bus driver said to me, and helped the white boy up from the floor. He looked at the other two brothers and said, "Go sit down," and pointed to the back of the bus.

They didn't say anything, and quietly went to their seats following the direction of the bus driver. Everyone on the bus was dumbfounded, and Cecilia sat frozen in her seat. The bus driver helped the third brother to a seat in the back and got behind the wheel and started the bus to continue the route. Dad never got out of the car. When we got to school, Dad parked his car and walked over to the bus to see what happened.

Dad climbed onto the bus after most of the students had departed and asked, "What happened? I saw one boy that looked like he had a busted lip." He looked at me.

"Yeah, your son hit one those boys when he called him a nigger," the bus driver said as he looked around. "That boy's a little retarded, and is always causin' trouble, so he deserved what happened to him." The bus driver looked at me with a little admiration, "Your son done good, sir. You should be proud of him."

"Are you okay?" Dad looked at me again.

"Yeah, I'm fine." Dad escorted me from the bus to my classroom and told Mrs. Pritchard what happened as well. That was a heck of a way for Dad to meet my new teacher. Dad then went to the principal's office to inform them of what happened and spoke to Mrs. Winters. I didn't get in trouble from Dad. I think he was proud of me, and I didn't get into trouble with the school or that boy's parents. Strangely, I never heard of that incident again; nor did those boys ever bully me or call me "nigger" again.

At the tender age of eight years old, in the fifth grade, I had learned to fight and gained some of my own self-respect in the process.

I finally fought back.

CHAPTER 5

Self-Respect

Successful people are successful because they are confident in their ability to accomplish their goals. One of those keys to personal success is self-respect, knowing yourself, being comfortable with yourself and striving to be better. I had been a cocky little kid coming out of Whittier. I was smart, athletic, and popular with my classmates at school. I felt good about myself and thought I could do anything.

In contrast, my experiences in New York helped to eat away at how I felt about myself. Those kids succeeded in making me feel like less of a person, and in response, I developed a protective shell that caused me to be distrustful of people and their motives; more caustic in my comments to people; more defensive in my response to people; and much more introverted.

Baseball and bowling helped as far as my belief in my physical abilities amongst my peers, but still didn't solve the issues at school. The one-sided fight on the bus helped to move me forward as far as my self-perception as a victim. I would no longer be a victim, regardless of the circumstances, and I'd stand up for myself to do what it took to carve out a place in whatever situation I found myself. This transformation didn't happen overnight but began on that second morning bus ride to Cambridge Elementary School in Belton.

My classmates, none of whom were on the bus, found out I had decked that kid on the bus. A few asked me about it, and I told them that I had hit the kid because he called me a "nigger." This was long before the politically correct term of "the 'N-word'" became a popular way of saying "nigger" without offending anyone. No, I just said, "Nigger." My classmates, all uniformly bigger than me, got the message. I was never again called "nigger" by anyone in my class or at the school, at least not to my face. I earned their respect by sticking up for myself and knocking the crap out that little white boy.

Every day we had a physical education period, something unheard of in New York. In New York we had music period, or recess or lunch, but not P.E. During P.E. at Cambridge we engaged in various activities such as square dancing;

running various distances; playing various games and sports. Albeit October, it was still warm, and we played co-ed softball, the girls with the boys. I had played T-ball and baseball, but not softball, and I was not experienced with slow pitching. Inexplicably, I had a unique knack for pitching slow pitch softball and because of my baseball experience, excelled at the rest of the game. After a while, I became one of the first picked when we chose teams once everyone found out I could pitch, hit, and field. I became more than just the "token" or the class "mascot," I was a popular player on the softball field. I loved it.

Everyone also played basketball, a sport I had never played. One day, within a few weeks after my arrival and advent at the school, my mother had a parent-teacher conference with Mrs. Pritchard. And since she dragged me up to the school, and left me outside, I had nothing to occupy my time. One of my classmates, who they cruelly called "Bubble Butt" because of his kind of big round butt and the way he walked, sort of a rolling gait with his butt sticking out, was out shooting hoops after school. His real name was Brian and he'd always seemed like an okay guy. He was kind of chubby, but not really fat, and several inches taller than me. He had brown hair that fell over his eyes as he dribbled the ball, and had a face full of freckles. He wore jeans, gray sweatshirt with the sleeves cut off, and high-topped black tennis shoes. He brought his own ball to practice with at the school, and was dribbling and shooting all over the court. He looked pretty good playing out there, as if he knew what he was doing. I stood on the side of the court watching when he called over to me and asked what I was doing at the school.

"My mom is meeting with Mrs. Pritchard." I said.

"Well, she'll probably be in there for a while, so you want to play?"

"Sure, but I really don't know how."

"C'mon, I'll teach you how to play."

"Okay." My first lesson in basketball would be administered by a white kid… how ironic.

He showed me how to hold the ball, how to pass the ball, and how to dribble the ball. Finally, he showed me how to shoot the ball. A mere eight years old, and not very tall or strong, I shot the ball in the direction of the basket with maximum effort, and didn't even hit the hoop. But, I had fun out there and we played for about an hour while Mom remained inside with Mrs. Pritchard. Thus began my love for street basketball and awakened my desire to get better at every aspect of the game.

Inside, unbeknownst to me, Mrs. Pritchard voiced her concerns to Mom about my behavior, inattentiveness during class, and my poor scores on the Iowa Basic Skills Test.

One of the things I couldn't get used to was the Missouri accent. That nasally "New Yawker" way of talking, and the much faster pace of New York speech was my norm. Here, the people spoke slower, with a southern accent that took some getting used to. In my opinion, it had the effect of making them seem less intelligent, and I really didn't pay much attention to the teacher.

Anyone who spoke with that type of accent couldn't have much to teach me; and unfortunately, because they lagged behind the New York school system, the class covered material I covered the year before. I found it all boring, and brought books to class and read while Mrs. Pritchard conducted her lessons. In her attempts to trip me up, she asked me questions about the material and I would always answer correctly, which really frustrated her. There wasn't much she could say except, "Put down that book and pay attention." I would put it down for a bit, but pick it back up when I got bored, which was most of the time.

Ostensibly, the reason Mrs. Pritchard called my mother was due to my scores on the Iowa Basic Skills Test; a standardized, multiple-choice, and timed test administered every year to determine the progress of students in grade school.

I had always done extremely well on such tests, and for that reason I was eight years old in the fifth grade. That was something else Mrs. Pritchard had concerns about. Mom later told me how the conversation went with my teacher.

"Mrs. Pittard, I think you may want to consider putting Chris back in the fourth grade." Mrs. Pritchard began the conversation with that show-stopper.

"Why would you say that?" Mom said.

"I think he's too young for the fifth grade. I have the results of the Iowa Basic Skills Test right here, and Chris did not answer one single question."

"You mean he didn't get any answers correct?" Mom asked with some incredulity. She knew I'd done extremely well on such tests and it was almost inconceivable to her I hadn't gotten any answers correct.

"No, I mean he didn't answer any of the questions." Mrs. Pritchard reiterated.

"Let me see that," Mom demanded, and reached for the test results.

Mrs. Pritchard handed over the blank Scan Tron sheet to my mother and waited for Mom's response. Mom checked to see if it had my name on top.

"This is unbelievable," Mom exclaimed. "He's never done this before."

"Well, I saw him doing the work, and even using a piece of paper to work out the math problems, but he didn't make any marks on the Scan Tron, as you can see."

As many will undoubtedly attest, in order to get credit for a correct answer, you actually have to darken the circle of the multiple choice answer you select on the computer-fed Scan Tron sheet; and each answer has to be darkened in completely in order to get credit for the answer. I had failed to mark any of my answers; so apparently, in Mrs. Pritchard's eyes, I was some sort of moron.

"What can we do about this?" Mom asked.

"He can retake the test tomorrow, and based on his results, we will make an assessment as to what grade he should be placed in." Mrs. Pritchard stated with some finality.

"Okay, Christan will retake the test tomorrow and I'll make sure he knows to fill in the circles on the Scan Tron." Mom had no concerns about my ability to perform well on the test. But, If I failed again, I would be put back in the fourth grade. Huh, no pressure at all.

While I was outside playing basketball with good ol' Bubble Butt, and having a great time, Mom and Mrs. Pritchard determined my fate for the next year.

The next day I took the test for the second time, and this time, based on my mother's stern advice, I made sure I marked my Scan Tron appropriately. And yeah, I passed it at a higher grade level. I passed the reading at the seventh grade level and the math at the sixth grade level. In other words, as I had shown in class, I was more advanced than my pedestrian classmates who remained mired in the red mud of the Missouri school system. Mrs. Pritchard, much to her chagrin I'm sure, had no choice but to keep me in her class.

Unfortunately, my advanced levels of reading and math did not translate into great grades. I think I was so bored I really didn't try very hard and that just drove Mom crazy. Maybe I was getting back at her for that humiliating experience from my previous fifth grade class. She kept giving me the "You know you can do the work if you try, so if you want good grades you have to try" speech.

I really didn't care at that point, so I continued to get lower grades. I preferred to play basketball and softball; and away from school, touch football, bowling, and hanging out with friends my age on the base.

One of the other activities I did not participate in while we lived in Missouri was Cub Scouts. Mom found out who the troop leader was for the Cub Scouts for the officer's kids and introduced me. I attended one meeting of the troop, but there was a wrongness to the vibe I got from the other Cub Scouts. This troop, exclusively made up of officer's kids, was all white. Because of the lack of Black officers at RGAFB, I was the only Black kid at the meeting. I felt like an outsider and decided not to participate in scouting that year. I never went back to scouting. Instead, Dana and I found other outlets for our desire to hunt and explore.

⬦   ⬦   ⬦

One of the things that we did extensively, particularly after the Christmas of 1966, when Dana and I got our high-rise handle bar, leopard-skinned banana-seat, really-cool, bronze Stingray bikes, was to "patrol" around the base. On Saturdays during the school year, and all the time during the summer, we gathered our "essential" supplies, and filled our canteens full of Kool-Aid. We learned our lessons from Fort Totten and prepared ourselves like Tommy. We procured little pocket knives, ropes, mini-binoculars, and magnifying glasses from junk sales at the school. We even out-did Tommy's stuff because we now had walkie-talkies, and toy rifles from our birthdays and Christmas, and anything else we could think of that made sense to boys between eight and ten years old. We still had our Army surplus backpacks, so we looked the part. Once we got loaded up on our supplies, we bid Mom goodbye and went to explore the base.

She said, "Be careful," of course, and we would take off. Dana and I had great fun just riding all over post, from the creeks to the airfield to watch the huge cargo transport planes take off and land, and watch the fighter jets as they came in as graceful as swans landing on a placid lake. We went over to the golf course to check out the ponds for frogs, crawfish and turtles, which, if we caught any of them, would proudly bring them home to our mother. She really dreaded us returning with our prizes.

We got to know the base like the backs of our hands and used to plan "missions" to accomplish on our patrols. We "reconned" various sites, like the big blockhouse where Dad worked, or the airfield, and various other structures around the base, and plan on how we would attack them if given the opportunity. We planned ambushes of military vehicles as they passed by and imagined ourselves at war with the military personnel on post. At times, we pretended we were evading the MPs, and on occasion, based on our location, we actually had to evade some of the military police.

There was a pasture, either on base or immediately adjacent to the boundary of the base with several head of cattle. One fine summer day we decided to jump the barbed-wire fence surrounding the pasture, taunt the cattle, and maybe taunt a bull or two. Yeah, I know, not very bright, but we were young and watched way too much *Combat!* You know, the 1960s-era World War II television show starring Vic Morrow. We loved that show and tried to emulate some of the actions of the men during our patrols.

We scaled the barbed-wire fence fairly easily and ran through the pasture avoiding the "cow patties" that permeated the ground, and had fun yelling and screaming at the cows. After a few minutes, someone came out of the barn area and yelled at us and threatened to call the MPs if we didn't leave his property. We sort of ignored him until we saw a MP car ease up to the far end of the pasture, opposite from where we had hidden our bikes. Once we saw the MPs pull up we knew we had to get out, and quick. We ran to the barbed-wire fence closest to our bikes and scrambled over the fence. Unfortunately, I was not as graceful going back over as I had been getting in earlier. I cut open a pretty deep gash in my left palm that started bleeding pretty heavily. I screamed in pain, and started to cry. But my sense of self-preservation prevailed and I got over that darn fence!

Once we got to the little glen where we had hidden our bikes, and we were out of sight from the farmer and the MPs, Dana came over and looked at the gash in my hand. Once he saw how badly it was bleeding, he looked in his backpack and grabbed a little first-aid kit that we carried with us. We tried to clean the wound as well as possible in that little wooded area and wrapped some gauze and first-aid tape around it. But it continued to bleed. We dreaded having to tell Mom what happened.

She wasn't happy, but relieved nothing worse had happened than a cut hand. She took us to the base hospital emergency room, where the nurse clucked over the wound and the doctor decided it needed stitches. That was like major surgery to me. I gritted my teeth as they cleaned out the wound, and stuck me with a needle about the length of my arm to administer a local anesthetic so they could sew up my hand. They also stuck me with another needle for a tetanus shot to guard against infection because I cut my hand on a rusty barbed-wire fence. I watched the procedure with a clinical detachment and saw the doctor use this little special needle with a special plastic thread in a cross-stitch pattern.

I wasn't nervous once he started and it didn't hurt, so I found it easy to watch him do his work. With stiches in place, the doctor congratulated me on being a "brave boy" and sent us on our way.

I had survived a rather harrowing experience. My self-respect continued to grow with each new experience in and out of school.

The summer of 1967 we spent a month in Philadelphia with my grandparents, and more importantly, that summer we learned how to swim, finally.

CHAPTER 6

Swimming and Cycling

In the spring of 1967, during Spring Break, Dad had gone on temporary duty to Fort Bliss, and on this occasion brought the family along. During our visit, the Caros—long-time friends of the family—invited us to their house. Their daughter, Becky, a pretty girl that I had fallen in love with at the age of five, was my idea of the prettiest girl alive. A brown-skinned beauty, with dark eyes and straight black hair, and at 11, already developing curves. She and her family visited us the previous year in Missouri, in their really cool Jaguar XKE, and we were returning the favor. Becky, even though one year older, had been the first girl I ever kissed, so, you know, I was in love.

Becky, like many young girls, liked to be impressed, and Dana and I tried our best to impress. Unfortunately, we weren't that successful on that trip. First, when we rode her bike, we tried to show off our skills in doing "wheelies," at her behest, on her long-lined Schwinn bicycle. She challenged us to do a wheelie on her bike, although she never attempted one. For the uninitiated, a "wheelie" is the art of raising the front wheel or tire of the bicycle so that the rider is riding only on the back tire or wheel. The point of a wheelie competition is to see how long the rider can ride on the back tire or wheel. That is a real art. We tried our best, but we couldn't manage to get that front wheel off the ground. Up to that time, we hadn't really attempted to do wheelies on bikes. That was something you saw on TV, and we hadn't mastered that particular skill. Our complete lack of ability in that area apparently greatly amused Becky and she had a great laugh at our expense; my first embarrassing moment in front of a girl. Well, it wouldn't be the last, not even the last that day.

The second time came after dinner when she asked us to go swimming in their backyard pool.

The Caros had a beautiful two-story house in a very nice area of El Paso called Cielo Vista. Their house was the first we had seen with its own pool. It was a beautiful kidney-shaped pool with a spring diving board at the deep end. After dinner, Becky invited us out to the pool. She had some extra swim trunks, so we went out to the pool with some trepidation. Once we got out to the poolside patio, we stripped down to our borrowed trunks and walked to the shallow end of the pool. We gingerly walked down the pure-white concrete steps into the cool water. The weather in early April was really nice and warm. As Dana and I dipped our toes in the shallow end, Becky went to the deep end, and cleanly dove off the diving board into the pool. We were amazed that she could dive into the pool that well and were further amazed as she swam effortlessly to the shallow end of the pool to talk to us. I was most amazed by how good she looked, at almost 12 years old, in her bikini. Wow, she was really cute in that bathing suit. I had a crush on Becky for most of my young life. Yeah, I had it bad at 10 going on 11. Dana had just turned 8, and we were out of our league socially. What a crushing blow to our egos as we watched Becky flit around the pool like some young water nymph. She seemed so comfortable in the water, as comfortable as we felt uncomfortable.

I hadn't gotten over my fear of deep water and putting my face in the water, and Dana hadn't even attempted to learn how to swim. We were so humiliated, as only young boys can be in front of a pretty, popular, older girl. Dana and I looked at each other and the same thought passed through our minds at the same time, never again.

We voiced that sentiment by promising ourselves that when we got back to Missouri we would master the art of performing wheelies with our high-end bikes, and learn how to swim like fish, even better than Becky. We needed to restore our self-esteem and self-respect. We couldn't live this down, and we pledged not to see Becky again until we mastered those skills.

✧   ✧   ✧

As soon as we got back to Richards-Gebauer we started learning how to perform wheelies. While talking to some of our friends, we realized that part of the secret rested with the bike itself. The longer the frame of the bike, the more difficult to raise the front wheel off the ground. In El Paso, we used the longer Schwinn bike to try to show off our lack of wheelie skills. In Missouri, we had the shorter-framed Stingray banana seat bikes with the y-shaped handle bars, ideal for "popping" wheelies. We made it a neighborhood competition with our friends, Gary—who we nicknamed "Der Wiener Schnitzel," and George Sevier, to see who could learn how to pop wheelies first and best.

I won that competition. I figured out by process of elimination that the slower I rode my bike, the easier to raise the front wheel. In El Paso we rode the bike too fast, and based on the physics of the weight of the rider, and the inertia of the bike, it made it more difficult to raise the front wheel. I employed an innovative way of raising the front wheel of the bike. I used the edge of the entrance to our driveway with the slight hump to help lift the front wheel of the bike. As I rode the front wheel against the slight bump I would lift up the front wheel by pulling back on the handle bars. I felt exhilarated the first time I got that front wheel off the ground and rode several feet on the back wheel of the bike! Oh yeah! Take that Becky!

Once I had perfected that technique, the other three guys began to imitate me. As they struggled to perfect that technique, I worked on raising the front wheel without the aid of the driveway bump. I finally accomplished that feat by riding my bike almost at "stall" speed and then pulling back on the handle bars as hard as I could. Wow! I felt like I had defied gravity and was floating in mid-air! It felt great! I popped a wheelie without the crutch of the driveway bump, and was able to keep the wheelie going for several yards. The other guys looked on in amazement.

Once I had figured out the method, I showed everyone how to do it, and within a few days we popped wheelies at will. As we worked on perfecting the technique we were able to pop wheelies in unison, and in formation. That was pretty, to see the four of us popping wheelies on command and keeping our bikes up in the wheelie position for several yards in a slow-motion formation, almost like the famous Air Force Thunderbirds performance team. Dana and I had mastered doing wheelies. One task down, one to go.

Running concurrent with our efforts to learn how to do wheelies were our plans to learn how to swim. As soon as we got back to RGAFB, we pestered our Mom to find out how we could take swimming lessons on base and when was the earliest we could start. She was both surprised and pleased at our persistence to learn how to swim, since we really hadn't shown much interest even though she had suggested it the year before. Nothing like being embarrassed in front of a pretty girl to motivate young boys! But she didn't know that; all she knew was we wanted to learn how to swim in the worst way. And thanks to her, our training would begin the week after the school year ended.

The base had two large pools, one at the Officer's Club, and the other located near the center of the base. The Officer's Club pool was reserved for the military officers and their families and the larger base pool was for everyone's use.

The swimming lessons were to be held at the larger base pool, and they began the Monday after school let out for the summer. Dana and I were ready. Scared, but ready. We were determined to see this through and become one with the water.

On that Monday morning the sun broke out in a crisp and clear blue sky. Lessons began at 8 o'clock in the morning, and Mom drove us over to the pool. I had never been to this pool before and I was impressed by its size. It was an Olympic-sized pool, 50 yards long and about half as wide with eight swimming lanes marked by black lines painted on the bottom of the pool.

On the far side of the pool, at the deep end, were two diving boards, a "low dive" or one-meter board, and the "high dive" or three-meter board. I couldn't imagine myself on either board, but it was exciting to see.

The morning was cool, and we dreaded getting into the cold water. We were dressed in our little matching swimsuits and tee shirts and had white towels from home. Ironically, these were the same swim suits we had worn at Becky's house. The pool was surrounded by a four-foot chain link fence with a gate near the shallow end. Mom dropped us off and wished us luck as we got out of the car and walked through the chain link gate. We stood there shivering as we watched the car drive off. We were the only Black kids of the twelve or so in the class, but all the kids had that same anticipatory look of dread. This was the first day of two weeks of lessons, each day from Monday through Friday for two weeks. We had two instructors, a young man and woman in their early twenties. Both dressed in red, lifeguard swimsuits and white tee shirts. He was tall, and brown haired, while she was a little over five feet and blonde. They introduced themselves as Luke and Jennifer, or Jenny for short.

The first thing Luke said was, "Everybody line up and get in the pool."

Dana and I took off our tee shirts and dropped them and the towels on one of the beach chairs surrounding the pool.

We lined up next to each other and exchanged looks as if to say, "*This is it,*" and with the other kids, bravely climbed into the chilly water at the shallow end of the pool.

The first lesson of the day required that we get used to putting our faces in the water and holding our breath. I had been through swimming lessons a few years before, so this came easy. Dana handled that part pretty well, as did some of the other kids. At some point, it became obvious that the class had to be divided into two groups—those that would move forward at a faster pace, and all the others. They placed Dana and me in the faster paced group and we moved on to learning how to perform the scissor kick while hanging on to the side of the pool. The first day's lesson ended with us attempting to put our faces in the water and perform the scissor kick at the same time. So far so good, we were ready for the next day.

We looked forward to each day's lesson because each day we learned something new. Like the first time I had taken swimming lessons, the first week I stayed exclusively in the shallow end of the pool as we learned the "Dead Man's Float," which was a technique where we learned to float on our stomach with our faces in the water. Our instructors taught us to move forward in the water with our arms in front of us, faces in the water, and using the scissor kick to propel us across the pool. The fourth day they taught us to dog paddle, and by the fifth day we learned the basic over hand Australian Crawl or freestyle technique. The first week went well, but the deep water lessons, my previous Waterloo, loomed for the following Monday morning.

All that weekend, I wrestled with the thought that on Monday I would be in the deep end, literally. I found it hard to sleep Sunday night. Dana didn't seem to be as worried; then again, he hadn't been thrown into the deep end as I had at Fort Totten. As Monday morning dawned, my stomach roiled and I felt queasy with the thought that today I would be in deep water. As we drove to the pool I felt like I was walking my "last mile" to my own execution, but Dana just chatted happily about going off the deep end. I'm glad someone looked forward to the experience, because I certainly didn't.

When Mom dropped us off I almost cried as she drove away. No turning back now, we were in the advanced class, and it was now or never. The thought of Becky swimming around us, laughing at our inability and fear of swimming in the deep end of her pool kept me moving forward to the deep end of this pool—one of the longest 50 yards I had ever walked. With that thought in mind, I squared my little shoulders and told myself I would get through this and really learn to swim.

The experience this time was significantly different from my previous experience at the deep end. First, Jenny was in charge of our next phase of swimming lessons, so I knew she would not throw me in against my will. When we had all gathered near the lower diving board she told us she wanted us to get into the water and just hang on to the side. And second, I had Dana with me. Side by side, two skinny little Black kids, we got into the water and hung on for dear life.

Once our hands were pried from the side of the pool, the instructor went over what we had learned the week before, but in the deep end of the pool. The scariest maneuver that first day was holding our breath and dropping to the bottom of the nine-foot deep area. Nothing felt as good as coming up out of the water and breathing that first great big gulp of air! Once we overcame that fear of going down to the bottom, we began swimming back and forth across the pool using the freestyle technique. That first day in the deep end was great! Not only had we survived, we actually began to like swimming in the deep end.

The next two days we concentrated on learning to tread water in the deep end and to continue perfecting our freestyle technique. Treading water became easier once I understood the concept of *economy of movement* to keep my head above water. I developed a rhythm to moving my arms in a kind of butterfly pattern and my legs like I rode a bicycle. Fast enough to keep my head above water, but slow enough to conserve energy. Economy of movement. Learning to tread water probably became the most important skill of all.

The fourth day she taught us a new technique—diving from the edge of the pool. Yeah, that was pretty awkward, trying to get in a position with your hands sort of in front of your face, arms outstretched, knees bent, head down, to propel yourself in some fashion out into the pool.

That first time was scary because you had to orient yourself in the water after the dive, and swim to the edge. To prepare us for that part of the exercise, the instructor taught us to jump from the side of the pool down to the bottom, and then, again propel ourselves up to the surface and swim to the edge. That became so much fun, that we didn't want to get into diving. But diving was fun also and made us feel like real swimmers.

The final day consisted of three parts. Part one, *jump* off the one-meter diving board. A piece of cake! Part two, *dive* off the one-meter board. Not too bad, a little higher than the side of the pool, but doable and even enjoyable. Part three, and oh my god, *jump off the three-meter board!* They made it optional, but Dana and I egged each other on and decided we could to do it, as sort of a climactic graduation to our successful swimming lessons.

Jenny called out our names, and we climbed the ladder. We had been watching the previous few kids climb up the ladder and gingerly walk to the end of the board and jump. Some of them held their noses as they jumped, some just jumped. One little girl ran to the end of the board and jumped out as far as she could. That was impressive!

I didn't know if I could do that, but she embarrassed us into getting up the ladder. As I looked up, it seemed to be miles in the air; and as I began to climb up the ladder ahead of Dana, each rung seemed to be three feet apart from each other, and the ladder endless. As I continued to climb, my muscles seemed to tighten up and it became more difficult to keep a hold of the railing and climb the ladder. The higher I climbed, the more difficult to look down. With Dana right below me, I had to continue to climb or be embarrassed by crawling back down a coward. After what seemed an interminable period of time, I finally reached the top of the ladder where the railing was larger and rainbow-shaped.

I climbed up on the rear edge of the diving board and felt the rough surface of the board on the bottom of my feet. I tried to stand up, but it felt more comfortable to crawl to the edge of the board, but again, that would have been humiliating, as everybody watched from below, and Dana from below the rear edge of the board. I tentatively stood up on the board, and everything looked to be miles down. To the left I saw the poolside area, and in front and directly below, blue water, shimmering in the bright morning sun. It looked inviting and frightening at the same time.

As I stood there, Jenny said, "Okay Chris, your turn to jump!"

Oh no, this was it! I had to move forward on the board and jump. My heart raced, and my palms sweated, but I continued to walk forward to the edge of the board. The water looked so far down, and I seemed so high in the air. I saw everyone's face peering up at me. I stole one last look at Dana behind me, who had made it all the way to the top of the rear edge of the board and appeared ready to follow when I jumped. Both of us couldn't be on the board at the same time, so I had to jump. I could hardly breathe. I looked down, then out over the pool and just stepped off the board.

"Aaaahhhh!" I yelled all the way down and held my breath before I hit the water with a big splash. The next thing I knew my feet hit the bottom of the pool and I reflexively bent my knees and shot up to the surface of the water and opened my mouth for a big gulp of air. I made it!

I swam over to the edge of pool where the instructor waited, and she congratulated me on my jump. I looked up at Dana and he looked down with an expression of pride.

"Your turn Dana!" I yelled up at him.

"Okay!" He yelled, and took one big step and fearlessly jumped out over the water.

Dana had a much better jump than mine. He successfully came up out of the water and swam to the side where I waited at the edge.

We were both laughing and having a good time when Jenny asked, "You guys want to go up again?"

"Yeah!" We said in unison, and bounded out of the pool to jump off the high dive board again. In fact, we jumped off the high dive several times that day, and even dove off the high dive, overcoming both our fear of heights and deep water. When that last lesson concluded Luke and Jenny gave us nice little cards with the American Red Cross symbol that proved we had successfully graduated from the ARC Certified Course. Having that card allowed us to go to the RGAFB main pool and Officer's Club pool without our parents. Becky here we come!

✧ ✧ ✧

With my baseball season somewhat curtailed in 1967 because of the injury to my hand, the league still designated me as an all-star little leaguer that year and every other year I played in Missouri. I made it as an all-star at shortstop, third base, and second base. When it came to competing against my peers, I was always extremely competitive. My performance on the baseball field proved that. As an experiment, my dad, the coach, started training me as a pitcher, and that's how I ended the 1968 season. During that same season, one of the teams in the league, the White Sox, broke up and the players were farmed out to other teams. Our team, the Yankees, got one of three brothers. Yep, those same three brothers. The one I'd knocked to the floor of the bus ended up on my team. Dad needed someone for me to pitch to in practice and this kid became my catcher in practice. The irony was not lost on me or Dad.

CHAPTER 7

Catchin' Critters

The rest of the 1967 summer beckoned to us, as we began the process of becoming better swimmers and divers. We swam every day we weren't playing baseball. We stayed in the water and became a fixture at the Officer's Club pool. Now confident in our ability to swim in the deep end, dive off both heights of the diving boards; with the credentials to prove it, and experts at popping wheelies, we were ready to beat Becky at her own game!

We spent the rest of the summer improving on all those skills and exploring the base. We also became adept at hunting and killing frogs, and capturing snapping turtles, and crayfish, or as they're called in various parts of the country, "crawfish" or "crawdads."

We had a couple of friends, George and Jimmy who liked to go with us to hunt these various amphibious creatures. George, a blond kid, with freckles and walked pigeon-toed, had a really fine-looking fourteen-year old sister. Jimmy, a skinny little guy, with dark hair and a pointed nose, whose dad was the Provost Marshal for the base, was from Louisiana, and spoke like he was from backwoods Louisiana. He really knew his way around creeks and ponds when it came to hunting frogs, turtles and crawdads. Yeah, I guess we had a habit of hanging out with the provost marshal's kids wherever we went, but they seemed to know more about doing stuff in the woods, and that made them fun to hang out with.

When we all got together to go hunting for swamp critters we had different stuff in our backpacks, like small fishnets for the crawfish, bigger nets for the turtles, along with long sticks or poles, and sharpened sticks for the frogs. Some of the time we would try to capture the frogs, and other times we would try to "gig 'em," a polite way of saying stabbing them to death, rather than capturing them.

We hunted in the several creeks that flowed through the base, along with the ponds at the golf course, which were rumored to not only have the biggest bullfrogs, crawfish and turtles, but also the mythical alligator or two. The other ponds, bordered by the aforementioned pastures with the cattle, were more accessible. In fact, those ponds fed the creeks and the water supply for the cattle, so when we went to those ponds, we were right up against the base boundary.

On a typical summer day, we would load up our backpacks with the requisite equipment when hunting "critters" in the various waterways around the base. We used to watch a lot of *The Beverly Hillbillies* and *The Andy Griffith Show*, and were pretty familiar with the concept of hunting and capturing "swamp critters" like these. We also knew they could be eaten, but Mom wouldn't consider cleaning, cooking and eating our catches of frogs, crawfish and turtles. We'd hunt them earlier in the morning or later in the evening because our research and folklore told us those would be the times when they might be most active and easier to catch.

On a typical day, we scouted the most likely spots to catch one of the three. Sometimes, we saw crawfish just sort of crawling along the bottom of the creek, and we'd stay there long enough to try to catch as many as possible. If they had an inkling of danger, the little buggers would quickly dart away. We had to be patient.

One way to catch crawfish was to use a small fish net on a slim metal handle to quickly dip the net into the water before the crawfish knew it was there and started running. Unfortunately, you had to be very quick with the net or you would catch nothing but water and air. The most reliable method of catching crawfish one at a time was with your hands. Of course, that required really quick reflexes to anticipate where the crawfish would run and get your hand in the water with fingers open and then be able to quickly close your hand over the targeted crawfish. You also had to have your body in a position to be close enough to the water to stick your hand in the water without falling in. Most of the time we'd lie prone next to the creek close enough to see down into the water to discern the little creatures' hiding place. Usually, the water stayed clear and made it easy to see where the crawfish hid or swam or crawled along. Sometimes they might be under rocks and you could barely see their tails or claws, or they might be hiding under the darkness of a shadow in the water.

We waited quietly until we saw them crawling to an ideal position where we could shoot our hands into the water and grab one. Not an easy task with these quick little buggers. And as soon as you tried to grab one, the silt and mud at the bottom of the creek would get stirred up and mask where they had gone. You had to be quick and sure when grabbing for one of them. Of course, with the larger ones, you had to be careful of their claws, because, like little lobsters, they could cause some painful injuries to smaller hands. You had to be certain when you grabbed one. I tended to use my right hand, my dominant hand, and I had the most confidence in catching crawfish with that hand. Sometimes we used diversions to herd the crawfish into position. As an example, we might drop a "dirt clod" into the water on one end of a section of the creek and frighten the crawfish into either the little fish nets or our hands. Most of the time I was pretty successful in catching crawfish.

On one occasion, as I shot my hand into the water, I slashed the top of my middle finger on my right hand against a sharp underwater rock where I saw several crawfish crouching. That was painful and bloody, and required another trip to the ER to get it sewn up with a few stitches and another tetanus shot for possible infections and bacteria in the water. Yuck! I think Mom was getting used to taking us to the ER with our minor cuts and abrasions. A consequence of growing up, learning the ways of the woods, and catching edible critters.

On other occasions, when we hunted frogs, we resorted to other methods to catch or gig 'em. Frogs usually hung out along the banks of the creeks and ponds, hidden by the brushes along the banks, under the hanging roots, and cuts in the bank above the water for quick access to the water.

When the frogs heard us coming they all jumped into the water in unison, like there was a bull frog alarm or something. So, we had to resort to sneaking up on them in order to capture or kill them.

One way was to use these little binoculars we'd picked up at a school-sponsored yard sale. They were 5x-power lenses that came in a flat black case that opened up into binoculars that adjusted for better viewing. They were probably good to about 100 yards, and plenty good enough for our purposes. We wanted to be able to see the frogs before they jumped into the water, so we would focus on their croaking to pinpoint their location. At the golf course, it was actually easier to slip up on the frogs because the rough area around the pond was still a lot better than the wild undergrowth, rough terrain, and other obstacles that lay in our path near the more natural ponds and creeks.

At the golf course, we resorted to getting on our stomachs and low crawling towards the croaking that identified the positions of the frogs. When we got closer we jumped up and threw our larger nets over the frogs before they could jump into the water. We were successful about half the time. The other half of the time we watched the frogs leap into the water and swim away using their natural "frog stroke" to get as far away from us as possible. Well, that tended to be bad luck for the frogs, because that's when we would pull out the sharp sticks and would try to gig 'em in the water. Yeah, I know, extremely cruel, but that was what we did if we couldn't catch them on land. We weren't always successful at gigging them either, and sometimes they got away altogether. Lucky them.

Despite our frustration at not capturing the frogs or gigging them, it was always fun to watch them swim in the ponds and creeks. In fact, from watching our favorite cartoon series, *Jonny Quest*, and various war movies and shows, and watching how these frogs moved in the water, Dana and I started working on our underwater swimming techniques. By the end of the summer, we had developed a pretty fair imitation of what we called the "frog stroke" involving pushing away the water in front of us to either side with our hands and kicking our legs away from each other like huge frogs under the water. Another skill added to our repertoire of swimming and diving. Yeah, take that Becky!

Turtles were a different matter altogether. Larger and more ornery than either frogs or crawfish, the snapping turtles would actually fight back, so they had to be handled carefully. You couldn't just grab them from the side of the pond or creek, you had to use sticks with hooks and larger nets to capture turtles of any decent size, and you normally couldn't do it by yourself, it had to be a team effort. In our case, we would first have to figure out where the turtles hung out in the pond or creek.

The creeks were shallow, and it was fairly easy to see the turtles underwater. We'd lay our nets in the water ahead of the turtle's direction of travel and use the longer sticks to herd the turtle into the net. Once the turtle crawled onto the net, we'd lift the net from both sides and capture it. These tended to be somewhat smaller, maybe eight to ten inches in diameter, and could fit into a large ice cooler. The bigger turtles were normally found in the ponds where they could grow to a much larger size because of their age. You could tell a turtle's age by the markings on its shell and the size of the shell. So, the older, bigger turtles could be found in the ponds and were always harder to catch.

We only tried to catch the bigger snappers on a few occasions, and were rarely successful; but, the one time we had success, was pretty exciting.

That day began as a typically warm one, with a few clouds in the sky and the sun shining bright. We gathered on the far side of the bigger pond, over by the pasture, the pond where we'd had a lot of success hunting larger crawfish, and frogs, as well as turtles. Jimmy wanted to go after the bigger turtles and came prepared. He opened up his backpack and began pulling these overall-looking things out and put them on. I'd never seen those before, but they resembled rubberized overalls with boots built into them, a kind of olive drab color.

"What are those?" I asked.

"My waders, I use them when we go fly fishing." Jimmy replied in his nasally accent.

"What are they used for?" Dana asked.

"We like to get in the water to do the fly fishing and we use the waders to go in the streams and creeks to fish." Jimmy answered.

"Okay, so why do you have them on today?" Dana persisted.

"We're gonna catch one of them big suckers today!" Jimmy exclaimed.

"So, how do those things help?" Dana insisted. He was getting annoying.

"We're going out in the pond and grab one!" Jimmy said with some exasperation.

Dana and I looked at each other, the same thought going through our heads, *We're not going in the water. We'll let the crazy white boy do that.*

So I verbalized, "Umm, I don't think so. I think we'll stay here on the bank."

"What, are you chicken?" Jimmy taunted.

"Begawk!" I made a noise and flapped my arms like a chicken.

"Okay, okay," he said, "I'll go out in the water and you guys stay here. I'll take the net with me and if I can it get over a turtle, you guys pull it to the bank, okay?"

"Yeah, we can do that." Dana grinned.

Jimmy continued to put the waders on over his jeans, and when he finished, he unwrapped the larger net from the seat on his bike and gave it to me. Dana and I unfurled it so Jimmy could take it out in the water.

"How do you know where the turtles are out there?" I asked.

Jimmy shrugged his shoulders, "I figured I'd just wade out there and scare 'em up to the surface and just grab one."

"Well," I said, "maybe there's a better way?"

"Like what?" Jimmy asked.

"Well, don't turtles have to come up for air? Why don't we wait until one of them comes up or shows itself and then grab it?" I explained.

"Yeah, that sounds like a plan," Jimmy said, and Dana agreed.

So, as we had when hunting frogs, we laid out on the bank looking into the water, waiting for a turtle to come to the surface. While we waited, we saw some pretty big crawfish swimming by and resisted grabbing them. Frogs croaked around us and the cicadas sang in the trees. The sun beat down on our backs and after a few minutes we felt like we were baking. The grass around the pond was pretty high, and as we laid in it we could feel the bugs and insects crawling around us. The smell of summer got in our nostrils—you know that mix of dirt, grass, and water only found around ponds and creeks. We loved that smell and inhaled it like an intoxicating fragrance.

Jimmy saw it first, a huge-looking turtle about 20 feet out in the water.

"I'm going after that sucker! Get ready!" He exclaimed.

He jumped up and slithered into the water not to alert the turtle that his executioner lurked nearby. Luckily, where Jimmy waded the water wasn't too deep, and he easily kept his chest above the surface which freed up his arms. The unsuspecting turtle was just minding his own business as Jimmy snuck up behind him. The turtle started to angle towards us and came within about four or five feet of the bank. We stood breathless and wide-eyed on the bank as Jimmy stalked the turtle; and when Jimmy got within a few feet, he threw the net over the turtle. Wow! We'd never seen a turtle react like this one! This turtle started thrashing and tried to dive down into the water.

"Pull the net! Bring him in!" Jimmy yelled.

We had the ropes that connected to the net and started to haul in the turtle. This one fought hard. He rolled over and over in the water, trying to free himself of the net. I was almost afraid to pull the turtle up on the bank because I didn't know what it would do once it got on solid ground. Jimmy followed behind the net encouraging us to pull it out of the water. As it got closer, we realized we didn't have good leverage on the turtle because of the way the ropes were tied to the net. The net needed to be brought under the turtle in order to properly pull it out of the water.

"You need to get the net around him so we can pull him out!" I yelled to Jimmy.

"I ain't getting close to that joker, he's pretty mad!" Jimmy shouted back.

And yeah, you could say that. The turtle snapped his jaws at whatever got near him, and he appeared twice as big as any turtle we had previously captured.

"Let me get out of the water, I can get one of the sticks and maybe I can maneuver him into the net!" Jimmy yelled.

"Okay," I said, "but hurry, he's getting heavy!"

Dana and I struggled keeping this thrashing, snapping devil-turtle in the net. Jimmy leapt out of the water and ran to our bikes and got a fireplace poker he brought for the occasion. Apparently, Jimmy had come prepared for bear. The poker, made of wrought iron, had a sharp point and a hook on it for moving fire-hot logs around in a fireplace. When he got back to the water, he began poking the turtle to try to get it to turn over so we could get a better hold it.

"Where did you get that thing?" I yelled.

"The garage," he answered, and continued pulling at the turtle with the hook part of the poker. With Jimmy's help, the turtle began to turn over. When it turned over, I let go of my side of the net and quickly grabbed another part of the net to get the turtle further into the net and give us better leverage in getting it out of the water. Once we got the turtle further into the net, Jimmy dropped the poker on the ground and grabbed another part of the net.

"Okay, let's pull it out now!" Dana said.

"On the count of three…one…two…three!" Jimmy directed.

We all pulled at one time with a mighty tug, and the net and turtle came out of the water on the bank.

Now what? This thing on the bank was not your typical little cute turtle you keep as a pet. Nope. This mean, snapping, pissed off animal would snap off the arm of an unsuspecting little kid, like us. This monster, almost 18 inches across its back, was spitting mad. Jimmy started poking it in the mouth with the poker to have it snap at it and to feel the force of its snapping jaws.

As it continued to thrash and snap in the net, I yelled, "What are we going to do with it?"

"We can take it home." Jimmy suggested.

"It's not going home with us!" Dana said, and I agreed.

"What do you want me to do, put it back? Doggone it I worked too hard to get this thing out to put it back in!" Jimmy said.

"Hey!" I said, "We worked pretty hard too, but what're you going to do with it? You can't keep it in your house and I don't think your mom would want it in the yard. It's too big."

"Yeah, okay," Jimmy conceded, "You're right; we'll put the sucker back in the water."

All the while the turtle was still kind of pissed, but because we had stopped poking it while we discussed its fate, it sort of quieted down and just looked at us with a quizzical look on its face, like, "Well, what you gonna do?"

We got around it at a safe distance, and began pulling it back towards the water. The turtle didn't fight this time, maybe it sensed the return home. At the bank we ran into a little problem because we had to unfurl the turtle from the net. Although it had stopped fighting, it watched warily and we didn't want to get within range of those snapping jaws. Jimmy hit on the plan to use the poker to get the net off the turtle.

"Hold that end of the net, and I'll pull this part of the net away from the turtle." He said as he orchestrated our efforts.

"Okay," we chorused, and began pulling on our part of the net.

The plan worked pretty well and we began to free the turtle, and it began to struggle to get out of the net. Like the Wicked Witch of the West said in the *Wizard of Oz*, this had to be done "delicately." We didn't want this thing loose on the bank mad at us. So, as it began to struggle, Jimmy used the poker to begin pushing it back towards the water, and then as it got close to the water we pulled the net off and Jimmy pushed it into the water where it landed with a big splash. Dana and I ran to the edge of the water and watched as the biggest, meanest, turtle we had ever caught swam off into the pond. This was great! The highlight of our frog, turtle and crawfish hunting days. We never captured a turtle quite that large again.

All these summertime experiences helped me regain my self-respect. No longer a defenseless victim, I would continue to fight back.

CHAPTER 8

Snooping and Pooping

During the 1966-67 school year, I attended Westover Elementary School as a sixth grader. Westover was a K-6 school, so the sixth graders ruled as the big dogs at the school. We ran the school. Except, of course, in my case I was fairly new, although I knew a few people in the school from the base and from bowling; I hadn't attended the school the previous year as had Dana.

I immediately noticed the lack of overt racism by my classmates and the students in general. We had a 100% population of military kids, and they were a lot more enlightened than their small-town counterparts. A lot of African-American kids attended the school, and many had distinguished themselves on the playing fields.

One of the more interesting developments occurred when Dad ran for PTA president at Westover that year and won. Dad became the guy who ran the parent-teacher association, and may have been the first African-American to do so. Our next door neighborhood, Cecelia's mom, ardently supported and admired my Dad and campaigned ceaselessly on his behalf when he ran for PTA president. Although I came to the school as a new kid, I wasn't an unknown kid. Dana, now a second grader, and my father in charge of the PTA, gave my family a nice foothold at the school.

This represented a different experience for me. Gone was the bullying, taunting and name-calling from the past two years. The students accepted me in the class, even though, again, I was the only Black kid. I did make a couple of good friends, Wayne and Bernard. Wayne, a slender little white guy, wore horn-rimmed glasses, and had a round head with dark brown hair in a bowl haircut. He loved the *Space Ghost* and *Herculoids* cartoons as did I, and we got along famously. Bernard, a new guy to the area, had previously lived in Germany. He looked like he needed friends, and Wayne and I befriended him. Bernard, a large kid, was kind of slow and spoke slower than most kids. He had kind of a big square head, covered with tousled black hair, but was a really good guy to have at your back in tough times.

During that same year, Dana and I met the Smiths, a Black family that had recently arrived at RGAFB. The father, an Air Force captain, had recently married the former Mrs. Scott. The father had two children of his own; Wanda, a few years older than me, and a grade ahead; and Joey, also in the sixth grade with me, and two years older. Then there were her kids; Larry, in the sixth grade with me and also two years older; and Billy, my age, and at least two grades behind me at Westover. Dana and I got along great with Wanda, Joey and Larry, but Billy…that was another story.

I hated Billy as only a nine-year old can hate another nine-year old. Probably because he was just about everything I wasn't. Both cocky and athletic; he could play the guitar; he could play pool; he could bowl better than I could; he was bigger than me; and he could dance. And he always made fun of me, and…I…*hated*…him.

Unfortunately, my parents liked his parents, so we ended up at his house on several occasions. He and his brother Larry had a father who, apparently, would give them whatever they wanted, so they had professional quality guitars, drum sets, a pool table, bowling balls, and electronic equipment. Whenever we went down to their basement we entered their world and I always felt diminished and humiliated. Our parents stayed upstairs and couldn't save us from these guys. Hell, they encouraged us to be around them, probably because they felt we needed to be more seasoned around Black people as part of our education— although we had spent two years in a predominantly Black part of a major urban center in Philly.

Well, I certainly learned I didn't like Black kids from New Jersey. Billy was the original trash talker…all…the…time. He wouldn't let up. He incessantly talked about himself and how much better life was in New Jersey, and how much better he was than me. I wish he had stayed in New Jersey to relieve me of this torture. I hated him. No, really, I can't say it enough…I…*hated*…him.

I'm not sure why I became his personal whipping boy. I didn't see him at school because I was two grades ahead of him, but maybe that was part of it. He had a slightly darker caramel-colored skin color than me, and me being a little, light-skinned boy, with green eyes, maybe that was part of it; or maybe because my Dad outranked his step-father. I don't know, but this kid had it out for me. I…*hated*…him, with all my being. Did I say I *hated* him?

This went on for the 1966-67 school year, and then the following year they thankfully moved away, and I didn't have anything to do with him…ever…

again. But there were two good things that came out of this year-long torture. First, because Dana and I felt so embarrassed we couldn't dance, we begged our mother to show us how to dance. And second, we learned how to play pool. Both these skills would be well utilized later in life, so I have to give credit to Billy for forcing me to learn them. But I still hated him!

As kids, Dana and I were not very big. We were destined for that real late growth spurt, which tended to make us even smaller than our age peers. So we tended to be the butt and target of other kids' jokes and ridicule. Each time we ran into adversity from some kid, we found the fortitude to learn how to beat that kid at whatever they had used to try to humiliate or tease us. In this case, dancing and pool. I wasn't faster than Billy and wasn't as big, but I could compete in other things. I competed in bowling eventually, although he started off better than I did. I worked on my game and practiced whenever I could, so I could compete with him, and that proved to be successful. These important lessons Dana and I would take forward in life. Like James Brown in the *Big Payback*—it starts with the setback, then there's comeback, and finally, the big payback.

At school during that school year it was a different story. Maybe because of my Dad, or because I was more accepted, or because I was getting older, but I began to challenge the rules more than I had in the past. Everyone in my class knew I was the youngest by two years, and initially they treated me like a little kid. But as time went on, I became much more accepted as one of the guys, so I began to hang out more with them. This led to me attempting to push the envelope a little as far as challenging authority and rules. At first it was little things, like sneaking into the girl's bathroom after school had let out—I was just curious at what it looked like, and I went in after school one day. Luckily, there were no girls in there.

During recess or during lunch, Wayne, Bernard and I would sneak back into the building ahead of everyone else—just to see if we could get away with it—and we did. We didn't vandalize anything or cause any property damage, just doing little things that gave us confidence through snooping and pooping. That confidence from the 1966-67 school year translated to the fun Dana and I had during the summer of '67 in our patrolling and pushing the edge on base.

The following year, after the three of us had graduated sixth grade, we reunited at Belton Jr. High School, in the seventh grade. The three of us didn't see each other over the summer of '67, but we quickly got together at Belton JHS.

My seventh grade year I experienced a dichotomy. On the one hand, I had my friends from Westover to hang out with; and on the other hand, Cambridge and other Belton elementary schools fed into Belton JHS, so I was re-exposed to the backwards thinking of these small-town bumpkins. In one particular class I had one white tormentor, Jonesy, a short, chubby blonde kid from one of the other elementary schools that fed into the junior high school. He would make fun of me because I was younger and smaller; and of course because I was the only Black kid in my history and English classes—the classes I shared with him. Luckily, his torment consisted of jokes at my expense, and after a while he became a buzz in the back of my head, like a mosquito you want to swat, but can't quite get to. He was ignorant and I treated him as such and ignored him most of the time. Unfortunately, I couldn't avoid P.E.

This was my first experience where I had to shower and dress in front of my male peers. Again, as in most classes, I was the only African-American. The only class where there was another Black student, Denise, was in my Beginning Art class, a class I shared with Wayne and Bernard. Otherwise, as far as other Black kids, I was on my own, as usual.

In P.E., the instructor was one of the football coaches, a large, redheaded, freckled man with a very deep voice and not much patience for smaller, weaker, kids. When I competed against kids my own age, I did very well, but when matched up against boys maturing at a faster rate, and at least two years older, I didn't stand a chance. That year our physical education included running various distances up to 880 yards, high jumping, broad jumping, doing push-ups, sit-ups, basketball, football, soccer, softball, and wrestling.

I hated P.E. I tried my best, but that wasn't good enough. I got humiliated daily during class, and then humiliated again in the locker room because of my lack of musculature, and penis size. And yeah, guys look and compare, and at that age especially, make fun of those who aren't quite as well-endowed in that department. Of course, my time would come, but at the age of 10, compared to 12 and even 13-year old boys—some of them were pretty stupid, and probably the result of inter-marrying amongst relatives, I mean we *were* in Missouri—I was pretty puny and small. At one point I stopped showering after class, and just went to class smelly and sweaty. I didn't care, I refused to expose myself to that kind of ridicule from these white boys.

Interestingly, Wayne was in the same P.E. class and he suffered from some of the same degradation that I had been subjected. He and I bonded even more, and looked for opportunities to get back at everyone. We included Bernard in our plans because he caught hell too, primarily because he was a little different from many of our classmates. Again, the three of us hung out and planned mischief.

During lunch, students were strictly forbidden to be in the main classroom building. We had two classroom buildings. The smaller one, a one-story building, had the cafeteria. The second, an older two-story building, the main classroom building, and where our first class after lunch, the Beginning Art class, was held. Student hall monitors patrolled the corridors to prevent students from coming into the building during lunch. We didn't really need to get into the building, but we devised ways of getting in during lunch. Sometimes we would bluff our way in depending on who guarded the door or in the hallway. On other occasions we created a diversion with one of us while the others snuck in behind the monitor. Other times, we actually timed their rounds and just boldly snuck into the building while they walked somewhere else, then hid in one of the classrooms until the bell rang for the first period after lunch.

The point of the exercise wasn't necessarily to get into the building for any particular reason; but to challenge the authority keeping us out, and give us the opportunity to plan these little break-ins like little thieves. We weren't always successful getting in. Sometimes we got caught trying to sneak in and told to get out, then they became more vigilant and it was almost impossible to get back in that day. Other days, they had more monitors and it made no sense to even try; but, we had a fifty-percent success rate, and it was fun.

The experience of "snooping and pooping" and planning various "covert" operations to "infiltrate" the school house taught me some valuable lessons on how to penetrate enemy defenses, and how to plan for that kind of operation. Yeah, okay, we weren't conducting a raid behind enemy lines or infiltrating an enemy stronghold, but the basic idea was the same. Who knew that might become important some day?

❖   ❖   ❖

On April 4, 1968, the world came to a stop, and all the hopes and dreams of Black people in America were dashed by a single white assassin's bullet. I had seen protests, marches, sit-ins, and violence against Blacks on TV. I had even seen the Ku Klux Klan marching and burning a cross alongside a dark and lonely Indiana highway on our way to Indianapolis. But the night they murdered

Martin Luther King, Jr., was unlike any other night in my young life.

My parents, like most Black parents, kept us inside that night. Black people rioted across the country expressing their frustration at the system that took away their only hope for equal rights, their Messiah. Blacks put torches to many a neighborhood across the country; shots were fired, and people hurt and killed. Even in Kansas City, the closest large metropolitan area, had its own riots. The next day I saw cars that had bullet holes and heard stories from combat vets from Vietnam about how scary a night it had been in KC.

As I watched his funeral, I thought about everything that MLK had meant to Black people, and how it would affect us going into the future. The idea formulated in my mind that I wanted to do what I could for civil rights, and that's when I thought about being an attorney. That would be my chosen profession at some point. I finally found my calling and what I was going to do in life—the law. I now felt like I had a purpose in life.

❖　❖　❖

As the 1967-68 school year came to a close Dana and I found out Dad had been assigned to another Air Force installation, this time in Corvallis, Oregon.

Oregon?

What's in Oregon? We would travel from the Midwest, right above the Mason-Dixon Line to the far Northwest. I had endured a lot here in Missouri, it had to be better in the far Northwest, right? Right? Well, we were about to find out.

CHAPTER 9

Oregon

We had to find Corvallis, Oregon, on the United States atlas our parents had purchased for the trip. One of the skills my brother and I acquired as military brats was the ability to read road maps and to decipher all the symbols on the maps from the map key and the legend found on every map. We got so good at it that our parents tended to use us as navigators. Not only did that make us feel important, but showed that we actually knew how to do it. I guarantee Dad would not have trusted me to give him directions on a road trip going anywhere if he didn't feel I knew how to navigate.

Dana and I learned how to orient a map using the directions on the map, and comparing them to our location on the highway. We didn't have other landmarks or terrain features to orient the map, only the names of towns, mile markers on the interstate and on the map, intersections, and signs showing upcoming towns.

Dana was nine years old at the time, and would start the fourth grade when we got to Oregon. During that summer Dana was inspired by a *National Geographic* article and picture of General Dwight D. Eisenhower as the Supreme Allied Commander in Europe during World War II. Dana read that article and took it to heart. He had a mission in life—to go to the United States Military Academy at West Point, to eventually become a general, and lead men in combat. Me, I played at being a little soldier, but had no real intentions of serving in the military. But, the map reading exercises were fun and imminently helpful in our immediate travels and eventual careers. Coincidentally, we were both inspired to pursue our eventual professions within a few months of each other during the spring and summer of 1968.

Our route took us across Kansas, through Colorado and into Wyoming and Utah. We drove into Casper, Wyoming, and Dad decided to stop to get something to eat. There weren't many choices that morning, but one looked reasonable, a diner. Dad parked our blue and white Chrysler 300 near the front door, and we got out and walked to the front door. The diner was part of a group of storefronts that faced the main street through Casper. The door was shiny aluminum set in a brick façade. There was one picture window off to the left, but the curtains were closed, so we couldn't see inside until Dad opened the door. As we entered onto a white linoleum floor I saw a metal and wooden counter along the right side of the room with red vinyl-covered round stools bolted to the floor. The counter ran around to the right and joined the wall. The rest of the diner held several four-person tables with wooden chairs and red-vinyl cushions. The diner was well lit and about half full of white people, mostly men and a few women. Everything stopped when we walked in the front door.

The disbelief by the all-white patrons of our invasion into their restaurant was palpable. Almost every head turned in our direction. I'm sure we were a sight to see. One they hadn't seen in there, maybe ever. My very tall and dark-skinned father, my very short and light-skinned, red-haired mother, and two little Black boys instigated this invasion. I guess to them, they had been invaded. That was one of the coldest and hate-filled environments I had ever been in, even more so than in Missouri where I had been introduced to the word "nigger" on more than one occasion. The hate was almost a physical thing coming from those white patrons. It reached out towards us and tried to infiltrate the pores of our skin. I shuddered at the feeling it evoked from me. I thought we had left all that behind us, but unfortunately, I saw that bigotry existed everywhere and knew no state lines.

I'm sure my parents felt the vibe in there as well, and rather than creating a potential confrontational scene, Dad ushered us out of the diner and back out to the car. Farther down the street, near the outskirts of the town, was a familiar national restaurant chain, Howard Johnson's, where we had stopped several times in our cross-country travels. We could always depend on HoJo's for service. We enjoyed a great breakfast there and didn't discuss the earlier incident like it never happened.

We continued the drive northwest to Oregon, and soon after crossed into the state of Oregon. The scenery began to change, and we drove through lush green hills and mountains covered by tall evergreen trees. Beautiful! I had never seen such greenery! And yeah, this was the land of Sasquatch (otherwise known as "Big Foot"), and we started looking for that mythical beast from the moment we got to Oregon until we finally left the following year.

Our first living quarters was a first-floor apartment in the visiting officer's quarters. That was temporary until our permanent quarters became available. Dad being the ranking Army officer on Adair Air Force Station, and, coincidentally, the ranking and only Black officer on base, was authorized a five-bedroom house for the person occupying that slot. We had to wait for that family to move out before we could move in.

Again, Dana and I had an interesting status on base. We were the only Black Army officer's kids on an Air Force station, and the sons of the highest-ranking Army officer on base—second only in rank to the base commander. Yeah, a definite step up in prestige on base.

Our friends tended to be other officers' kids, primarily white, but we tried to bridge that gap once we moved into our permanent quarters. Until then, we remained stuck in the VOQ.

Word must have gotten out in the Black military community, both on and off base, because soon after we arrived several people came by the apartment. Mom met this one Black woman at the Base Exchange and she told Mom she was the wife of an Air Force LTC who had been deployed to Korea, and that she had a really cute 11-year old daughter. Yeah, right, we'd heard that one before! Of course Mom bragged on her two sons, so that following Saturday, Mrs. Betty Blades came by with her daughter Joan. From the moment I laid eyes on Joan she became my girlfriend, even before she knew it…heck, even before I knew it, but we instantly connected that day. Joan was the second prettiest girl I had known. I still had it bad for Becky, but Joan had a different look. Joan was slender, light-skinned, brown-eyed, with long light brown hair. She had a very cute face and wonderful personality. She wasn't mean or vindictive, which at times could describe Becky. Joan was the sweetest girl I had ever known, and she liked to have fun. She and I were about the same age. My birthday fell in December, and hers fell on Ground Hog Day, very easy to remember, but I was two grades ahead. I would start the eighth grade at the newly built Cheldelin Jr. High School, and she would be starting sixth grade at a different elementary school in Corvallis than Dana's.

That first Saturday at our apartment Joan and I had fun dancing, laughing and listening to records. She taught me to appreciate the music of the Queen of Soul, Aretha Franklin. We developed an instant bond that gave me hope for the rest of the year. Of course, one of the reasons we bonded so quickly was because we found ourselves in similar situations and suffered from a lack of options, but the one option we did have, each other, looked good. And yeah, this time, the mother had it right; she did have a really cute daughter.

Yep, so far, so good, in Oregon, until school started. There were two African-Americans in the eighth grade at Cheldelin, Jackie Jackson and me. I met Jackie on the first day of school on the bus. She and I were the only Black kids on the bus, so we began talking and sitting with each other. I told her about me, my age, and where we had just come from; and she told me that she had been at Cheldelin the year before. Once we got to school, we found out we were not in the same class, but would be able to see each other during the day at recess and lunch.

Jackie, a brown-skinned "sista' girl", with a fairly large Afro, at thirteen she was older and larger than me, and larger than most boys in our grade. She took no shit from anyone. Her dad was a non-commissioned officer/sergeant, the head chef at the Officer's Club at AAFS. She and I got along fine, and she became my protector during that year, almost like a big sister.

We developed a social life away from school. I used to go over and hang out at her house and listen to records, and, thankfully, like a big sister, she approved of Joan. She understood my need to be with someone my own age. Even though Jackie didn't have many options there in Corvallis, we were good friends. Her younger brother, Walter, was in Dana's class in the fourth grade, and was the fastest kid in the fourth grade. He and Dana became good friends too, so when I went over to the Jacksons to hang out, Dana normally went with me to hang out with Walter.

Although Jackie was in the same grade, once again, I was the only African-American in my home room, which was also the English class. This meant that I would be the only Black kid in all my classes for the rest of the year. Here we go again. But it couldn't be as bad as Missouri, could it? Yeah, it could. In fact, it could be worse.

⟡ ⟡ ⟡

On the second day of class, during lunch, we were playing four-square, a game I'd just been introduced to the day before at recess. The game is played outdoors on a blacktop marked by four equal squares that are connected, so that each has a corner meeting in the middle to make a larger square. Each square has a number and the object is to hit the ball, a special red four-square ball, into someone else's square in such a way that they can't return it, and so they're eliminated from the game. The player can only allow the ball to bounce once in his square or be eliminated; or the player could be eliminated by hitting the ball out of the four-square game surface. The person in the number one square is the initial server and thus has an advantage in trying to eliminate another player. The server rotates to the next number based on which player gets eliminated.

Players can use different methods of hitting the ball out of your square including two handed, causing the ball to curve, or hitting it hard like a volleyball slam.

I learned to play the game the normal way, by being told the rules as I got my butt kicked. But I was a fast learner, and by the third or fourth game, I was beating other people. In this case, my smaller size actually worked in my favor because I was able to nimbly use more of the square than most people and I had quick reflexes. I also had an uncanny ability to almost anticipate where a person was going to hit the ball and could get to where I thought the ball would go almost as fast as the person hit it. Of course, if I guessed wrong, then I would get eliminated, but that didn't happen very often.

On this fateful second day, I played four-square with some white kids not in my class. One of them, much larger than me, wasn't a good player, and resented being put out of the game by me. He thought he was a lot better than he really was; so, of course, when I eliminated him, he called me a "nigger" and then started walking away laughing, thinking he got the best of me. Unbeknownst to him, my parents had given me permission to take appropriate action in these circumstances; and because he was bigger than me, I picked up the four-square ball and threw it at the back of his head as hard as I could…BAM!

Hmm, maybe in hindsight not a great idea, but I was angry at the time and took immediate action. As a former pitcher, I was both accurate and deadly.

I hit him in the middle of his dirty blond head, and when he turned around, his normally tanned face was a bright red…red with hate and anger.

"You stupid nigger! I'm gonna kick your black ass!" he screamed.

"You gotta catch me first!" I yelled back, and I took off running in the opposite direction around the concrete playground, crossing several four-square games, tether ball courts (you know the game where a volleyball is hung from a pole by a chain and two people play at knocking it around and around the pole), basketball courts and eight-square games (eight-square was a bigger version of four-square).

I got a pretty good jump on him and had an initial lead of about 50 yards; however, although I was fast, he was bigger and faster and began to make up some of the distance. Uh oh! Time to get inside where I can find a teacher, guard, or somebody who might give me some protection from this guy. Now, I don't know how the word got out, but every time I tried to get inside, the white kids near that door blocked it. This happened twice, and each time they laughed at my predicament. Finally, at the third door, the guy caught up to me and grabbed me from behind.

That's when Jackie burst out of the door and yelled, "Let him go!" With her fists balled up, she looked ready to fight! She made quite an imposing figure and a godsend for me!

"He hit me with a ball and I'm gonna kick his butt!" He yelled.

"No you're not! I know what happened and you're not going to do anything to him or I'm going to kick your ass!" Jackie yelled back.

Apparently he believed her because he let go of me and said, "Fuck you!" and walked away.

"And don't bother him again!" Jackie yelled at his retreating back.

The guy just shook his head, muttered something to himself, and kept walking.

I turned to Jackie with great relief in my voice, thanked her and then asked, "How did you know he would back down?"

"These kids know me. Last year, I beat up one of the bigger boys, and when they came after me, my big brother came down to the school and stopped all that nonsense. I haven't had any problems since then. Now they know you're under the same protection, so they should leave you alone."

Mystified, I asked, "How did you know he was chasing me?"

"I didn't until I saw all these white kids at the door laughing about some little Black kid about to get his ass kicked and I figured it was you." She smiled.

"Well," I said, "you were right, and thank you."

She asked what caused the fight and I described what happened. She said, "Yeah, I'm not surprised, a lot of racist people up here, so you need to watch yourself."

"Okay," I said, "it's just like Missouri, all over again." Too bad, I just started to like Oregon.

CHAPTER 10

Enduring Oregon

In our society today, with the Internet, so many school-age children are connected through the social media outlets like Facebook, Twitter, YouTube, Instagram, Snapchat, and others. The federal and state governments, along with schools, are passing laws to control "cyber bullying" because of how students use social media and the internet to facilitate such bullying. Schools have "zero tolerance" policies for bullying and will expel students for physical bullying, and even label such activity as assault and charge it as a crime.

Not in 1968. Every two-bit bully in my homeroom class, and in my P.E. class targeted me, and I had to endure that in silence, or deal with it in my own way. So I decided to handle such conduct in my own way and not depend on teachers, school officials or my parents to help me. I observed my homeroom teacher, Mrs. Blowhard…yeah that was her name, but she pronounced it differently than it's spelled…watch as my classmates made fun of me and did nothing about it. I knew there was no help in that direction. As a result, I waged my own campaign to counter the bullying and gain my own level of self-respect and respect amongst my classmates.

The bullying occurred almost every day, and particularly between classes in the hallways where teachers or monitors couldn't see what was going on.

I need to describe how I looked and how that invited such bullying.

First, my clothes. I love my Mom to death, but she had no clue how much grief I took at school because of the clothes she bought for me and forced me to wear. She dressed us in the most unfashionable straight pants and button down short-sleeved and long-sleeved shirts imaginable. During that time, bell-bottomed pants and jeans were the fashion, in many different and exciting colors and paisley patterns. In contrast, our clothes were straight-laced and drab. They tended to be in earth tones, brown and tan button-down cardigan sweaters, and brown suede-brush Hush Puppy shoes.

I took my books to school in a brown briefcase with the strap over the top, the most conservative-looking briefcase in the store. I attended junior high school, in a city where a Division I university, Oregon State University resided, and whose mascot is the Beavers. So, all the junior high and high school kids emulated the college kids and what they wore on campus and around town. Everybody at my school wore vibrant colors, jeans, bell bottoms or flared pants, shirts with paisley patterns and Nehru jacket shirts with medallions and pendants. I fit in like a skunk at a Shriner's convention—not well at all, and my classmates made fun of me mercilessly. I hate sweaters to this day for that reason. I was a "dweeb" a "dork" who wore "dorky" clothes and looked like a "turd."

Dana and I begged Mom to buy us more contemporary clothes, and finally she broke down and bought us nice little Nehru shirts, more colorful pants, and each of us got a little medallion for Christmas. Finally, I was able to wear some clothes with a little pride, clothes that didn't cause me to feel embarrassed to wear to school. However, it didn't matter what I wore, the other boys always found something wrong with me. At least the girls seemed to appreciate the small changes and let me know they liked them. That's what probably pissed off the boys in the class, that I actually got some traction with their girls. They hated that—hah!

Next, they attacked my hair style. No Afro, just a flat top haircut. That's the way Dad had it cut, and there was no argument. You could land a jet aircraft on my head! Hell, I hated it, so you know I took grief because of it at school.

I had three main tormentors, Fred, David (yeah, another David), and a big red-headed kid named Brad. I hated those guys, and they fed off each other, trying to top one another on how much they bullied me. Fred, the smallest of the three, had freckles, a round head, tousled brown mousy hair, and a kind of chubby body. Again, probably the kid everyone had picked on before me, so he was happy to direct everybody's attention to me. David, the pretty boy of the class, had blond hair and dark eyebrows. His blond hair was probably dyed. He was taller than me, and the girls all thought he had the cutest face with his straight nose and Hollywood-like pretty-boy features.

He also wore all the right clothes, all the "cool" clothes and was my greatest clothes critic. And when he wore a sweater it was around his shoulder and tied by the sleeves in front. Kind of gay if you ask me—which I pointed out to him on several occasions. The last guy, Brad was just a big dumb red-headed, befreckled country hick, who wore jeans and plaid work shirts to school. He just didn't like me because I was "colored" and made no bones about it.

In fact, Blowhard asked me in class one day, what I preferred to be called, "Black, "Negro" or "colored." I really wanted to be called "Chris" but she was trying to be politically correct, so rather than create a lot of waves, I answered, "Negro." Obviously, the term "Black" was fairly controversial then, and no one had heard of "Afro-American" which probably would have caused a riot. I refused to be "colored," so I settled on "Negro." You could almost hear the sigh of relief from the class, they had a "good one." Anyway, back to the bullying.

Part of the problem with these three guys wasn't that they would just say things about my clothes or hair, they would actually touch my head, or try to trip me to watch me fall down and dirty up my clothes, or cause me to drop my briefcase. One of the tactics I learned to defend myself was using my brief case. It made for a very effective weapon.

I carried all my books in my briefcase and I had pretty good balance, so when Fred or one of his cohorts—yeah, he tried to get others involved which made it harder to detect where the trip might come from—threw their leg out to trip me in the hallway I used the momentum of the trip and the balancing weight of the briefcase to not only keep me upright, but would come around in a horizontal windmill motion with my body as the fulcrum, my arms as the blades, and the briefcase as the end of the spinning blade. As I would come around, I aimed my briefcase at whoever had tripped me and would hit them in whatever part of their body was closest, head, arm, leg, whatever, as hard as I could muster. And with the weight of my books, I packed a hell of a wallop! And that's what I did, I walloped them whenever I could, and dared them to do something about it. It took me a few weeks to develop this method of attack. Initially, they tried to trip me on a daily basis, then it became a couple of times a week, then it disappeared by the end of the year. They finally learned the most important lesson—that the consequences of potentially getting hit by my briefcase outweighed the thrill of tripping me. Eventually they stopped trying.

I wasn't always successful in defending myself, but I sure as hell tried, and I was always feisty. On one occasion, in early spring, in homeroom class, Mrs. Blowhard wasn't in the classroom, and Brad took it upon himself to begin making fun of my hair, and ran his hand over my head.

We sat in our assigned seats near the back of the classroom, sort of away from everyone else and I told him, "Quit touching my head!"

And he replied jokingly, "What are you going to do about it?"

That's always the invitation to fight, and it was no different in this case. Well, I didn't want to fight this guy. I mean he was huge, like a redheaded ogre or something. He had a unibrow, and his eyebrows protruded out over his eyes like an overhang on a cliff, which gave him a definitive Neanderthal look. He looked like one of those posters we had in class showing the evolution of man, like one of the earlier troglodytic phases of Man's evolution—an evolutionary throwback of sorts. He also had this reputation of being crazy, and having an uncontrollable temper, which had resulted in him being kicked off the football team.

Hmm, he had such a bad temper that he got kicked off the football team, a game of controlled violence, and he was too violent. This guy would probably grow up, climb a tower on a major university campus and start gunning down his classmates with a long-range rifle, he was very scary.

All this ran through my mind before I responded to his challenge, so I simply said, "Just leave me alone."

He ran his hand over my head again and that pissed me off. So I hit his arm and said, "I said stop it!"

He yelled, "You little motherfucker!" jumped up from his desk, and picked me up with both his hands, out of my desk, and twirled me around so that I was upside down and he held me by my ankles.

At this time I got sort of scared, but I yelled, "Let go of me!"

And he said, "Fine I'll drop you on your fucking head!" And he did just that. Luckily, I wasn't too high up when he dropped me, and I managed to break my fall with my hands which saved my head from serious injury against the hard linoleum floor. But no one in class came to my aid; in fact, all the kids just stood back, watched, then laughed when he dropped me, Fred and David the loudest. I hated those white kids and vowed to someday get my revenge on all them, but it would have to wait until I was in a position of strength. Strangely enough, I think my display of anger and braggadocio had an effect on Brad, and he pretty much left me alone after that. I think he may have also been worried that I would report him to Blowhard or someone else, and he thought better of bullying me any further.

Unfortunately, there was still P.E. and I had no defense to being one of the smallest and weakest in the class. But this year, unlike the seventh grade, I wasn't the smallest or the weakest, thank God. Lucky for me, Fred was almost as small and weak, and Winston, they called him Winnie, very unfortunate for him, was comparable to my size, but slower and weaker than me.

I knew I could look forward to getting bigger based on my father's size and his family's general height and girth; but these other guys were probably going to be small the rest of their lives.

Dad always told me he had a late growth spurt, after he turned 16, and I hoped that was the case for me. I kept that hope alive and it kept me going. I would be bigger and better than these guys, and I would show them some day.

I developed a huge chip on my shoulder, one that would grow with each encounter with someone who picked on me. I may have been smaller or weaker, but I vowed that one day, I would cash in that chip in a big way.

However, that day hadn't come yet, and I had to live in the present, and in the present, I was still one of the smallest and weakest in my P.E. class. This tended to manifest itself almost every day we had to do something athletic, like run a mile or wrestle, or do anything which pitted my smaller, weaker body against the bodies of my larger, stronger classmates.

Unfortunately, a convergence of events in the track and field area caused me further embarrassment. In 1968, a student at Oregon State University, right there in Corvallis, developed the high jumping style eventually nicknamed "the Fosbury Flop" after its inventor, Richard "Dick" Fosbury. The Fosbury Flop consisted of a different method of high jumping rather than the old tried and true method of jumping and straddling the high jump bar face first, the traditional "Western Roll."

The Flop envisioned going over the high jump bar with your back over the bar and your head leading, and then kicking your legs up so that they didn't knock down the bar. This unique way of high jumping won Fosbury the Olympic gold in Mexico City in 1968, and became the rage with budding high jumpers, especially in the town of its birth, Corvallis.

Yeah, we were introduced to it as a matter of course, and when I thought it couldn't get any more embarrassing at the height I tried to jump over the high jump bar, it became worse when the P.E. coach "encouraged" me to try the Flop. And yeah, I flopped! It was also kind of painful, because if you didn't know how to land, even with that big over-sized mattress, you could hurt yourself, and I did end up with plenty of bruises. Thanks a lot, Dick!

Speaking of dick, the constant and embarrassing episodes in the boy's locker room continued. Like in Belton, there were always the comparisons of "packages." Unfortunately, the myth about Black guys being so much larger in that department didn't seem to apply to me at that age and at that time. That would come later, but at the age of eleven, I was much smaller than my thirteen and sometimes fourteen year old classmates. Brad looked like someone about thirty, and looked like he had been kept back a few times in school. So, in P.E.

class, my smallness became a subject of much laughter and embarrassment, again.

My erstwhile tormentors also introduced me to the practice of "towel whacking." One of the boys would take his wet towel, roll it really fast in front of him so it looked like a fat whip, and then whip that sucker towards his unsuspecting victim with a loud "Thwack!" Quite painful if you were on the receiving end, and unfortunately, at least at first, I was on the receiving end fairly often. And, oh yeah, if you think complaining to the P.E. teacher would have been helpful, think again.

The P.E. teacher, Mr. Connolly, seemed to not only condone that sort of behavior, but seemed to encourage the bullying. He was a large, balding, auburn-haired white man, with a high forehead and bony protuberances that enclosed his hazel-colored eyes in twin caves surrounded by his reddish-colored eyebrows. By any standard, he was an ugly bully who took it out on the weaker boys. Not just me, all the weaker boys. He looked like he could have been Brad's dad—he had that Cro-Magnon, troglodytic look like Brad—and that same sort of mean streak reserved for those of us who he perceived to be weaker than the others. Sort of like when the lions separate the slowest, weakest member of the herd of zebras to attack and kill. That's sort of how it was for the smaller and weaker boys…no mercy.

Again, I had to learn to fight back.

❖　❖　❖

During the first few weeks of school, I didn't fight back, except the four-square episode. But as with the tripping in the hallways, it got to the point where I had to fight just to keep them off me. After the first few weeks I would go home and practice with a wet towel, the motion of rotating the towel so that I could make into a tight spiral, almost like a rope with a pointy tip. I also would wet the tip for maximum snap and "thwack" when it hit its target. Then I worked on the snapping motion to get the maximum snap and "thwack" out of the towel. I walked around the house snapping my towel at multiple targets, like the door or my bedroom, chairs, tables, and of course Dana. Yeah, he didn't really enjoy it too much, but I had to get an idea of how the towel sounded against a human body and he happened to be handy. In deference, I showed him how to spin up the towel and use it as a whip, and then we would have towel fights. At home it could be fun…at school it was war.

One fateful day, after P.E. class, I stood by my locker getting dressed, like everyone else. I had my towel on the bench next to me as I faced my locker waiting for someone to approach me with a wet towel. Fred didn't disappoint me. He tried to sneak up from behind while my back was turned, but I could see him in the reflection of the locker in front. As he got closer, I suppose to aim for my behind, which I covered with more than one pair of underwear for protection, I turned quickly around and snapped at his face with my towel.

"Oww!" he yelled in pain and surprise, as my towel made contact with his chest.

"I'm going to get you!" he yelled, and I deftly dodged his towel and snapped him again in the legs, once, twice, three times in quick succession.

"Fuck!" he yelled, and scrambled away from me. I didn't chase him, but I laughed really loud and hard.

Yeah, I had beaten him at his own game, at least this time. And, yeah, I had witnesses to this little tableau, who, I think enjoyed watching Fred get his butt kicked by me. After this incident, he was very wary about how he came at me in the locker room. Fred tried a few more times, but he never caught me without my trusty wet towel within arm's reach, and after a few months he gave up altogether.

I became a feisty little guy and I learned not to take any crap from these bigger, older white guys, regardless of the circumstances, and to stand my ground. In some ways, I think I earned their respect, and after a while they left me alone. Eventually, my homeroom class elected me as student council representative; I attended school dances, where I never danced with anyone, and, after a fashion was accepted by my classmates.

Yeah, at the end of the school year, Fred, David and Brad all signed my yearbook. I had survived the bullying, and in their little minds, a sort of rite of passage, and by signing my yearbook showed that, in the end, I was all right. Huh, imagine that.

⟎ ⟎ ⟎

Living at Adair was not as difficult as going to school. I bowled on base in the youth leagues and was fairly successful. I bowled in the city tournament and won a medal, and then broke the middle finger on my right hand, my bowling hand, and didn't bowl in the state tournament. Dana and I made friends with several of the other white and Jewish officer's kids, particularly Joey, Kenny, and

Barry. We played *Risk* with them, a board game of global domination; chess; football; and bowling. Joey was a really good bowler for his age, nine, and his older brother, a second lieutenant in the Air Force, competed strongly with Dad. They were the best two adult bowlers on base.

In addition, we played football. Usually amongst ourselves, the officers' kids, and then in hotly contested games against the NCO kids. When we had those games, I played quarterback for our team, and another eighth grader, Kevin, who was much bigger than me quarterbacked the NCO kids. Of course the NCO kids' team featured Walter Jackson, one of the fastest kids on base, and very hard to cover. The NCO team featured more Black kids, and they were always a tough cover as well. This was also the summer of the Apollo 11 landing on the moon. I remember playing football that evening waiting on our parents to call us in to see the moon landing. What a great night for us and the country.

The vast wooded area on this base was its most interesting feature. The wooded area included ponds, creeks, and small trails and paths throughout.

We built a fort deep in the woods called "Mammy, Woof, Woof, Woof," named after a phrase from a *Flintstones* episode. Yeah, I know, not very inventive, but that was our secret code to get in—you had to know the code phrase, or you couldn't enter. Like in New York and Missouri, whenever we went to the woods exploring, we packed our backpacks with various supplies and equipment, along with our walkie-talkies and traveled on our Stingray bikes. We also learned how to fish, and went fishing for bluegills in the stocked ponds on the base.

We also honed our skills in capturing various reptilian and amphibian creatures. Falling back on our experiences in Missouri, we knew how to capture frogs, and now we hunted salamanders, garter snakes, bull snakes and the green snakes that populated the base. We became pretty good at catching these harmless reptiles, but Mom wasn't really thrilled with us bringing snakes to the house. She became less thrilled when one of them got loose in the house. Yeah, that ended bringing them in the house, so we kept them in wooden boxes out in the yard. We lost our fear of snakes, well at least the non-poisonous variety, and actually did a lot of research on snakes to make sure we could recognize the poisonous from the non-poisonous ones. No poisonous snakes existed in that area of Oregon, so there was little danger, but we still remained careful.

We also tried our hand at tracking various types of animals. We always held the belief that Bigfoot might reside in the area, so we pretended to track him and any other large beasts that might be in the woods. We looked for spoors in the woods, and tracks around watering areas like the ponds and creeks, and looked for other telltale signs that large animals had passed through the area. We never saw Bigfoot, but it was fun thinking that somewhere out there he watched us.

Finally, I played little league baseball through the Boys and Girls Club in Corvallis. I was the only Black kid on the team, and joined the team late. I rode the bench most of the season and barely played at all. I didn't really enjoy playing until we went up to Seattle, Washington, to participate in a regional-level tournament that had we won, would have led to the Little League World Series. Needless to say, we didn't win, but I actually played some significant minutes, and played well. I think the coach wished he had put me in sooner in the season, but I also believed there may have been pressure from other parents to let their kids play even though I may have been a better player. But the summer ended on a high note with the regional tournament as one of the last events I participated in while living in Oregon.

Then, we left Corvallis for El Paso.

CHAPTER 11

Eastwood High School and Jr. ROTC

In the summer of 1969 we moved from Corvallis, Oregon, in the Great Northwest, to El Paso, in the desert of the Southwest, the westernmost city in Texas. El Paso bordered Ciudad Juarez, Mexico, so there was a significant Mexican and Hispanic population in El Paso. We returned to the home of the Air Defense Artillery, Fort Bliss, Texas, where Dad would retire from the Army as a Lieutenant Colonel. Mom and Dad planned to rent a home while we had a home built. While in Oregon, my parents asked me and Dana where we would like to live after retirement and we picked El Paso. We were also so taken by Becky's pool that we asked if we could have an in-ground pool too, and our parents agreed. YES!!!

Again, as in the last several years, I lived two lives—the life of a 4'10", 12-year-old freshman in high school; and the same 12-year-old who interacted with his peers in a much more confident and cocky manner. My confidence in interacting with my age peers was enhanced by my experiences competing with my older classmates.

In the past two years I climbed the ladder of seniority in each of the two junior high schools I attended. At Belton Jr. High School I went through the rites of passage as a seventh grader, the lowest rung on the ladder. At Cheldelin Jr. High School I chaffed at the second rung of the ladder, only one rung down from the "Frosh," the highest rung on the ladder in junior high schools. In turn, I looked forward to being at the highest level as a freshman in the junior high school system.

I would be disappointed again. I learned to my dismay that El Paso, and many other places in Texas, did not have junior high schools, but middle schools. Middle schools, or modified junior high schools, had either the sixth, seventh and eighth grades or just the seventh and eighth grades, but not the ninth grade. This meant that the high school had four grades and the freshmen, the "Frosh," were the lowest rung on the four-year ladder at the high school. So, here I found myself again, at the lowest rung beginning my freshman year at Eastwood High School. Damn.

The one advantage, though, to being in high school was the JROTC program. JROTC allowed me to avoid gym class and the embarrassment and humiliation I had endured the past two years. JROTC also seemed to have the advantage of actually teaching me some skills and preparing me for a potential career in the Army, if I so chose, unlike P.E. or gym class which, in my opinion, had no redeeming qualities. I looked forward to beginning my JROTC career at Eastwood High.

⬦ ⬦ ⬦

Junior ROTC served as the high school version of the ROTC program found in many of the colleges and universities around the country. Obviously, the main difference is that successful completion of ROTC at the college level would result in a cadet's commissioning as an officer in that service. The Army, Air Force, and Navy all had collegiate ROTC programs. There were reciprocal programs at the high school level; however, successful completion of four years of JROTC would not get you commissioned as an officer, but it could get you a promotion to E-4 faster than your peers if you enlisted in the armed forces. That wasn't my goal at the time. My goal at the time was just to avoid gym class, learn something about the Army, and maybe make my Dad proud of me because I was sort of following in his footsteps.

My first day of JROTC came on the first day of class. The JROTC department was positioned under the concrete football stadium with several classrooms, offices, and an armory full of M-1 Garand rifles, M-14 rifles, .22 cal target rifles, and eventually M-16 rifles. There was also a range built for shooting the .22s, where the Rifle Team practiced their sharpshooting skills. All under the stadium, very impressive.

That first day, the new cadets, not all of us freshmen, met SFC Kittlested, who ran the program as the Senior Army Instructor, and 1SG Patino, the Assistant Senior Army Instructor. Interestingly, even though Patino outranked Kittlested, Kittlested held the senior Army instructor position at Eastwood. This was Patino's first year and somehow that made him junior to Kittlested. Eastwood also housed the offices of LTC Garcia, the District Army Instructor, or DAI, who was in charge of the JROTC programs for the entire Ysleta Independent School District, to which Eastwood High School belonged.

That first day, as SFC Kittlested gave his canned speech to new cadets and outlined the program, the expectations, and what we would learn during our time in JROTC during the first year and beyond, I finally felt I belonged somewhere. I hadn't felt that way since leaving Philadelphia five years earlier, and it felt good.

That first day of JROTC, they issued us our uniforms, including the Class "A" greens with blouse and trousers, the overseas cap or "cunt" cap, and the saucer cap with brim. I didn't know what the slang term "cunt" even referred to at the time and just thought it a colorful way of describing the overseas cap. The black shoes and brown poplin shirt we had to buy on our own. They also issued us a short-sleeved khaki shirt to wear as our "B" uniform with the green trousers, a black webbed belt and brass buckle along with the brass insignia of "ROTC" and the little cloth rank we had to wear. The one individualized piece of equipment was our engraved black name plate that we wore over the right-upper pocket flap on our uniform blouse. Each was engraved with our last name and really looked cool. The supply sergeant sternly told us we had to sign for each of the items and we were responsible for the items of clothing we received, and would be responsible for returning said items in reasonably good condition at the end of the year. The supply room, once again, you wouldn't expect to be located under the football stadium, but there it was. The JROTC department made good use of the space under the stadium and even had an area for official military vehicles. Quite impressive!

The next several days the cadre oriented the new cadets to the rigors of JROTC, including teaching us Drill and Ceremonies from FM 22-5, the official Army manual on how to march. The instructors taught us how to march in formation, how to keep cadence with our fellow cadets, how to salute, how to stand at attention, the positions of "parade rest" and "at ease." They also taught us how to wear the newly-issued uniforms. Each Friday was "uniform day" at school, and I especially looked forward to being in uniform and showing off my JROTC status.

That first week they also told us at what length to keep our hair—no more than two inches long and tapered at the back. No girls could participate in JROTC at that time, but we had what they called the "Sponsors," a special corps of junior and senior girls with "honorary" rank as officers.

All of them were officers and we had to salute them unless we outranked them. My "play cousin" Jeri was a Sponsor and helped me get in good with all those good looking junior and senior girls. Did I mention that SFC Kittlested personally picked these girls from all the applicants for the Sponsors? And, oh yeah, he had a good eye for young feminine beauty, and these girls were some of the cream of the crop at Eastwood. Almost all of them were accomplished in other areas, and almost all of them had been Homecoming queens and princesses; and Eastwood-In-Elegance queens and princesses; and prom queens and princesses. So, to say a lot of these girls would say "hi" to me, a lowly freshman, was certainly a feather in my cap!

In preparation for that first day of wearing the uniform, which started the second Friday of the school year, SFC Kittlested gave us a chance to prepare our uniforms and get a proper haircut. In my case, I thought I had an inside track because my Dad was an Army officer and knew how to put together a uniform, shine shoes and shine the brass accoutrements. On second thought... not so much.

Dad didn't really seem to take that much interest in helping me out, although he did give me some advice on polishing the brass and bought me "Brasso" to clean it. He also showed me how to brush shine my black shoes, but he didn't seem to know how to put a "spit" shine on the shoes; and no, spitting on the shoes didn't quite do it. He did help me put the brass on the uniform so that it looked straight and made sure my uniform appeared clean and fresh looking. I learned to iron, because it was my responsibility to iron my own shirt, either short-sleeved or long-sleeved. Dad did teach me how to tie a tie (which we had to buy ourselves) the "Army" way, in a triangular shape. Finally, Dad took me down to Estelle's barber shop for my first military haircut. When Estelle asked me how I wanted it cut, Dad answered, "Flattop." Hmm, it seemed like I had been there before; oh well, all for a good cause, and it made it easier to put on the overseas cap.

On that first "Uniform Friday" I finally felt like a little soldier. I got up early that morning after having ironed my shirt the night before under the watchful eye of my mother; shined my brass; shined my shoes; and put what little brass I had on my uniform—the ROTC torch on a round brass plate, and the initials "R.O.T.C." surrounded by a wreath on my overseas hat—and laid out my uniform on its hangers.

That previous night, I had just stared at the uniform and couldn't stop grinning,—I would look like my Dad and I wanted to wear that uniform proudly to school the next day.

Dad woke me up promptly at 6 a.m. in anticipation of leaving the house at 7:30 that morning. I jumped up and went to the bathroom to get cleaned up for this very special Friday. After doing all my morning ablutions, I put it on. I savored the feeling of putting on the uniform piece by piece. First, the thin black socks, one foot at a time. Next, the short-sleeved shirt, button by button until it felt snug against my neck. I spent the next several minutes tying my new black tie. It still took me a few minutes even though I had practiced all week on tying it just right. I thought that, maybe, I should leave it tied the rest of the school year, that way I didn't have to keep tying the darn thing. Once I had the tie on, I looked in the mirror and saw the beginning of a new me, albeit without any pants.

Next came the pants. They fit kind of loose, since they had to order special small pants for me. They would fit well enough. I sat on the bed as I pulled them up to the top of my thighs, then I hopped off the bed and I hoisted them up to my waist. I tucked in my shirt and made sure the "gig line" was straight. The gig line was the straight line from the seam of the buttons on my shirt, through the edge of the brass belt buckle, and down to the zipper. Once perfect, I had to actually fasten the pants. Like other suit pants they had a three-way closing system, the strap that came across the inside with a button, the little metal slip-on clasp at the waist, and finally, the button on the waist. I had to adjust the pants again to make sure I had a straight gig line. The last item for the pants was the belt and belt buckle. I hadn't practiced putting on the belt and buckle without smudging the buckle—not as easy as it may look. I had to grasp the belt on either side of the buckle to slip the brass tip of the belt into the buckle and then press the fastener down to cinch the belt in place and make sure it was nice and tight. The right edge of the buckle was supposed to be even with the gig line so that if you looked at me, you would see a straight line of the seam next to the buttons, down to the belt buckle and the zipper. The belt had a brass tip, which had to be lined up next to the buckle, and I had to be careful in handling the tip as well as the buckle. I also discovered that in putting on the belt buckle, I had to use a clean cloth to ensure I didn't smudge the nice shine I had put on the buckle and the tip the night before. I also used the cloth to keep the buckle and tip shiny all day, so the cloth stayed in my pocket.

Finally, time for the jacket or blouse. This is the only time it's okay for a guy to wear a blouse, when putting on a uniform. Again, the jacket was a bit large, but the smallest they had, and it was still a little too big. That's okay, it belonged to me, and I would wear it proudly. Before I put on the blouse, I carefully placed the name plate that said "PITTARD" on the upper right pocket flap, and centered it on the flap. Oh yeah, that was the best part of putting the uniform together, putting my name on it! After I pinned the name plate, I put on the jacket and slowly buttoned each of the brass buttons. And there I was, fully dressed in my uniform. To top it off, I put on the overseas cap and admired myself in the mirror, looking at my reflection from the front and each side, happy with the result. I was ready to go to school.

The uniform seemed to give me a different kind of confidence and power. Dad dropped me off at school and told me good luck on my first day in uniform. I thanked him and walked proudly into the school. I went to my first class, English with Mrs. Carolyn Wolterstorff, whose husband had served with my dad in Korea. She had always been supportive of me and immediately complimented me on my uniform. I beamed. I felt really good, even though I had my detractors in that class, all these white guys who took P.E. and liked to make fun of guys in JROTC—but not that day. That day they remained strangely quiet and didn't have anything to say to me. No problem, I was happy to be in class and in uniform.

I had JROTC class during fifth period and by that time, the uniform had gotten a little wrinkled from sitting and standing and walking all day. But I stood inspection and passed for the very first time. I beamed with pride because not everybody passed.

In addition, my platoon leader, Brian Collins, approached me and asked if I wanted to be the company guidon bearer. He said I was the right size and I had impressed him and the company commander, Dennis Holt, with my marching, my discipline, and the way I presented myself on that first uniform day. In addition, he told me that becoming the guidon bearer would result in my immediate promotion to corporal, that's two stripes, when all my new cadet peers would be no-stripe or one-stripe or one-up-one-down privates, or privates first class.

I immediately jumped on the opportunity and said, "Yes!"

They immediately promoted me and taught me how to handle the eight-foot tall company guidon. The guidon is the staff by the company commander that had the company flag on the top and was used to help identify the company and to make sure the cadets knew where the commander was at all times. I took great pride in this honor and I really strutted to my sixth period class because now I had slipped on the cloth rank of a two-stripes-up corporal, the highest ranking freshman new cadet! Of course, later on I found out that each of four companies, Alpha, Bravo, Charlie (mine) and the Headquarters company, had a guidon bearer. So there were three more corporals, John Hendrickson, Greg Smyth, and James Haas, and for a while, we ruled the new cadets.

I always walked home from school, but that day I almost skipped home. When I got there I proudly announced that I had been promoted to corporal and that I was the "C" Company guidon bearer. Mom and Dana were very proud of me, but Dad remained sort of non-committal. He congratulated me, but didn't really get into the moment like I thought he might. He still seemed sort of stand-offish about me being in ROTC, and I never really figured out why, even now.

The following week our cadet squad leaders finally taught us the basics of drill movements with the rifle. Initially, we used the M-1, and eventually we transitioned to the M-14 as a drill rifle. We learned the intricacies of standing at attention with the rifle, at parade rest, and at ease. We learned how to hoist the rifle up to our shoulders in the "right shoulder" position, the "present arms" position, "port arms," and my favorite, "inspection arms." I say that with a bit of sarcasm.

The inspection arms movement required the cadet to bring the weapon up to the port arms position in such a way as to pull back the bolt with the blade of your right hand and to lock it into place while simultaneously looking down into the chamber, ensuring there no round remained in the chamber, hence the "inspection" part of inspection arms. You needed some upper body strength and some arm strength to accomplish this task and yours truly didn't have enough of either to adequately accomplish that task. Fortunately, I was the guidon bearer, so I didn't have to actually perform that maneuver during inspections like everyone else. I just had to look pretty with the guidon and make sure my uniform looked good, which it always did. But that was an eye-opening week and showed me an additional aspect of the military. I was really looking forward to four years of ROTC.

CHAPTER 12

Trouble at School

The following Friday, I proudly wore my Class "B" uniform with the short-sleeved khaki shirt, and new corporal stripes to each class so that everyone could see my new rank. The previous week, only the students in sixth period had seen the rank, and this week everyone got to see my new rank. However, there was some jealously by one of my Black classmates, Bill Benford. Benford stood about six feet tall, brown-skinned, with short black hair, was a freshman and new cadet. He had been going around telling other cadets and students I didn't deserve my new rank.

I didn't have him in any one of my classes except ROTC, and it was during fifth period that he took my overseas cap. I didn't know he had taken it until the end of the period when I went to retrieve it from where I had laid it down. Someone told me he had taken it. When I confronted him about my cap between fifth and sixth period, he denied having it. Well, I knew his locker number and I was determined to get my cap back.

So after sixth period I went to his locker and found it unlocked. Almost as soon as I opened his locker I saw my cap and grabbed it. About that time, Benford snuck up behind me, and slapped me on the head hard enough to knock me down. Damn, that hurt!

He screamed at me in his high-pitched voice as he towered over me, "What the fuck are you doing in my locker?! I'm going to kick your ass little boy!"

He had called me "little boy" before, and knew that it pissed me off. I'm not sure why this guy had it out for me so early in the school year. I didn't know him, didn't want to know him, but for some reason I pissed him off, which led to him taking my hat. I'm sure it was his jealousy of my new rank.

All that was moot at this point. I prepared myself to fight someone who towered over me, and probably outweighed me by fifty or more pounds. I was determined not to let this guy kick my ass.

Just about that time, a white male teacher came up on us and asked angrily, "What's going on here?"

"He stole something from my locker, and I was getting it back!" Benford lied.

As I pulled my body up, the teacher asked me, "Is that true?"

"No," I said, "I was getting back my overseas cap that he took and put in his locker to hide it from me." I showed the teacher the cap in my hand with my name in it, and he asked Benford if that was true.

Surprisingly, Benford admitted that he had taken my hat as a joke and didn't mean anything by it. I think he got scared he would get in trouble and decided to come clean about what happened. The teacher looked at us both and asked for our names. He wrote them down and said that if we caused any more problems he would report us to SFC Kittlested and get us kicked out of ROTC. I said it wouldn't happen again, as did Benford. The teacher told us to go in opposite directions. And we walked away from each other. Of course, since we both rode the same bus home, we couldn't always avoid each other, but on this occasion, we kept our distance from each other on the bus.

Unfortunately, this encounter led to another, but this time with a Black girl and a white girl.

Benford was that type of guy that I couldn't stand—the type of guy that talked about you behind your back and got people riled up against you. Like a little bitch. He would whisper in girls' ears spreading rumors or saying things to get people pissed off, and he did a good job of that on the bus on the way home.

I sat about halfway back on the bus trying to keep some distance from him, and he sat in the very back talking to several people. Two of the girls he talked with were friends. Sort of unusual back then, but we lived in a pretty diverse neighborhood, so it wasn't totally unusual, a Black girl and white girl as friends.

In this case, Julie Burke and Benell Canavan, were freshmen like me, but I think they had been friends longer than just this school year. And of course, much older than me, probably 14 years old. Julie was taller, very dark-skinned, almost jet black, with straightened coarse hair that came below her jaw line. Benell was taller still, with a lot of freckles and short brown hair that hung above her shoulders. Benell had a fairly straight and sharp nose and spoke with kind of nasally whine in her voice. She could be irritating just in regular conversation, and could downright piss you off if she ever came at you with her voice. Well, this happened to be one of those days.

After we had been on the bus a few minutes, Julie walked down the aisle to where I sat during one of the early stops and said, "Why did you go into Bill's locker?"

"It's none of your business." I replied.

"Yeah, but he said you were stealing stuff out of his locker." She persisted.

"Did he tell you he stole my cap and I was just getting it back?" I was really tired of this crap.

She considered this for a moment, apparently he hadn't told her that part of the story, and said, "No, I don't believe he would do something like that."

By this time the bus started to move, and it rocked back and forth as it rolled to its next stop.

"I think you're just a little thief." She said accusingly.

At that point I'd had enough of this crap and yelled, "Shut up you ugly black bitch, you don't know what you're talking about! Why don't you go to the back of the bus where you belong?"

Yeah, I probably shouldn't have called her an "ugly black bitch," but her accusations really angered me. The bus got real quiet at that point and Julie just stared at me in astonishment and started to cry. That's when Benell decided to intervene.

She stormed down the aisle to my seat and pushed past the still crying Julie and screamed, "HOW DARE YOU SAY THAT ABOUT MY FRIEND!"

Well, this was just turning into a really peachy day for me. Strangely, I noticed that they dressed similarly, both wearing plaid skirts, brown or black low heel shoes, and Benell wore a white blouse while Julie wore a light-colored blouse of some sort, with very similar collars. This sort of went through my mind as I figured out my response. I wasn't friends with either of them, but I knew their names from riding on the bus for the past month or so, and I didn't really have any feelings towards them one way or another. I guess that would soon change.

This may have been the first time I used the word, and I certainly had never used it on a girl, but I think I used it appropriately, and since I had just learned to use it, I wanted to make sure I used it appropriately. I looked Benell in her eyes and said very clearly and calmly, "Fuck you."

If I thought I had pissed her off before, Benell became almost apoplectic.

"I'm going to kick your ass! Right now!" She screamed.

About that time we had reached a bus stop not too far from my house, but not hers or Julie's stop, so I pushed my way past her and hastily got off the bus, thinking I had avoided another physical confrontation. Uh uh, nope.

She and Julie followed me off the bus, and as soon as they got off, I faced them and Benell took a swing at me striking me on the side of the head. So, I balled up my fist and hit her, my first time hitting a girl. But this was self-defense and I had to protect myself. Benell being much taller than me and definitely outweighed me, I couldn't let her just beat me up. As soon as I hit Benell, Julie jumped into the fray, and tried to break it up.

By this time other kids had gotten off the bus and had formed a half-circle around us, as the bus pulled off in a cloud of black exhaust and gravel shooting back at us. Julie grabbed Benell and pulled her back and some other kid grabbed me and pulled me back. Benell was still yelling at me and I yelled at her, but we didn't strike at each other again. Thanks to her my uniform was all disheveled and I looked a mess, but at least my head may have been bloody but still unbowed, literally and figuratively. I picked up my cap where I had dropped it and wiped the dirt from it, and walked to my house while they began the trek to wherever they lived. I didn't say another word to Julie for the rest of my life, and didn't speak again to Benell until she made a critical comment to me our senior year in high school about my role in the Senior Play. That's another story.

And Benford, I had nothing more to do with him. Although he continued his whispering campaign against me for the rest of our time in high school, I didn't interact with him. He left ROTC after a couple of months when he made the freshman basketball team, so we didn't have much interaction. And because of after-school practices, he no longer rode the bus with the rest of us. And the following spring, 1970, my family moved into our brand new house in a different neighborhood and I didn't have to ride the bus anymore with those folks

❖   ❖   ❖

The new house, built in an area called New Eastridge, and situated on the edge of the desert was the furthermost east you could go in El Paso at the time. Nothing else existed out there but the desert and its many denizens.

Over the next four years Dana and I had the opportunity to explore the desert and become familiar with operating in that environment. We hunted snakes, lizards and jackrabbits out there. I had previously been taught how to run traps on jackrabbits, but didn't have the opportunity to do that myself. Most of the time we would scare them up and watch them scamper with cheetah-like speed away from us. Where was Wile E. Coyote when you needed him?

My parents had given me a BB-gun and I used that to hunt the smaller animals in the desert. On some occasions we would build fires and throw various small animals in the fire, including lizards, snakes, and grasshoppers. I actually tasted a grasshopper to see what it tasted like and it wasn't half bad. We had a lot of fun in the desert and it taught us how to conduct operations in that type of environment.

Yeah, we felt like the stars in our own version of *Desert Rats* and had a lot of fun exploring the outreaches of the desert near our new house.

CHAPTER 13

Drill Team

The rest of my freshman year in ROTC passed without incident, but I ended the year as I began it, as a corporal. They never told me there was no chance of promotion for me as a guidon-bearer during the year. My highest rank would remain corporal. Although I was initially promoted ahead of my peers, some of my more ambitious and militarily-skilled classmates passed by me in rank and ended up as sergeants and squad leaders by the end of the school year. This put them in position to assume platoon sergeant positions at the beginning of our sophomore year.

Probably the most up and coming of my classmates was John Tiffany, whose older brother Robert, served as the battalion commander of the Eastwood High School JROTC battalion and a cadet LTC. They eventually promoted Robert to Cadet Colonel. As his brother, John had big shoes to fill, and he was up to the task. He wasn't in my company, but I had heard about him. Not a very tall cadet, maybe 5'6" but a regular dynamo. By the end of our freshman year he was a Cadet SSG, and on his way to being a 1SG the following year, the highest rank a cadet sophomore could hold. Only juniors and seniors could be officers, but it was a sure bet he would be the battalion commander senior year.

One of the activities that students could try out for, other than rifle team, was the drill team. The drill team consisted of 16 cadets, highly skilled in drill and ceremonies, and able to wield a rifle with the best of them. Those guys had to be the best at rifle D&C and be able to do things with rifles that others could not do, such as throwing rifles in the air and catching them; spinning rifles in their hands; having rifles thrown to you and catching them; and being able to march in close formation doing marching movements, only limited by the imagination of the drill team commander. The drill team competed in interscholastic competitions in El Paso and Las Cruces, and performed at halftime during football games and at pep rallies. John joined the drill team as a freshman and became quite good. He would eventually be its commander.

I didn't have any aspirations of being on the drill team because I knew my limitations with the rifle. You had to be able to do inspection arms on command,

and I couldn't do it, so, no drill team. During my sophomore year, I got to know many of the drill team members and loved to watch them go through their routines. They practiced early in the morning and in the evening after school. I began playing basketball in the mornings before school and would watch them practicing. I found it all fascinating, but knew I couldn't compete for one of those coveted drill team spots.

During my sophomore year they promoted me to SGT, then SSG, and I ended up as a squad leader to round out the year. I became more and more adept in the military training to which we were exposed and really excelled. I loved to read military maps, and to conduct land navigation with the lensatic compass. I became very adept at running the platoon and good at calling cadences and giving marching commands. I developed very crisp and precise movements with the rifle, except for my one bug-a-boo—inspection arms, which I tried to avoid as much as possible. I turned out to be a good D&C instructor to new cadets and was given that task by my company commander, to be the primary instructor on teaching new cadets how to stand at attention, parade rest and at ease; as well as how to march in formation and execute the various movements. I loved it, all of it, and felt, once again, that I belonged to something greater than myself.

At the end of our sophomore year, SFC Kittlested promoted John Tiffany to Cadet Lieutenant and appointed him the Drill Team commander for our junior year. Apparently, one of the ideas John developed to enhance the drill team and make them more competitive at drill meets was the addition of a guidon bearer. He had seen other drill teams win drill meets using a guidon bearer and believed that gave them a winning edge. He wanted such an edge. That's where I came in.

John approached me near the beginning of our junior year during JROTC and asked me if I had ever considered being on the varsity drill team.

"No, I don't think I'm strong enough or big enough to make the team." I replied.

"Well, I'm looking at creating a position especially for you as the guidon bearer for the team." John said.

"What would I do?" I asked.

"Well," John replied thoughtfully, "You would be following me around, but you would also be operating outside the regular formation, you know, doing your own thing as we go through our regular routines."

Huh, I thought, *that might be kind of neat.* "What about the rest of the team, how do they feel about this?" I asked. I was thinking that, maybe, these guys might resent me coming on to the team without having earned it as they had through tryouts.

But, John reassured me that not only were they on board, they specifically recommended me when he asked the team members who might make a good guidon.

"Wow, okay, I'm in! What do I need to do?" I was kind of flabbergasted that these guys wanted me on the team.

"Well, the first thing is to come to tomorrow's practice at 6:30 and we'll start working on how you're going to fit into our routines," John replied.

"Great, I'll be there!" And I walked away feeling on top of the world.

The guys on the drill team were a pretty tight-knit group. They represented the elite performance team in JROTC and it took a lot of work and effort to attain the level of competence they had achieved. They had a lot of trust in one another because of the maneuvers they performed, from spinning full-sized, full-weight, rifles, and throwing those same rifles to one another, throwing them spinning into the air individually, or high in the air over the formation to another team member. These guys hung out together socially, had end-of-year dinners, and played tackle football together. This was my first time being with an elite precision team, and it would bode well for me as I moved through life, in and out of the military.

When I got home that evening, again Mom was excited because I was excited, although I don't think she really understood the significance of being on the drill team, but was willing to support me in whatever activity I chose. Dad did understand the significance and also understood that if I had to be at practice at 6:30 in the morning he would have to take me to school as early as 6:15, and that did not make him very happy. In the two years I served on the drill team, Dad never came to a meet or saw a performance. Somehow I thought he might be proud of me, but, again, he remained pretty noncommittal about my involvement on the drill team. I guess I just couldn't get it right.

Mom, however, did come see us perform at halftime at the Homecoming game both years. Thanks Mom!

The next morning, Dad woke me up promptly at 5:30, and got me to my first practice on time at 6:30. As I walked up to the JROTC building, the drill team members were drawing their M-14s from the armory. John had the armory keys and had his second in command, Jim Agee, issue the rifles to the team members. My guidon stood against the wall, separate from the company guidons which were kept in the classrooms. This one had a special flag on it that resembled a cavalry flag with royal blue on the top half and gold on the bottom half and crossed sabers embroidered in white in the middle. Too cool! Someone put some thought into this guidon, and it was mine to command!

Except, it sat on top of a normal eight-foot pole, with the chrome-pointed bottom end, and the chrome cap on top. I had to learn how to wield this thing in such a way as to integrate my movements with the team and enhance our chances against the competition. Not easy.

I stood less than 5'4", and the guidon towered over me with its height. As the team went out to the football field to begin this year's practicing, I went off to the side to work on routines with the guidon, and to learn how to manipulate it through my hands, and around my body, like a drum major. After about thirty minutes, John came over to me during a break and told me how he wanted to integrate me into the drill team.

Looking back over his shoulder at the drill team, he said, "I just want you to kind of follow me around as I give my commands to the team. There are a couple of routines where I go through a gauntlet where they are spinning their rifles and it takes perfect timing so I don't get hit. I want you to follow me through the gauntlet, so we'll have to work on the timing."

"Okay," I said, "You don't think that long ass guidon isn't going to be a problem?"

"Well, we'll see," John said, "But I think it'll work."

"Alright, let's give it a shot," I said with some trepidation.

John gave the team the commands to get them into position for the gauntlet. This was the most intricate maneuver prior to the big finale for the routine and it had to be perfect. When John gave the command, the guys facing us, began to spin their rifles. John quickly moved forward and just as the first two guys spun their weapons John moved past them, and moved through the gauntlet in that manner. On the far side of the gauntlet, John stopped and did an about face, and without any verbal commands, apparently they had been working on silent commands, the team members faced each other and began to kick up their weapons in such a position, in sequence so they could throw their rifles across the gauntlet to their teammate on the other side. When the first pair of rifles was thrown, John began marching down the gauntlet coming back to where I stood watching. Wow, very impressive! It went off without a hitch! Now we had to figure out how I fit into all that.

The first time we tried it with me going through the gauntlet, it was a disaster. The length of the guidon created a problem. The spinning rifles kept slamming into the guidon, BAM, BAM, BAM, with no way to avoid that from happening. We tried it coming back in the other direction, and the same thing happened. The rifles thrown across would hit it from behind and caused guys to miss the weapons or drop them. This was not going to work. John called a halt to the practice, and allowed the team to take a break while we discussed my role. Jim Agee, Donald Treadwell ("Tread" or "Halftrack"), Henry Ho, Richard Sabatini, Sterling Johnson (the only other Black guy on the team), Greg Smyth, and other guys jumped into the conversation with their opinions. The one opinion that mattered was John's and he favored keeping the guidon, but use it outside the formation, and not try any more walk-throughs. I breathed a big sigh of relief and looked forward to integrating myself into their routine.

We devoted the rest of the practice to perfecting the routine that had been developed during the summer and the beginning of the school year. The team had already performed at the first pep rally of the football season the week before, and John looked for something else to add to the team. Basically, John and I worked on our timing as I marched around the formation with him and determined the best position for me at each segment of the routine. My moment of individuality occurred during the gauntlet. Instead of me going through with John, I went around the formation twirling the guidon around my body and over my head, meeting John on the other side of the gauntlet. So, as he came out the first time, I was there waiting, and the same was true on the way back, so that when we finished that maneuver, I was by his side and the formation faced forward ready for the next command. The next command called for the entire team to get in line to do the finale, the Queen Anne Salute. An intricate movement of the rifles done in sequence down the line when each team member ends up with the rifle at a modified present arms position with their left hand held across their chest and in a kneeling position. Once all the team members finished, John and I did a present arms, him with his saber and me with the guidon. An impressive finale.

John and the team liked the way we integrated the guidon into the routine, a bit of non-intrusive fluff, that could give us that little bit of an edge to beat out similar teams. So, I was in, and we moved forward. Now, I needed to get my official drill team uniform.

All of us had been issued khaki short-sleeved shirts, but the regular cadets wore them in conjunction with the green pants. They also issued us khaki pants, but we rarely wore them, but the drill team wore them as a part of their uniform. The drill team wore the full khaki uniform with a royal blue scarf around our necks to cover the white t-shirt; a royal blue beret; a blue and gold braid around our right shoulder; a full-webbed pistol belt with holster; a .45 cal holster, and jump boots. Unlike the regular cadets, only the battalion color guard and the varsity drill team wore boots. We tucked the bottoms of our khaki pants into the top of the boots. This was when I learned a little about spit-shining boots, for drill meet inspections. We were the total package, and for the first time, on a Friday, I wore the varsity drill team uniform instead of the regular cadet uniform. We wore all our ribbons, marksmanship medals, brass, and rank, on the drill team uniform on Uniform Day. However, for drill meets, we didn't wear all the ribbons or marksmanship medals, just the brass and rank.

That first day, as I strutted down the hallway in my varsity drill team uniform, beret and all, Janice, one of the "cool" Black girls who was sort of in charge of the Eastwood Black party scene, told me, "Looking good Pittard!"

Yeah, I felt on top of the world. We next performed during the pre-game activities at the Homecoming football game. We were scheduled to perform right before the national anthem. The idea would be that we would already be on the field in the Queen Anne salute line with the color guard in position in front of us, so that when The Star Spangled Banner was sung, the singer would have both the color guard and the varsity drill team as her backdrop. In theory it should have looked impressive—in reality it was *really* impressive!

Homecoming drew an unusually large crowd that gathered pretty early, so we had an almost full stadium of onlookers as we marched onto the field. As the crowd settled in, John gave his first command in his parade-ground voice, and the stadium became relatively quiet. We went through our routine with cheers and gasps at the appropriate time. However, when we broke down into the finale Queen Anne salute, and I did my spinning present arms finale with John's saber salute, the crowd gave its loudest cheer. Oh yeah, that routine was a winner. And, more importantly, a crowd pleaser.

The color guard came out almost immediately and formed up in front of John and me, followed by the young lady from the Chorals, the school singing group, who had been selected to sing the national anthem. It went off without a hitch and when she finished we all got a standing ovation.

I felt I belonged right here, out on the field performing in front of crowds. In a unique situation, different from the other Black students at school. This was the first year there had been Black cadets on the drill team. Since there were only two of us on the drill team and I was a featured performer outside the formation doing my own thing, I got a lot of the attention from other Black students. And that year, the school had a lot more Black students than ever before.

CHAPTER 14

Transformation

Both Eastwood and I went through a racial transformation in 1971. At Eastwood the racial demographics had changed significantly between my freshman year and my junior year. In my freshman year, Blacks may have comprised one percent of the student population. By the beginning of my junior year that percentage had ballooned to close to ten percent.

That year there was an explosion of Black faces in the hallways. In the preceding two years there had been a steady influx of new Black students as more African-American families moved into the district, and more and more students graduated from the feeder middle schools. But that didn't explain the veritable explosion of Black students in the fall of 1971. That year we had students who had moved into the district, others that had graduated up to Eastwood from the feeder schools, and what appeared to be a change in the lines for which neighborhoods were included in the area that fed into Eastwood. We had an interesting mix of Black freshmen, those who had transferred from Burgess, in the more middle-class Cielo Vista area, and wannabe gangstas from Bel Air, the school south of I-10, with a predominantly Black and Hispanic population.

For me, my transformation began when I read *The Autobiography of Malcolm X*, as told to Alex Haley, during the spring of 1971, my sophomore year. I didn't know anything about Malcolm X before then, but the book was on the list of books we could order through our English class. My English teacher, June Carroll, almost choked as she read the book synopsis. Ms. Carroll, a young white woman, was either uncomfortable or unfamiliar with the concepts of Black Muslims, Black nationalism, pimps, thieves, and prison, all words used on the back of the book. She mumbled most of it as her voice trailed away during the description of Malcolm X's life, and death. All that intrigued me and I immediately ordered the book, the only one in my class.

The book opened my eyes to other aspects of the Black experience in America that I had heretofore not known. I had known nothing of the Nation of Islam, or the rise of Malcolm X, or the concepts of Black Nationalism. My head was spinning! The book changed my perspective of my place in America as a Black person, and made me distrustful of white people in general. Although I had lived through the riots of '67, the assassination of MLK, and witnessed the treatment of Blacks in the South, and had my own experiences to fall back on, this book changed my view of everything. This began my slow transmogrification from being feisty to being militant.

When we spent the summer in Philly that year and I was exposed to the all-Black culture of North Central Philadelphia and Germantown, I had a different perspective of Black people in that environment. Interestingly, while visiting my grandmother in Philadelphia my brother and I were "inducted" into the Cumberland Street gang, made up of young brothers who carried knives, chains, and zip guns—homemade guns that would shoot one or two rounds. These were not "wannabes" they were the real deal and we had to swear fealty to them while we lived on that street. Fortunately, we never had to fight in any gang wars that summer…yeah, not sure how that would have turned out for us.

Our education into Philly continued as we heard gunshots at night; with the night air filled with the sounds of emergency vehicles responding to whatever violence had erupted in the neighborhood. The neighborhood had changed since we had lived there as kids.

As a different feature of that culture, we went to several house parties in various parts of Philly and learned the newest dances from Philly girls who found us attractive. Philly girls, at least in our experience, could be pretty aggressive and if they liked you they made no bones about it. So, we had an interesting experience over the summer that would have baffled the likes of some of these Black kids at Eastwood.

My transformation continued as did that of Eastwood because these new Black students also brought their social scene to an otherwise white-bread party and prom scene at Eastwood. Many of the Black students went to house parties instead of the dances sponsored by the school, although that would eventually change. But at the beginning of my junior year, house parties was where it was "at;" and they were invitation only or if you happened to belong to that part of the "cool" or "hip" crowd you automatically got an invite.

I was not a part of that scene and, although I didn't realize it at the time, I wanted desperately to be an accepted part of that crowd. I had always been a "nerd," being short, and wearing glasses that year. I was vice-president of the chess club, and third board on our school chess team. I was in ROTC, played on no athletic team, nor did I dress very cool. I took advanced placement classes in math and English, without many Black classmates. Many of the other Black students viewed me as one of the "smart ones" who spoke and acted "white."

In my favor, I did play basketball on the courts every morning, and played tackle football at lunch. But I didn't dress cool, didn't fawn all over the jocks, and wasn't a "wannabe gangsta." So, I wasn't very cool, at least not in the eyes of most of the newer Black students. But that changed, thanks to the drill team.

Within a couple of weeks, after the Homecoming performance, that same Black girl invited me to one of her coveted house parties! Oh yeah, I was really in there, as a new entrant into the Black party scene at Eastwood, and it was due to being on the drill team. I had been noticed. And it was my appearance at this house party where it was discovered that, "gee, he can dance too." Yeah, I knew all the dances from the east coast, so, yeah, I could dance. So now, I was still short, but cute and I could dance.

The following week, on the way home, two very cute Black freshmen girls "ambushed" me because they wanted to meet me and get to know me better. Hmm, maybe because of my recent advent into the Eastwood Black social scene I was almost socially acceptable.

This happened late in October, and there was a bite of frost in the air, so I had worn my suede leather coat, gloves, and of course my Hush Puppies. I really needed to upgrade my shoes, but my HPs fit so comfortably, especially for that mile-walk home both ways every day. I hated to give them up for more fashionable footwear, hence the nerdy HPs.

My route home took me across a large, bare field that had a low-slung rock wall that traversed the entire field. For those of us who lived in the New Eastridge area or Eastwood Heights going up Montwood you either had to follow the street around the field or cut across. Most of us cut across because that would cut ten minutes off the walk home.

All the foot traffic across the field was funneled through the only opening in the wall unless you felt adventurous and jumped the wall.

On this occasion, there were two girls sitting on either side of the opening facing in my direction. Both girls were very cute, one slightly darker than the other. Both wore brightly colored jackets and gloves, with well-fitting jeans and oxford shoes.

As I approached, looking for some way out of this because it looked like they were waiting for me, the darker girl raised her voice, "What's happenin' Chris Pittard?"

Of course I had heard the phrase before, but was still unsure how to respond. Typically, I'd heard the greeting from guys and I just responded with "what's happening?"

I learned that in Philly, cause you always had to appear cool, or they'd be on you. But coming from a girl, and a cute one at that, threw me for a loop. And, yeah, I did speak "white," and did not speak Ebonics, or jive or slang, or cool or hip talk. I was very proud of how I spoke the English language, but that wasn't helpful in this case.

"Uh, I uh, what's happening with you?" I sort of mumbled back.

Vaudean, the darker one, said, "We've been waiting for you. Would you like to walk us home?" Oh boy, shades of Philly.

By that time I had come to a stop in front of her, and glanced over at her friend, Lenore. "Okay, you live near me?"

"Yep, just a couple of streets over from you," Vaudean said, as she got up from her perch on the stone wall. She was slender with a nicely-coiffed afro, with pretty dark brown eyes, and milk chocolate skin. Lenore, who had also gotten to her feet, was about the same height as Vaudean, with a similar build. Lenore was more mocha-chocolate with lighter brown eyes than Vaudean. They were both freshman, so they were about my age even though I was a junior. I had seen them around the school, but because they were two grades behind, I didn't see them very often. Obviously they had planned this, had thought through this "ambush" at the wall, and equally obvious, Vaudean led this train.

As I passed through the opening, Vaudean shifted her books to her left arm, and looped her right arm in my left arm. Lenore took her place on my other side, locking me in a nice sandwich. We were all about the same height. I had never been between two such nice looking girls that weren't relatives. A nice feeling.

"You're cute, you know?" Vaudean began the conversation as we walked across the rock-strewn field.

"Uh, thank you," I said, "um, so are you." I mumbled again.

Lenore giggled at my discomfiture. I was uncomfortable with the situation, and they both must have known it. Even with my little experience in Philly, I was ill-prepared for this situation. But I still enjoyed it.

"I heard you can dance, too." Vaudean teased. I blushed at that.

"Yeah, a little bit." I said, again uncomfortable, but silently thanking my mom for the dance lessons and my experiences that past summer.

"And you bowl with Sterling, right?" Vaudean asked. She was Sterling's little sister. Sterling was the other Black guy on the drill team and a transfer to Eastwood from Burgess as a junior. He was a cadet major and the battalion S-1; participated on the varsity drill team, the varsity basketball team; and was a championship bowler that I knew from my participation in travel league. Sterling bowled for Center Lanes at Fort Bliss, and I bowled for Red Rooster, near downtown El Paso.

"Well, I sort of bowl against him," I said, "but we're on drill team together."

"Yes, I know." She grinned.

Lenore laughed out loud then. Lenore seemed to enjoying this way too much.

We continued to make small talk all the way to Vaudean's house, only a couple of streets over from mine. I left both of them there as I made my way to my house. That was one of the most enjoyable walks home I'd experienced and one of the best times I'd spent with a girl my age since Joan.

Joan had lived in El Paso during my sophomore year, and we had reignited our relationship. She was in the eighth grade, so I only saw her on the weekends, as often as I could, but she didn't attend Eastwood, so I only saw her occasionally. Once she moved away in late spring during my sophomore year, I hadn't dated any other Black girls. There hadn't been any my age at school until my junior year when all the freshmen girls showed up.

I didn't think much would come of all this, but it was nice to know someone found me cute, themselves also very cute and around my age.

I dated Vaudean for a few months, going to the bowling alley, to dances, and to the movies. But after a while we just kind of drifted apart. Nothing dramatic, we just stopped "going together," or "talking." No fuss, no muss—probably the easiest break up in my entire life. The experience had been a real confidence builder and I walked with a little more of a swagger in my step.

None of this happens if not for me being on the drill team and being sort of cute. I mean I was 14 years old now, and a junior in high school, but the difference in uniform and the fact of being on the team helped a lot socially. I was sort of a "cool" ROTC guy, and enjoyed a little status at school.

CHAPTER 15

Kickin' Ass

We competed in our first drill meet that fall at the University of Texas at El Paso (UTEP) and it was the first time I had attended such an event. Every team competed in three areas for scoring: the inspection; standard manual of arms/drill and ceremonies; and the exhibition drill team portion of the competition. I participated in all three parts of the competition with varying degrees of involvement.

In the initial inspection, in which every team participated, the inspectors looked at every team member. First, they inspected me and John at the front of the formation. When John gave the command for the team to open ranks for the inspection, I just stayed up front by myself while he accompanied the inspectors through the ranks. The second part of the competition didn't involve me at all, and I sat on the sidelines while the team executed the rigid manual of arms and D&C required of every team. Then there was the exhibition portion—that's when I had my time to shine along with the rest of the team. I also got a chance to watch other teams, particularly those with guidons, and grade their performance, and potentially learn from those better than me. The only one that outperformed me came from Odessa Permian, the Panthers. He did something that I hadn't thought of at the time. But, first, I need to describe the Odessa Permian drill team.

Odessa Permian High School, in 1971, was the bad boy of West Texas high school football. They had won multiple state championships and were thought to be almost invincible. Wrapped in black and white, with the emphasis on black; they always looked intimidating, kind of like the Oakland Raiders. Apparently, the Odessa Permian drill team took a page from the football team because they had all-black uniforms. Black shirts, black uniform trousers, shiny black boots, and topped off with shiny black helmet liners. They were baaaad, and knew it. You could tell by their swagger they came to win and they acted like it.

The OP guidon was this short little white guy who also used a full size guidon and performed amazingly well in wielding it around his body and over his head like me. But when they did their finale move as a part of their exhibition drill team phase, he executed a jazz split with the guidon and a left hand salute at the same time his team executed their Queen Anne salute. Impressive!

I knew that I couldn't integrate that move into my repertoire of moves by the time we were to perform. However, I vowed that by the time I either performed or competed again I would be able to execute a jazz split, and maybe come up with some twists of my own.

Later I found out jazz splits were not as easy as I thought. I'd never done jazz splits before and it meant having to learn how to stretch and then how to actually execute the jazz split. First by itself, then with the guidon, and then in unison with the drill team's finale. So I first practiced at home until I felt comfortable performing a jazz split on command. Then I began practicing on the field with the guidon, over and over again until I could do it with no hesitation.

Within a week I could perform a jazz split with the guidon and at the following drill team practice, I surprised everybody by executing a jazz split with the guidon at the same time the team ended the Queen Anne salute. When that last team member hit the ground, I threw my left leg into the air and went down in a jazz split and extended the guidon behind me on my right and brought my left hand up in a salute across my chest with my head bowed forward. My performance even impressed John. Now I was ready.

Our final competition that school year was at the Ysleta ISD Annual JROTC Drill Team Meet held at Riverside High School. There were five high schools in the Ysleta District: the Eastwood Troopers; the Bel Air Highlanders; the Parkland Matadors; the Ysleta Indians; and the Riverside Rangers. Riverside was a comparatively new high school, having only been open a few years at that point. Consequently, their JROTC program was really in its infancy, but they hosted the meet, maybe in an attempt to gain respect and credibility for their JROTC program. Well if that was the idea…sorry, it didn't work.

Their drill team was pretty awful, and the meet seemed a bit disorganized. Teams not knowing where to line up; not enough judges for the various events; no place to practice before going before the judges; and just a feeling of tasks not being done the way they were supposed to be done. Anyway, we came in second to the Bel Air varsity drill team who adorned their gray uniforms with navy blue berets and white braids on their shoulders. They looked good and they drilled well. They had a boring guidon, with no eye-popping moves. In contrast, the Bel Air rifle-wielding members had some outstanding moves, and the one that probably won it for them was the blindfolded-over-the-formation rifle throw executed by their two best rifle throwers. Very impressive! We threw rifles, but not that far back and not blindfolded. What also gave me a source of pride was that half the Bel Air team was Black, and it was good seeing Black cadets performing well in that environment. But our team still lost and second place in our own district wasn't good enough. So, our goal next year was to win Ysleta.

❖ ❖ ❖

We came back my senior year with a different attitude towards winning as a drill team. One of the ways we decided to change our attitude and make us feel and look more aggressive was to change our uniforms to better compete with teams from Odessa Permian and Bel Air. Instead of the all-khaki uniforms, we went to an all navy blue uniform and navy berets and gold scarves. Second, we began calling ourselves "Black Jacks," after General of the Armies John Pershing. As a high school drill team we could not belong to the Pershing Rifles which was a collegiate drill team organization, so the next best thing was give ourselves a name associated with General "Black Jack" John Pershing. Finally, to add some more pizzazz to the team my guidon position evolved into a "baton and saber" guidon which meant that I manipulated either a wooden baton about three feet long or a saber (you know, a sword), again, outside the formation. I would do various routines including jazz splits and I got pretty good with both the baton and the saber.

We competed in Las Cruces, at New Mexico State University, in the first month of our senior school year. By that time we had added a few new members to the team, Moises and Paulo Piralta, both black belts in Tae Kwon Do, had just moved back to the States from Panama. In addition, I started training a freshman, Andy Bland, to eventually take my place on the team the following year. Andy, a young African-American whose dad was an Army officer, had just moved to El Paso. He reminded me of me and I had recommended him for the guidon position in his company, like me, so he could get the automatic promotion to corporal. He was a skinny little guy, chocolate-colored complexion, with black hair in a short afro, big teeth and a ready smile.

We hung out, even away from school, particularly the next spring after I got my driver's license. We used to follow cars, randomly, just to see if we could keep up with them, and it would also improve my driving skills. We stopped that practice after we followed this one car off the beaten path late at night to a secluded dirt road. When the driver pulled over to the side and pointed a handgun out of the driver's window, we drove off in a cloud of dust and in a hurry! We didn't track any more cars after that, but it was pretty fun while it lasted.

So, at the Las Cruces meet, Andy was there to observe, to get an idea of what I did during meets and to watch the team perform. During the inspection portion of the event, I used the full-sized guidon. I didn't participate in the mandatory D&C competition; and, for the first time, I broke out with the saber in the exhibition portion of the competition. In order to become proficient with the saber, I had practiced with a blue and gold tape-wrapped wooden stick, about three feet long. I learned how to manipulate the stick through my fingers on both hands and over my hands, around my legs and back, and over my head.

When the team performed at the first pep rally I used the wooden stick instead of the full-sized guidon, in eventual preparation for the saber. What little criticism I received after that performance was that I looked like a majorette captain twirling her baton. Well, I wasn't a "majorette captain" but I was twirling a baton. I got the message—time to move on to the saber, which ultimately was more dangerous because of the potential for cuts and injury.

The difference between a saber and a sword is the blade. The saber has a curved blade, and the sword a straight blade. Unfortunately, we used sabers, which was fine for John, but for me it problematic when trying to learn to spin the damn thing. Initially I learned to use the saber through the manual of arms for sabers and swords. There is an actual manual of arms for the use of the saber, and John and I practiced that together. I learned "present arms," "order arms," and the "carry saber" position in which the saber is held while marching. I became good with manipulating the saber, but I needed to go beyond the normal manual of arms. I had to become its master.

Yeah, right. That proved to be difficult because of the curved blade. The weight of the saber was down on the guard and the grip at the bottom of the saber, away from the tip of the blade or the "toe" of the blade. And, to complicate matters, the curved nature of the blade made it more difficult to manipulate through my fingers and hands. The saber had no real center of gravity, so I had to make my movements small and quick, closer to the grip and handle.

Spinning the saber proved somewhat of a challenge. I had never seen anyone spin the saber. I've seen people manipulate the saber by the handle or the guard, in order to perform the manual of arms for sabers and swords, but not spin it through their fingers. I learned pretty quickly that manipulating the saber through my hands caused a lot of small little cuts on my hands and fingers that hurt like hell. After the first practice with the saber, I bought a pair of dress white gloves to relieve me of the pain and threat of continued injury. The gloves were a life saver, and I continued to wear them the rest of the year.

I also learned to "whip" the saber round and round in my right hand, and over my head in kind of a flinging motion, as if I was getting ready to lasso a calf or something. My moves had to be more exaggerated than John's, so if we did a present arms, I would do it with a flourish of a whipping motion twice before bringing it up to my face for the "present saber" position. The same with bringing it back down for the "order arms" movement, and then for the "carry saber" movement. Everything I did had to have a flourish or stylistic move to it in order to bring some pizzazz to the team and me.

So, at the Las Cruces meet I marched out there ready to go for the exhibition event. For my part, the routine went fine; I executed all the movements including my modified Queen Anne salute at the end, as the last guy to actually do the salute. In my modified Queen Anne I had to spin the saber on my right side coming from the carry saber position, then twirl the saber above my head by the guard, and then spin it down on my right side again, hit the ground with the toe of the saber then bounce the saber up to the carry position, then crash down into a kneeling position with the left hand salute across my chest and my head dropped into a quick bow to the crowd and hold it in position as my finale.

Disappointingly, the team didn't fare as well. We had been working on our version of the long over-the-formation throw as executed by other teams, and in our case, we had the two biggest and tallest guys, Tread and Jim Agee executing it with Tread throwing it back to Jim. After hours of practice they were able to execute it about 70% of the time. Unfortunately, this was part of the 30%. The throw, executed before the gauntlet, went off to Jim's left and almost hit Richard Sabatini. Luckily they averted a disaster. Jim actually caught the rifle, but it didn't look good. The rest of the performance was flawless, but one mistake can cost you the meet, and that's pretty much what happened to us. Ironically, Jim and Tread executed that throw flawlessly at both the pep rally and at Homecoming, but not in Las Cruces. Well, back to the drawing board.

During this 1972-73 school year, the team also began to engage in the martial arts. I had been introduced to the martial arts through my Uncle Harold Caro when he had volunteered to teach me Tae Kwon Do. He was a 2nd Dan black belt, trained in Korea, and when he heard about my earlier exploits with some of the kids at school, he volunteered to train me. He worked with me during the spring and summer of 1970, but as the school year began in 1970, I sort of lost interest and we discontinued the lessons. However, when a bigger white boy on my street challenged me to a fight, I ended up kicking his ass, which ended both his threat and the threat of anyone else challenging me for quite a while. I retained an interest in the martial arts and even had a Bruce Lee poster over the head of my bed at home; so it came as no surprise when John and other members of the team got into the martial arts, I was right there with them.

The interest was sparked by Moises (or Moses) and his younger brother Paulo, who were both black belts. They offered to teach Tae Kwon Do to the rest of us during lunch, and after school and after morning drill team practice. They told us they did not want to focus on teaching the various "hyungs" or forms, which are the stylized progression of movements designed to teach fighting techniques and various strikes and combination of strikes and kicks.

Instead, the brothers taught us various fighting techniques, using what's called "one-steps" or the use of hand, fist, elbow, knee, or foot strikes and kicks in response to a multitude of attacks by your opponent. This was designed to teach you how to quickly react in an attack or fight with a variety of hand strikes or kicks. In addition, we would engage in free sparring, without protective equipment, just the shoes on our feet, with no gloves or protective gear for our hands, shins, or heads. If nothing else, we would learn quickly how to block our opponents' strikes just to make sure we didn't get hurt too badly.

Many of our sessions became quite lively and painful at times, and developed into one more thing the drill team did as a group, different from any other group at school. This was long before high schools had organized judo or karate clubs or teams, so this was our only opportunity to get this kind of training and experience for free, well almost free, we did pay them some level of money for their expertise and personal training. Some of us got pretty good, and I know John eventually became a 2nd Dan black belt in Tae Kwon Do, and I eventually, many years later, became a 1st Dan black belt in Tae Kwon Do Chung Do Kwon, and a black belt instructor.

Another distraction for the drill team and the ROTC guys in general was our collective bids for elected office at the end of our junior year. John ran for Student Council president; Greg Smyth for Student Council VP; James Haas, also a varsity wrestler, ran for Student Council as the senior class representative; and I ran for Senior Class president. We were known as the "ROTC ticket." Of all us, only James was elected to office. I was told I came in second, but who knows. The big thing for me was that I had gained the confidence, through ROTC and drill team, to even contemplate running for office and then actually running for Senior Class president. That in itself was an accomplishment.

We were still the varsity drill team. One good thing about losing our bids for elected office as we entered the 1972-73 school year it allowed us to focus on our main mission, to win the 1973 Ysleta District JROTC Drill Team trophy.

✦ ✦ ✦

The drill team continued to work on its routine until we executed it without mistakes, over and over again, then again for good measure. The big throw was executed to the point of 90% success, where Tread and Jim could probably execute it in their sleep, and it remained the centerpiece of our exhibition routine. We were ready for the spring 1973 Ysleta meet to be held on our home field, at Eastwood High School—Home of the Eastwood Troopers.

In preparing for the Ysleta meet I experimented with using two sabers at one time; and also experimented with working Andy into the routine with an exchange of sabers, similar to that of the throwing exchange of rifles. However, after getting a saber in the throat, where it hung for a very long second, I decided against both of us performing together. It was still my show, and I worked on routines where I spun in place while catching the saber in the air after throwing it up, as well as spinning it through my hands and whipping it around and over my head. The flashing blade in the afternoon sunlight was quite impressive. I couldn't wait for the Ysleta meet.

The meet began under the umbrella of a beautiful El Paso day. The weather had begun to get warm that April, and would get even warmer before the end of the day. That morning it was nice and cool for the inspection and the mandatory D&C, both of which we maxed. Again, it was going to come down to the exhibition phase of the completion to determine who would win. We were in a virtual tie with Ysleta and ahead of Bel Air, so this was our opportunity to take this thing, once and for all. Eastwood had never won the Ysleta drill meet. Ysleta and Bel Air had always been triumphant, but this was our time.

Our drill team had worked tirelessly on "silent commands." Ordinarily, the drill team commander would give the commands for the team for each of the drill movements or maneuvers. The year before, Richard Sabatini, Mike King, and I had visited New Mexico Military Institute on two occasions, in the spring and fall, and on both occasions we saw a demonstration of the NMMI silent drill team. The NMMI junior college team operated with a combination of signals, steps and cadences, to take their cues for each movement. With their shiny black helmets with the NMMI shield and black shades, they were really cool-looking and very impressive. They ranked as one of the best in the nation, and it showed in their routines. When we came back following the first visit we told John about the silent drill team and thought we could integrate that into our routines. It developed slowly at first, but little by little we performed almost the entire show with only one or two commands from John. Again, we thought this might give us somewhat of an edge over these other drill teams.

So, in April, after working on the silent drill team routine for months, we were ready to win Ysleta. John gave the initial command to bring the team onto the football field for the exhibition phase, and from there until close to the finale, the team went through its routine without another command. A flawless performance.

The team performed slow drills; had spinning rifles; rifle exchanges; and intricate marching movements. At one point, as the team marched from right to left in front of the judges, John gave the signal for the over the formation throw—uh oh, here we go—and Tread hit it perfectly, whew! That was the hard part, now we had a real chance of winning.

Once that had been performed, John brought the team back around in a "counter column" maneuver that's not in the D&C manual, to the area directly in front of the judges as we got ready for the gauntlet. Differently than before, John wasn't the only one who went through the gauntlet, I went through too. Since I was wielding the saber and not that unwieldy guidon, I was able to follow him through both sides of the gauntlet. When he went through, I followed a couple of beats later in the "carry saber" position, and at the end, after successfully avoiding the spinning rifles, I turned with a flourish and spun the saber around my side and got into position behind John for the reentry into the gauntlet. This time as we went back through, the team members threw their rifles in an exchange behind and in front of us. Whew! We made it through a second time, so now for the finale.

As John got to his position in front of the judges, he brought the saber down to the "order arms" position, and as he did so, the team, waiting on that movement as their command to move, executed their move into the Queen Anne salute formation of the line and once the last member was in place, he hit the heel of his M-14 twice on the ground as the signal to start. The Queen Anne salute started, not with him, but on the opposite end of the line, and ended with the team member, Jim Agee, who started the salute with his M-14. Once we heard the last rifle and knee hit the ground, John and I both executed our versions of the Queen Anne salute—John with present arms, and me with the spinning and kneeling maneuver. That brought to a close a very long and hard drill team season—one where we had tried to be innovative with some success and dotted with failure as well.

On this day, however, we tasted the ultimate—the Ysleta District JROTC Drill Meet trophy for 1973 was awarded to...drum roll please...Eastwood High School! Could there be any doubt?

The following Friday night we had our celebratory dinner at Henry Ho's parents' Chinese restaurant, the Golden Dragon. We each paid $10 and we ate like kings. Henry's dad invited us to come just as the restaurant closed so we had the whole place to ourselves. Oh, we had a great time after having won Ysleta and the trophy right there for us to admire and to cherish. I was happy to be a part of this elite drill team, and happy to be a part of winning the Big One, finally.

I'm not sure what everyone else got out of their experience, but for me it taught me how to work as a part of a precision team, making intricate movements under great adversity, and pressure. I also learned how to operate outside of the formation, and how to improvise and come up with successful ways of doing my own thing in conjunction with the team. These served as important lessons and also served me well later in life, again, both in and out of the military.

CHAPTER 16

NMMI

In the four years of JROTC at Eastwood I had been inundated, as all of us were, by films about the Army and the Army as a career—a career as an officer or enlisted. Our instructors exposed us to various aspects of the Army to include Special Forces, Army Rangers, Army Airborne, armor, field artillery, air defense, and combat engineers. The film on Ranger School had a significant impact on me because it seemed to elevate Army Rangers to the level of being the epitome of Army soldierhood—the best of the best, and something for all of us to aspire to one day.

In addition to the recruiting films and films about the Army, recruiters representing various institutions of higher learning, including New Mexico Military Institute, located in Roswell, New Mexico, visited with us.

NMMI was a combination four-year high school, and a junior college military institution. Since we were already in high school, we weren't being recruited for the high school portion of the school, but the junior college. Central to the recruitment incentive was the possibility of attending the junior college and going through a two-year senior ROTC program instead of the normal four-year program. Additionally, there was the potential incentive of a two-year ROTC scholarship to pay for the whole thing; and even if you didn't get the scholarship, as a ROTC contract cadet in the two-year program, you would receive a monthly stipend of $100. Attendance at the ROTC Basic Camp at Fort Knox, Kentucky, voluntary for us, and the ROTC Advanced Camp at Fort Riley, Kansas, which was mandatory, where we would receive the pay of an E-4, were part of the recruitment package. The ROTC Basic Camp was mandatory for anyone entering the two-year ROTC program because it was like going through regular Army basic training, and it was run by drill sergeants. Fort Knox was voluntary for those of us who had three or four years of JROTC because we had learned the basics needed before entering senior ROTC; however, the recruiter, a nice young second lieutenant, recommended going to the ROTC Basic Camp because it really prepared you for the two-year senior ROTC program.

The final benefit for going to NMMI and enrolling into the two-year senior ROTC program was that you had the choice of being commissioned as a second lieutenant in the Army upon graduation from NMMI or deferring two additional years after obtaining your bachelor's degree from a four-year institution. Wow! What a deal! This sounded almost too good to be true. The final icing on the cake of recruitment was the recruiter's offer to visit the campus over a weekend in the spring. Yeah, that sounded real good, and I thought I might take him up on that very generous offer.

The recruiter also brought a video of the school which included footage of cadets marching in large formations on an immaculate parade field, like West Point, and it showed cadets in classrooms, and doing all kinds of extracurricular activities from football, to baseball, horseback riding, rodeo riding, golf, student center with a 10-lane bowling facility (which caught my eye), intramural sports, archery, rifle team, ROTC cadets in the field, and of course, the world famous NMMI Varsity Drill Team. Quite impressive, even on film! I looked forward to eventually seeing the campus and the drill team in person.

I took as much information about the school as I could to show my parents. I was all excited about going to visit NMMI, and infected my Mom with my excitement. Dad, again, remained pretty non-committal, but thought it might be a good idea to visit a college campus. Dad still had aspirations for me to go to a Historically Black College or University (HBCU), like Texas Southern University in Houston. He thought I needed to be exposed to more Black people…that I wasn't Black enough. I resisted the idea of going to TSU or any other HBCU, not because they weren't good schools, I just didn't think they were good fits for me. Since I would graduate high school at 16, I thought a more insular school with a smaller population might be better for me; and a military environment might be even better. I had been thinking seriously about NMMI from the moment I heard about the school.

The recruiter had come through Eastwood in March, 1972, my junior year, and told us the next scheduled weekend for the open house and the opportunity to visit would be in April, right after the Ysleta drill meet. Well, that sounded like a plan, so I passed that on to my parents, and they both agreed to me going to visit NMMI. At 15 years old, this would be my first college campus tour and I'd stay in the barracks with the college cadets, whoo hoo! Two other students from Eastwood expressed an interest in going to NMMI for the visit, and possibly to school—Richard Sabatini and Mike King. Mike, a chubby, red-haired guy, was a weapons enthusiast and loved everything about the military and police departments. He bragged that he'd seen the movie *Patton* forty-five times. Geez, get a life! Anyway, he joined me on the trip, as did Sabatini. Richard was in speech and drama, as well as on the varsity drill team and had come to Eastwood our sophomore year. Richard's mother was British and Richard loved everything British, a real Anglophile. He spoke quite suavely with a very cultured air, was a nice-looking guy, and all the girls just loved him. Huh, must have been the voice.

◊   ◊   ◊

We left early on a Friday morning, so we could get to NMMI fairly early. Roswell lies east of El Paso, a little more than 200 miles, so it would take us about four hours to get there at the posted speed limit of 55 MPH. We met at the school at 6 am and loaded up our luggage for the weekend in the car. Our driver and escort/chaperone was 1SG Robert Patino, or as we eventually affectionately called him "Dad." But not yet; he was 1SG Patino to his face. Patino drove a nice, new, big rental car, so we enjoyed a comfortable ride to Roswell. I guess Patino had been "volunteered" for this duty, but I don't think he minded. He seemed to enjoy having an opportunity to visit a college campus as well as hanging out with some of his cadets.

We dressed in civilian clothes on the advice of the recruiter, but later we determined that it would have been better to have been in our cadet uniforms. As we rolled up to the campus, we drove to the Sally Port entrance to the huge square-shaped barracks/dorms of the "Box." The barracks towered above us and encompassed a huge square full of running and walking cadets. This was the centerpiece of the campus and where all the high school troops and most of the college troops resided. A majority of the population of the school lived in the Box, and that was where most of the action happened, including musters of the entire Corps of Cadets, graduations, and other significant events.

The Office of the Commandant of Cadets was located in the headquarters of the Box, where we were to report. 1SG Patino went into the headquarters while we stared wide-eyed at the passing cadets, all in their uniforms consisting of the short-sleeved khaki shirts and khaki trousers, cunt caps and black low-quarter shoes, with their various accoutrements and cadet rank, going to class or attending to their business on campus. Man, I hadn't seen anything like this since my long-ago visit to West Point when we lived in Fort Totten. I got kind of a thrill looking at these cadets walking around, thinking that one day I might be among them.

When Patino came back out he had interesting news. The official open house was the following week, we were a week early; however, they would accommodate us because we had come all this way from El Paso. It also meant we would pretty much have the entire campus to ourselves, with no other visiting students to compete with the admissions department's attention. They herded us to the admissions office and gave us an initial orientation, and then took us on a tour of the campus.

Our walking tour took us to the various classroom buildings, the student center with the 10-lane bowling alley, to the mess hall, the natatorium, the gym and weight rooms, the small 10-bed medical clinic, the Cadet Store, and finally ended at "the Slab." The Slab was the location of the last three college troops. The name denoted the enormous concrete slab that fronted the barracks for Kilo, Lima and Mike Troops. The Slab also had the reputation of being the wilder of locations, probably because everyone was in college and most were of legal drinking age. The practice football field and track were in front of the Slab, and to the far side of the Slab was the primary parade field.

1SG Patino had made the tour with us, but once we made it over to the Slab, he brought the car around so we could get our luggage, and then he said his goodbyes until Sunday morning. The plan was for us to spend two nights on campus, in the barracks, and, as it turned out, in the Mike Troop barracks. Mike thought it pretty neat that we would be staying in the "Mike" Troop barracks and acted like a kid at Christmas. He roomed with Richard, and I ended up in a room by myself.

We were assigned to a squad, led by a first-class cadet, Cadet SSG Montoya, from Artesia, New Mexico. He was a contract ROTC cadet preparing to graduate and get his commission. This is when I found out you could attend the junior college section of NMMI and not be a contract ROTC cadet, but everyone had to take ROTC.

We got settled in our rooms and prepared for dinner. The dinner formation was to form up at 1745 hours. At 1730, Montoya came around to our rooms to make sure we were ready to "fall out" to the formation on time, and also to find out if we could march. Richard and I assured him we could march and that we were on our high school drill team. Mike assured him of his marching skills as well. So, still with some trepidation, Montoya had us fall out at the end of his squad. I had never taken D&C commands from anyone other than cadets trained by SFC Kittlested, and we had a certain cadence and timbre to our voices. We gave our commands a certain way, and understood one another. But this was NMMI, and at NMMI they did it a little differently…

We had been taught to give commands with inflection and projection at certain points during the given command, to ensure the cadet could hear the command and perform the commanded movement with the crispness demanded by the commander giving the commands. Apparently, the NMMI method of giving D&C and marching commands was to do it in an almost monotonistic manner, with little inflection or significant emphasis on any syllable or word in the given command. We found this really confusing and difficult to hear and understand the commands of the platoon leader and the troop commander. All three of us had the same problem and looked around at the NMMI cadets to follow their lead. The simplest of commands, "Right Face," and "Attention," became more difficult by the lack of inflection in the command voice, as was the command to "Forward March" and the cadences sung by the platoon sergeant. This frustrated those of us who prided ourselves on our ability to, not only march, but to be the best at performing D&C, except, not here. Yeah, not only did we look awkward trying to keep up with the inflectionless commands, but we were doing it in civilian clothes which made our stumbling and bumbling even more noticeable. We all felt sort of embarrassed by the time we got to the mess hall.

The platoon sergeant, who could see our discomfiture, commented, "I thought Montoya said you knew how to march."

Uh, hmm, uh, yeah, we knew how to march, just not the NMMI way; but we simply responded, "We were just getting used to the way you all give your commands, we'll do better next time."

He laughed, and said, "Yeah, we do it different here, and if you come here to school, you'll find out we do a lot of things differently than you're used to." He continued, "We're modeled from the "Old Corps" from West Point, so we have a lot of cavalry traditions and we conduct drill and ceremonies according to those traditions, so it doesn't quite match up with FM 22-5, the bible for drill and ceremonies."

Okay, whew, we thought it might be us, but, in fact, they purposely did things differently and it would take some getting used to.

We found Montoya and his squad's table as they got ready to sit down for dinner. We all stood at attention until Montoya gave us the command to be seated. Since this was the second semester of the second-class year, the freshman college students, no longer known as RATS (Recruits-At-Training), just second-classmen, were allowed to actually eat their meal without too much hazing. We had an opportunity to observe the high school new cadets who remained RATS the entire year, and saw how they had to eat "square meals," and how they were subjected to continuous harassment and hazing during the entire meal.

The "square" meal derives its name from the 90 degree angles from which the RAT must eat his food. He cannot look down at his food, but must keep his eyes forward. He sits a fist distance from the edge of the table and when he brings food to his mouth he has to do it in such a way as to bring the food straight up from the plate to mouth level, then bring the fork or spoon to his mouth in a straight line, thus creating the "square." He must then chew his food within three seconds. Any longer than that he could be punished with a large tablespoon of peanut butter from the jar that sat on every table in the mess hall. The squad leader might ask you a question and you had to answer within the three seconds or be subject to the dreaded peanut butter. That didn't look like much fun, but it was part of the ritual of the Old Corps here at NMMI.

The mess hall was a large facility that housed the entire cadet compliment of almost 1000 cadets. Each squad had its own table co-located within each platoon and troop. The troop guidon for the various troops stood proudly behind the chair of the troop commander's chair where he sat with his first sergeant, field first sergeant, and the platoon leaders. I found it curious the platoon leaders did not sit with their platoons. An interesting comment on leadership styles.

But, the meal actually tasted pretty good. They served the food "family style" on large platters and in bowls of meat and vegetables. Pitchers of milk, water and tea, sat on the table and each was served with the common heaping platters of food. We had fried chicken, mashed potatoes with gravy, green beans, and small pieces of apple pie for dessert. This was actually pretty good…and when we ran out of a particular menu item, cadet waiters, part of the work-study program, would attentively replenish the food or drink as required. This was pretty neat! I could definitely get used to this!

At the end of the meal they allowed us to walk back to the barracks on our own. Neither of our rooms had a television or radio, limiting our entertainment choices. Still, it was a Friday night, and we asked one of the second-class cadets what they did on a typical Friday night. The college cadets received evening passes and many of them went into Roswell to experience the night life. Hmm, like Denny's, or the movies, or just walking around, and if you had a car then you could go even farther away. Many of the first-class cadets had cars and girlfriends, so they had a social life. Less so for many of the second-class cadets. The uniform for off-campus forays was the Class A casual that allowed them to wear a white shirt and green trousers with saucer cap. The normal uniform for walking around campus was the khaki shirt and khaki trousers. The second-class cadet we asked suggested the movie on campus. There was some Clint Eastwood flick playing that night and it cost a dollar to get in, so that sounded like a bet.

We walked over to the movie theater with several of the cadets, saw the movie, and just sort of hung out with them the rest of the night. We went over to the student center to the bowling lanes, and the pool hall, located downstairs with the bowling lanes. The bowling lanes were of an ancient design with manual score keeping, and the bowling balls rolled down on top of the railing of the ball return as they came back to the bowlers—it really looked weird. I'd never seen anything like that before!

We sat around the snack bar upstairs eating French fries, and drinking sodas, talking about ourselves and learning a little about our hosts. Music played out of the jukebox, and a lot of laughing filled the air. Kind of a strange scene with no girls, I mean, no girls anywhere, that just seemed…odd.

The cadets we spoke to hailed from New Mexico and California. They had been drawn to NMMI because of the prospect of becoming commissioned officers after only two years. There was only one other school like that in the country, and of the two, NMMI was the best. They described a little of their RAT semester, but didn't really get into much detail, I think they were forbidden to discuss the hazing portions of their experience. They talked about Fort Knox and ROTC Basic Camp and recommended we go if we could. They felt it had really been helpful to them when they got to NMMI. One of them performed on the NMMI Goss Rifles drill team and said they would be practicing the following day at the parking lot outside the ROTC building. That sounded pretty good to us, and we told him we would be there. After an hour or so we went back to the barracks and went to bed. They served breakfast at 7:30, but on Saturday, breakfast wasn't mandatory. However, if we wanted to eat, we still had to march over to the mess.

We went to breakfast with the formation, and this time we did better in understanding the marching commands. Breakfast was the typical fare—eggs, bacon, pancakes, sausage, grits, milk, cereal, and various juices, but was not served family style like dinner. They served it more like a regular mess hall where we walked through a serving line and sat where we wanted. Once we finished we returned to the barracks where 1SG Patino waited for us.

He told us that we would return home that day because we had pretty much seen everything we needed to see, and there was no reason to wait until Sunday. We told him about the drill team practice, and of course he knew two of us competed with the Eastwood drill team, so he acceded to our request.

The practice was scheduled for 9 o'clock, so we walked over to where they formed up. Since this was practice, the drill team members dressed in sweats and wore boots with no helmets. They had a meet in a week and were just polishing up their routine. This was the first time we had seen a drill team performing pretty much without commands, a "silent" drill team. It looked great! This might be what we needed to put our drill team over the top. We couldn't wait to get back and tell John and the other guys what we had seen—these guys were good, and deserved the national recognition they had earned. Wow! We were transfixed during the entire practice and all agreed this was the best drill team we had ever seen, even better than the U.S. Army Drill Team or the USMC Drill Team—these guys were really good! I knew I could never be one of them, but Richard began dreaming of being on the NMMI drill team one day.

Talking and laughter about our visit and the prospects of coming back the following year dominated our ride home. We had been invited for a return visit, and we certainly wanted to go back, except this next time we would visit during an official open house and we would wear our uniforms. 1SG Patino agreed to come back with us, the three "brothers" and "Dad" were coming back in the fall.

CHAPTER 17

NMMI Again

I looked forward to my senior year at Eastwood. I had established a niche at school through the drill team, and that allowed my social life to bloom as well. This year was the year for us to win Ysleta, and this year the three of us would go back to NMMI much better prepared than the previous spring. 1SG Patino found out the fall open house occurred the first week of October, and made the appropriate plans for us to attend.

I didn't know if anyone else would be interested in visiting NMMI, we never asked, and neither did Patino. We were going to do this as our "thing" this year, and no one else need be invited. James Haas aspired to attend the Coast Guard Academy; Sterling Johnson applied to the Air Force Academy; and no one else seemed interested, within our senior class in going to a military academy or institution, so we didn't feel too bad in perceiving this trip as ours.

We planned to go in uniform this time, so we had to figure out which uniform. Both Richard and I were on the drill team and had authorization to wear the drill team "modified" uniform that included the blue beret, the blue and gold braid on the right shoulder, and jump boots. Mike, the newcomer to the drill team was also authorized to wear the drill team uniform on this trip, but he hadn't acquired the jump boots or the blue uniform. He ended up wearing the beret, the braid, but not the boots. Richard and I were both captains—I was the assistant S-1 under Cadet Major Sterling Johnson, the S-1, and Richard was the battalion S-2. Eventually, I would be promoted to Cadet Major after being assigned the position of battalion S-3, training and operations. Mike was a cadet First Sergeant, and wore his stripes proudly. This time we went with significant rank—all our ribbons, marksmanship medals, and other accoutrements—and not as some sorry-looking high school students in civvies, but as JROTC cadets who knew what they were about.

The only unfortunate side effect of going on that particular Friday, we would miss "Yearbook Day" where the school photographers took most of the pictures of various groups for the yearbook. Richard was a member of the Drama Club, the Speech Club, drill team, JROTC, and other clubs. I was still a member of the King's Men chess club, drill team, JROTC, Spectators, and other organizations. Mike was a member of JROTC, drill team and other organizations, so we would miss out on several pictures. As it turned out, the most significant pictures were the JROTC and drill team; the yearbook staff took many of the others on succeeding Fridays so we were able to be included in many of our organizational pictures, but not all of them. So, we would not appear as often as we should have for our senior yearbook. But the trade-off, going to NMMI again, made it worthwhile.

This time as we approached Roswell, rather than going straight to the campus we went to the hotel 1SG Patino had reserved for himself. We had travelled in civilian clothes so we wouldn't wrinkle our uniforms during the long drive. We changed into our uniforms at the hotel, and got mentally ready to invade the NMMI campus as outstanding JROTC cadets from Eastwood High School—sort of how Clark Kent turns into Superman.

We piled back into the government van 1SG Patino had procured for our trip and looked forward to the first sight of Sally Port, again. And there it was, rising up in the distance, like a tower in the desert, an oasis, like home. That's what it felt like—we were coming home. The Box was the site for the initial in-processing for the open house, so when we drove up we knew exactly where to go. This time we had our bags delivered to our assigned rooms rather than us lugging them around. The cadet cadre separated us and placed us in three different troops. Richard and Mike in the Box and me on the Slab, again in Mike Troop. I looked forward to being back there because all the second-classmen from the previous spring were now in charge and they would be surprised to see me again, especially in uniform. This was great!

After we checked in they divided us into tour groups. The three of us stuck together in one group, and were escorted around campus to all the hot spots from the year before. The difference was that we had seen everything before and were able to ask more intelligent questions about the activities, facilities and the campus itself. Many people within the tour group wore civilian clothes, and for them it may have seemed right, but we knew that for us, we needed to be in uniform.

We also experienced an interesting phenomenon while walking around campus in our uniforms—high school and college cadets of lower ranks, particularly the RATS saluted Richard and me. This year we had a chance to see the junior college RATS and how they were treated. They had to run everywhere; they ate "square" meals in the mess hall where they could not look at their plates while they ate; and they treated us with the utmost respect by saluting us. We hadn't expected this, but it was really pretty special and we returned each salute with as much crispness and aplomb as we could muster. We wanted the person to whom we returned the salute to feel special. Of course, if we ran into someone who outranked us we would deliver as good a "parade-ground" salute as we could, to show we knew what to do as well.

On our previous visit we had noted a difference in the way NMMI cadets delivered their D&C and marching commands, but this time we were more cognizant of how they wore their uniforms, and particularly their cunt caps. It seemed that everyone had tailored uniforms fitted to their bodies, much more so than our uniforms, although our drill team blue uniform was much more fitted than our normal JROTC uniform. The cadet officers and senior NCO's were allowed to wear a different kind of cunt cap than the regular issue. These overseas caps were made of a thinner material than the regular issue and had a natural crease in the middle that made the caps look like they had two peaks. And the cap itself, when worn correctly, appeared more rounded than the normal cunt cap. These caps were perched on the front of the head over the forehead, at a 45 degree angle at the front of the head. In actuality, they really looked cool and made you want to wear them because of how these cadet officers and senior NCO's strutted around campus with them perched jauntily on their heads.

As an added bonus, Airborne Rangers existed, right here on campus! The jump wings and Ranger Tab on a few select cadets' uniforms screamed, "I'm a stud, look at me!" It didn't matter what rank they were, if they had jump wings, or the Ranger Tab, that made them hot shit on campus. I had never met a real Airborne Ranger before, and like a unicorn they appeared right before my eyes. I couldn't believe it, and couldn't wait to talk to one of them.

The three troops on the slab made up the 3rd Squadron with an Airborne Ranger as the squadron commander. He was a cadet lieutenant colonel, and he looked the part. He stood a tall 6' 2" and looked in really good shape. He was a pretty large white guy, with brown, intelligent eyes, brown hair cut short and a sharp nose. Kind of what I had imagined an Airborne Ranger should look like. Strangely, I didn't see myself in that role, because I didn't seem to fit the mold of what I'd come to expect of an Airborne Ranger—especially at that time since I stood a diminutive 5' 4" and weighed about 100 lbs. Not quite the epitome of the image of Airborne Ranger seen on film and in song.

I didn't get a chance to talk to that guy; he was way over my head as a visiting high school cadet. But, I did talk to the Kilo Troop commander, cadet Captain Kaleho, a Hawaiian cadet who gave me a little history of NMMI.

We had finished the tour for the day and I had wandered over to the student center. Dinner was a couple of hours away, and hunger pangs made my stomach growl. I walked into the snack bar and saw Kaleho sitting by himself. I got a Coke from the machine and looked for a place to sit. Kaleho called me over and invited me to sit at his table.

"How're you doing?" he asked. "Enjoying your second tour?"

"My second tour?" I was flabbergasted. *How did he know this was my second time here?* I wondered.

He smiled when he saw my surprise. "Yeah, I remember when you were here last spring. I was a new cadet in Kilo and remember the three of you staying in Mike. You weren't in uniform then. You're from El Paso right?"

"That's right," I said. "I'm surprised you remember."

"Well, it's because of you. We don't get many Black guys other than football players."

"Why's that?" I asked.

He looked around, and lowered his voice, "Last year, maybe you don't remember, Kilo troop had a Black troop commander. They called him 'Captain Midnight' behind his back."

"What? Why?" I flashed back to my own racist experiences and immediately felt bad for the unknown Black cadet.

"Because NMMI only started admitting Blacks in 1968, and he was the first Black troop commander. There're still a lot of rednecks that go to this school and a lot of people, including parents, resented him commanding their kids. He caught a lot of shit as a troop commander. So, if you're thinking about coming here, you need to know that. It can be kind of racist."

"Ok," I said. "Thanks for the info." *Great, another racist situation.* I thought. I was still impressed by the school and also reached a realization, that if I wanted a military career, this may be my best opportunity. I had faced racism on a personal level as a kid, and I was not deterred by this new information. I was going to be an Airborne Ranger, and NMMI looked like my best bet.

I looked over Kaleho's uniform and didn't see either jump wings or a Ranger Tab. He had other doodads on his uniform I didn't recognize.

I changed the subject, "I notice you don't have jump wings or a Ranger Tab. Why not?"

"You're pretty blunt aren't you?" He laughed.

"Yeah, I have that reputation." I smiled.

"Well, at this school, if you want to go to either jump school or Ranger School you have to be a Distinguished Military Student or a Distinguished Military Graduate if you go after graduation."

"What are those?" I asked.

"The DMSs and DMGs are the best of the ROTC cadets, maybe top five percent. There're only a few slots for ROTC cadets at Ranger School and only maybe one or two for NMMI cadets, so you have to be the best of the best to be selected for Ranger School."

"I want to be an Airborne Ranger," I confided in him, "I want to go to Ranger School." I whispered.

"You know anything about it?"

"Only what I saw in the films they show you at school." I replied.

"Yeah, I've seen that movie. It's pretty accurate, but I can fill in some of the blanks."

"Okay." I waited eagerly to hear more about that almost mythical school.

"Ranger School lasts 59 days or over eight weeks long. It's divided into four phases," He intoned.

"The City Week phase is at Fort Benning, at what they call Camp Rogers. It's named after Major Robert Rogers who used Ranger-like techniques during the French and Indian War."

Wow, this was really cool. I put my chin in my hands and continued to listen.

"The training at Camp Rogers focuses on preparing Ranger students for the rigors of Ranger School through a Ranger Physical Fitness Test, hand-to-hand combat, and the infamous "worm pit" of punishment." He smiled, "That's pretty tough."

"What's next?" I implored.

"Camp Darby is the next phase, also at Fort Benning. Named after Major William Darby, who organized the first Ranger battalion during World War II. The Ranger instructors, also known as RIs, train the Ranger students in advanced patrolling techniques, including an airborne assault. At the end of the Darby phase is the Ranger Confidence Course, the five-mile run, and Ranger Water Survival Test. If you get past all that then you go to the next phase, the mountain phase." He paused. "You want something to eat?"

"Sure." I said, and he got up and walked over and ordered us some French fries. When he sat back down, we began to munch on our fries, and he continued his description of Ranger School.

"The Mountain Phase is conducted at Camp Merrill, near Dahlonega, in Northern Georgia, near the Tennessee Valley Divide. Named after General Merrill who led Merrill's Marauders during World War II in the South Pacific, Camp Merrill is where the RIs teach basic and advanced mountaineering techniques along with patrolling in a mountainous environment. In addition, the Ranger students have to execute an airborne or air assault insertion into mountainous terrain. It's pretty tough going up and down those mountains in the TVD." He looked at me. "You think you're tough enough for all that?"

"Well, not now," I said, "but maybe later. Isn't there a Jungle Phase?"

"Yep, the final phase is the Jungle Phase at Camp Rudder, located at Auxiliary Field #6, Eglin AFB, in the panhandle of Northern Florida. Named after James Rudder, who commanded the second Ranger battalion that scaled the cliffs of Pointe du Hoc during D-Day. You would think his name should have been used for the Mountain Phase." Kaleho mused.

"Yeah." I said impatiently, waiting for him to continue.

"Anyway, the Jungle Phase is centered around a 12-day patrol that begins after an airborne insertion, and includes SERE training."

"What's SERE?" I asked.

"Survival-Evasion-Resistance-Escape training, where the RIs teach you how to hunt and kill game, evade capture behind enemy lines, how to resist torture and escape from confinement."

"Sounds dangerous," I said, secretly hoping I could go through that.

"Yeah, it is, along with many aspects of Ranger School. You know you're out there with real reptiles and amphibious creatures, so you could be stung, bitten or eaten by anything." He laughed.

"Ok, ok." I said. "What else?"

"The RIs train you how to track targets through jungle-like terrain, and you have a "survival" day where Ranger students capture, kill and eat their own food, if they want to eat that day. That's part of the survival training."

Sounds like fun! I remember that from the movie. I wonder how I would survive that? I thought and looked down at my French fries.

"Once you graduate you can proudly wear the coveted Ranger Tab, you know, the one that's black and gold in a half-moon shape." He said in an ironic tone.

Obviously, he had really wanted to go to Ranger School and the disappointment showed in his voice.

"If you don't go to Ranger School, where do you go?" I asked.

"Well, Ranger School is in place of the normal 6-week ROTC Advanced Camp the rest of the cadets attend. After your first year of contract ROTC you are required to go to Advance ROTC Camp—there are three: one at Fort Bragg for cadets who live on the east coast; one at Fort Riley, for cadets who live in the middle of America; and one at Fort Lewis for the west coast and Hawaiian cadets."

"I guess I would to go to Fort Riley?" I asked.

"You're from Texas right? Then yeah, you would go to Riley. Cadets can also attend jump school at Fort Benning, particularly if you were slotted to go to Ranger School."

"What happens if you don't pass Ranger School? I heard a lot of people fail." I said.

"Yep, the attrition rate is pretty high, especially among ROTC cadets. If you don't pass Ranger School, but get through at least the first two phases, it counts as having completed Advanced Camp, so you're given credit for Advanced Camp."

"Ok," I said.

"In addition, you're awarded the RECONDO badge. It's a poor substitute for the Ranger Tab." As he explained about the RECONDO badge, he pointed to a little doodad on his chest.

The RECONDO badge was an arrow-head shaped badge with the point facing down and a gold-colored ROTC torch ensconced in its center.

"So if you don't go to Ranger School and fail, how do you get that?"

"Cadets at the Advance Camp can earn the RECONDO badge by qualifying at least as a "sharpshooter" with the M16-A1 rifle, scoring at least a 400 on the Army Physical Fitness Test and passing the military stakes."

"What's military stakes?" I asked.

"It's a series of military skills tests including disassembly and assembly of the M16, the LAW throwing a hand grenade, OPFOR identification, obstacle and confidence courses, and other skills." He explained.

"LAW, OPFOR?" I inquired.

"Light Anti-Tank Weapon, and Opposing Forces." He patiently explained.

"Ok." The RECONDO badge was a nice badge to earn for the normal cadet, but it seemed a poor substitute for the coveted Ranger Tab.

"You really know a lot about Ranger School, why's that?" I asked. He had shown an almost encyclopedic knowledge of Ranger School

"I got all the way through the first three phases, but failed in the Jungle Phase. That's why I wear the damn RECONDO badge." He said with more than a little bitterness.

"I'm sorry," I said, "I didn't think you had gone to Ranger School." I was obviously wrong. This guy had been through that crucible known as Ranger School, and failed. I felt bad for him.

He got up from the table, and looked down at me, "One piece of advice, don't let them stop you from your dream of becoming an Airborne Ranger. Don't let them make you think you're not as good as they are. Just be yourself and you'll be ok." Then he walked away.

What the hell was I getting into? This guy looked like he was "squared away" and in great shape, and if he didn't make it, I wasn't so sure of my chances of ever being an Airborne Ranger. Yeah, that was sort of depressing, and it sounded really hard, like something that wasn't going to include me; but I could always dream about being an Airborne Ranger.

At least at that point, being an Airborne Ranger seemed to be somewhat more attainable than it had sitting in the dark watching those movies for the past three years. I mean, I had seen one and spoken to a guy who almost became one. I didn't know how I was going to do it, but I remained determined to become a United States Army Airborne Ranger some day!

The next day, Saturday, the NMMI Goss Rifles Drill Team treated us to a real exhibition of their prowess, not just a practice like last year. Again, we stood and watched in our modified drill team uniforms with the blue berets and jump boots, but I felt like a slacker compared to the way those guys wore their uniforms. First, these guys were in good shape, and almost uniform in both height and build—all about six feet tall with slim, but muscular builds. They all had washboard abs and thick wrists that were very muscular. Kaleho was right up front and looked sharp. Second, their tailored uniforms fit tightly on their bodies. The blouses were short-sleeved khaki and the pants were olive green tucked into gleaming black Corcoran jump boots. The uniform was topped off by the glistening black helmet liner highlighted by the gold NMMI crest and custom leather chin straps. They all wore mirrored sunglasses that were just too cool. And the routine! Even better than what we had seen practiced the year before with their burnished rifles and bayonets flashing in the sun. These guys went through their silent routine as if they were born to it. I had never seen such precision in drill movements—these guys were perfect! No wonder they reigned as national junior college champions and were recognized nationally even against the four-year schools.

Richard appeared as mesmerized as I was, and he confirmed it by telling me that he wanted to be out there next year. I told him he could do it, but secretly felt "no way…" but why tell him that and ruin his dream. I didn't tell him I wanted to eventually be an Airborne Ranger—that had to remain my secret. So, the two of us had a dream for the following year when we both would return to NMMI. But first, we had to get past ROTC Basic Camp at Fort Knox, Kentucky—our first real military test.

CHAPTER 18

Fort Knox Here I Come!

After we returned from the second NMMI trip, I began the process for applying to NMMI as my first choice. I took the SAT and passed with enough points, and kept my grades up to be accepted. In fact, I maintained a 3.5 GPA my senior year, the highest of my high school career. I took Advanced Placement English, Advanced Trigonometry, Advanced Spanish, typing, ROTC, and government. I enjoyed all my classes, and looked forward to going to college. One of the happiest days of my life occurred when I received the acceptance letter from NMMI! That was a great day, and at that time my desire to become an Army officer crystallized. I had been thinking about it, and working towards it, but it never really hit home until I received that letter. Not only was I going to college, but I would become an Army officer, yeah, all 5'4" of me. Too short and young to get into West Point, I had found another way—NMMI, and its two-year ROTC program.

The NMMI ROTC department, in its infinite wisdom, accepted me into the two-year program soon after NMMI accepted me. The ROTC acceptance letter included an explanation of the program and its commissioning potential after two years. The explanation provided a choice—whether to attend Fort Knox Basic ROTC Camp, or not. As a four-year graduate of JROTC I was eligible to enter the two-year ROTC program without going to Fort Knox. Other cadets, entering the two-year program, either as freshmen at military institutes like NMMI, or juniors at four-year institutions entering the two-year program with no ROTC or military experience were required to go to Fort Knox.

One of the attractions to going to Fort Knox was the opportunity to compete for a full two-year ROTC scholarship and save my parents the money to pay for NMMI. As a part of the program, I would receive the pay of an E-4 for the six weeks I attended Basic Camp at Fort Knox, and also earn a $100/month stipend during the school year for being a two-year ROTC contract cadet. Finally, the ROTC department recommended we go to Fort Knox to gain the experience of ROTC Basic Camp which would translate into becoming a better officer.

Both Richard and I opted to go to Fort Knox for all of the above reasons, and maybe just to find out what it was really like and if we measured up to the task.

The packet for Fort Knox included a description of some of the things we should be doing to prepare for Basic Camp. One called for us to get in shape physically. The APFT required cadets to run two miles and do sit-ups –none of which I had done in quite some time—and something called the Run, Dodge and Jump; the inverted crawl and the horizontal ladder. It became incumbent on me to prepare myself physically for Fort Knox. Although not on the PT test, the letter suggested getting in shape with push-ups. That motivated me, and I began to run and work on sit-ups and push-ups.

I started the process in April with a report date in mid-June, which gave me about two months to get in some sort of shape, at least in running. The distance from my house to Eastwood was approximately one mile, so that became my route to run on a daily basis. Of course, I didn't start running a mile right off the bat, I had to work up to it. I began running in the neighborhood to start developing my stamina and endurance. As I gained confidence in my ability to run up to a half mile, I began slowly running to school and back.

Drill team practice still began at 6:30 in the morning, so I would run to school with a backpack on my back with my books. The same on the way back each day. If we didn't have drill team practice I ran to school at about 7 o'clock to play basketball. The additional weight on my back helped increase my endurance and stamina and continued to prepare me for the rigors I would be facing at Fort Knox.

I got my orders in early May and I had to get my Dad to translate what they meant. They said I was to report to Fort Knox on June 15, 1973, between 0700 and 0800 at a building number on post. The orders also provided a voucher for air travel back and forth to Louisville, KY, so we didn't have to worry about paying for airfare. Unfortunately, there was no voucher for transportation from the Louisville airport to Fort Knox.

The orders also stated I was assigned to Bravo Company, 13th Training Battalion, 4th Training Brigade, and confirmed I would be paid at the grade of E-4. That was pretty much all the orders said. Luckily, my parents had friends from Louisville, the Fergusons, so the two families arranged for me to fly into Louisville on Sunday the 14th, and stay with Aunt Ann Ferguson's mother. One of her friends, who worked at Fort Knox, would drive me the approximately 32 miles to Fort Knox to my reporting building. Now I had a target date, and my preparations intensified.

I started doing more push-ups and sit-ups along with the running. I wasn't sure about the other events on the APFT, the Run, Dodge and Jump, and the Horizontal Ladder, and inverted crawl since I didn't have any way to train for them. I would just have to figure it out once I got to Basic Camp. On the weekends, now that I had turned 16, and all of 5' 4", I would drive down to school and run around the track—four times equated to a mile and eight times to two miles. I planned to work up to two miles, and I eventually did, just not very fast. I didn't know how to really train to run distances, so I just did my best. I also had no idea what a good time was for two miles, but I knew it had to be faster than what I ran at that time. But I was out there trying to get in some sort of shape to survive the ordeal of ROTC Basic Camp, which loomed in my immediate future.

The time from when I received my orders to June 14th passed pretty quickly, almost too quickly, because the 14th was right there and I had to go. This was my time to finally go out on my own and do something for myself without parents and without knowing anyone else. This would be an adventure and part of my moving forward as a man and as a future Army officer.

Early Sunday morning, Mom drove me to the El Paso International Airport, and saw me take off for the first time on my own. As I sat on the plane I got really excited contemplating the future as we speedily winged our way to Fort Knox. I was on my way! But I felt really nervous too, and at times could hardly breathe thinking about Fort Knox. What would it be like, and would I do well? I wasn't sure of my physical capabilities and hoped that my limited physical fitness training would allow me to be successful.

Well…I would soon find out.

CHAPTER 19

Beginning Basic

Louisville was just a blur. I stayed at Aunt Ann's mother's home and regaled her with stories of my high school career—she appeared politely impressed. The next morning her friend from Fort Knox came by at 6 am, honked the horn, and I said goodbye to my host. Off we went to Fort Knox. Garrulous would not begin to describe my newest friend. He had all kinds of stories about Fort Knox and the time passed quickly.

Sooner than I thought, we rolled up to the front gate of Fort Knox, Home of the Armor School, and Home of Armor for the United States Army. If the intent was to impress, it worked—I felt suitably impressed, and just really excited, and a little bit afraid. This would be my home for the next six weeks, wow!

Then reality hit…I was really here, at Fort Knox. Damn.

I had lived on various posts and bases all my life, but driving through Fort Knox struck me as being different. Here I wasn't going to be the "colonel's son" I would succeed or fail on my own merits. This was a real Army post and people here trained for combat, for war. You could feel it in the air, you could see it on the ground as tanks and troops rolled and ran by in long columns. This was for real.

We pulled up to a non-descript building that my newest host declared was where I was supposed to report. He told me he worked at C.I.F. and that he might see me later that day since that's where we would be issued our uniforms and equipment. I had no idea what he was talking about, but thanked him for driving me to Fort Knox.

As I got out of the car, I realized that I may have brought one bag too many. I had brought one suitcase, and maybe stupidly, one bowling ball for possible recreational free time. I unloaded my stuff and said goodbye to my driver, and dragged my suitcase and bowling ball into the gym. A lot of people sort of stood milling around inside trying to figure out where to go and who to see. I saw a drill sergeant with the distinctive "Smokey Bear" campaign hat that denoted him as someone in charge, so I made my way over to him.

Being no stranger to rank, I addressed him properly, "Excuse me sergeant, do you know where I'm supposed to report?"

He looked at me as if I was a piece of dog shit on his shoe, and growled, "Over there *caydet*! Look for the letter of your last name and stand in that line to report in. And what the hell are you doing with a bowling ball *caydet*?"

"Uh, nothing sergeant, I was hoping to get some bowling in while I was here," I quivered.

"You think this is some sort of resort *caydet*? You're going to learn this is no picnic, boy." He laughed really loud.

Terrific, now I've made a hell of an impression.

"Yes sergeant!" was my only response and I got the hell out of there and over to the reporting-in table, and stood in line in front of the table with "M - S."

"Next!" Someone called out, and I moved up one place in line.

"Next!" Then I moved up another place in line, and so on until I finally got to the front of the line.

"Orders!" the little specialist barked at me. I gave him my orders.

"ID?"

I gave him my driver's license.

"How old are you?" he asked incredulously because he already knew the answer.

"Sixteen," I said, sort of embarrassed. Everyone in earshot stopped and looked around.

"Sixteen?!" One of the other sergeants said as he turned his head to look over at me. He walked over to my line, stood next to me and peered down at me, "What are you doing here?"

"I'm attending ROTC Basic Camp Sergeant, like everyone else," I replied.

Oh great, I thought, *they're not going to let me even start this thing.*

"You're too young to be here," he said, "Let me look at those orders!" he demanded.

I handed him my orders and he was somewhat flabbergasted. He looked incredulous, but everything looked in order, so he couldn't deny me from in-processing like everyone else.

"You're probably not going to make it—you're going to have problems keeping up with all these older, bigger guys, and you'll probably fail." He warned me, then swaggered away.

Thanks a lot, I thought, *encouraging words, to say the least*. I bit my lip and didn't say anything; I just got my assignment, got my bags and moved out.

Apparently, word spread pretty quickly, because when I walked over to where my drill sergeant, SFC Carroll, was gathering and organizing his cadets for travel to our first destination, the barber shop, he asked me, "Are you really sixteen?"

"Yes, Sergeant," I said, already weary of the question, knowing I would hear it more often than I wanted to.

"Okay, well you must think you're pretty special, but you'll get no special treatment here." He assured me.

"Yes, Sergeant." I didn't know what else to say.

"That's **DRILL** Sergeant to you, understand?" He barked.

"Yes, Drill Sergeant!" And so it began.

SFC Carroll lined us up and marched us over to the barbershop, where we got about a ton of hair lopped off onto the ground. The natural reaction for most was shock because it was done so quickly and dispassionately, like an assembly line. Almost each time, the new cadet wiped his hand over his newly bald head in disbelief, marveling at his new baldness.

Next stop was Central Issue Facility (CIF) where they issued our uniforms and equipment (TA-50)—from our khakis, to greens, fatigues, and socks, boots, belts, buckles, tent halves, tent pegs, and everything we would need to survive the next six weeks. I craned my neck as I went through the facility but I didn't see my new friend. Oh well.

They measured our feet for the shoes and boots, and took our measurements to make sure the uniforms fit reasonably well. With me, it was pretty much "small" everything, and even then, most of my uniforms were a little big on me. My boots never quite fit right. I had to wear two pairs of socks to make them feel right. We signed for everything, including a duffel bag to carry everything which caused us to have to drag our duffel bags and our luggage, and in my case, that damn bowling ball, to our new home for the next six weeks—our platoon barracks.

Drill Sergeant Carroll led the way to the first floor of the barracks where our platoon, the 1st Platoon, would bunk. These consisted of two-storied WWII-era wooden barracks, with no apparent air conditioning, and open windows on each floor. As we entered we saw an open bay area on each floor, with our platoon on the second floor. On each side of the bay area was a row of ten metal bunk beds with a pair of metal wall lockers separating each pair of beds. And each bunk bed had a foot locker on each end, one for each of the bunk bed occupants. We were ordered to find our assigned bunk beds; and as it turned out I was bunking with one of the few Black guys in the platoon, Howard Williams, from Northeastern Louisiana State University. Hmm, I didn't think that was a coincidence, but it was fine with me. I didn't particularly want to bunk with any of the white guys in the platoon.

There were two other platoons and with several other Black guys sprinkled amongst the platoons. The platoons were almost evenly distributed with the Black cadets, again, probably not a coincidence. We didn't have much opportunity to talk when we dropped off our bags—DS Carroll rushed us in and out because we had a schedule to keep. He formed us up and had us on our way to the mess hall for our very first Army meal. One thing we learned pretty quickly, that we were always on a schedule, and even though many times it seemed as if we had to "hurry up and wait" we normally stayed on a tight schedule during the weekdays. So now, on to the mess hall.

We met SFC Carroll's assistant drill sergeants, SSG Thompson and SGT Youngblood at the mess hall. Both younger than Carroll and much more aggressive. They would prove to be the bane of the platoon, and me in particular.

We stopped in front of the mess hall and DS Carroll gave the command to "Fall out!" Which most of the cadets didn't understand, but for those of us that understood, knew it meant to dissolve the formation and move out to the mess hall. Drill Sergeants Youngblood and Thompson directed us into the mess hall and told us how to line up in the cafeteria-like line, where we found trays, silverware, the dessert tables, and juice and milk dispensing machines. Just as important was where to dispose of the used trays, dishes and glasses. We were told we had 30 minutes to eat, so we had to move pretty quickly to finish our lunch in time to move out. The penalty for being slow meant not finishing your lunch and maybe going hungry.

We had very little opportunity to talk during that first lunch, so we spent most of the time figuring out the location of everything and gulping down our first meal. The lunch wasn't bad, but we didn't have much chance to enjoy the meal because we scarfed it down so quickly. And yep, thirty minutes later we got the command to put our trays away and "fall in" outside back in formation. So, many of us still eating had to gulp our food and just throw the dishes into the KP area and get outside as quickly as possible. Those late getting in formation did push-ups. Yep, this was definitely going to be interesting.

The drill sergeants marched us back to the barracks to change into our khakis and prepare for our initial meeting with the company evaluator, an active duty captain. In the barracks, the drills showed us how to put on our uniforms, and how to arrange all our uniforms in the metal lockers and the foot lockers at the base of the bunk beds. They taught us how to make our bunks using two sheets and a green wool blanket. And yeah, they actually bounce a quarter off of it to see how tight the linen is on the bunk. They also taught us the routine for reacting to the presence of either an officer or drill sergeant on the bay floor.

They started the process of showing the newer cadets how to stand at "attention," "parade rest" and the "at ease" position. This apparently was the "soft" approach to teaching these positions, rather than the more extreme aggressive approach of the drill sergeants getting in your face and screaming at every opportunity. Well, that would come later, but right now it was fairly civilized.

Our first chance to respond to an officer on the bay floor came when our company evaluator showed up that afternoon to give us our first real orientation on Basic ROTC Camp and his role in the process. Our company evaluator, CPT James Lieteau, an African-American Armor officer, wore silver jump wings on his chest, but no Ranger Tab on his shoulder. He wasn't that tall, maybe 5'6" or 5'7", but still taller than me. He had black curly hair, had a lean physique, with chiseled features on his mahogany colored face.

When he entered the platoon bay, DS Carroll yelled out, "ATTENTION!" And everyone popped to the position of rigid attention.

"At ease," CPT Lieteau bellowed. "Take your seats." As he sat down in a chair at the end of the bay, we attentively perched on the edges of our bunks and foot lockers.

"I'd like to welcome all of you to Bravo Company, 13th Training Battalion, 4th Training Brigade, and the ROTC Basic Training Camp at Fort Knox."

We waited with bated breath to hear what he would tell us about the next six weeks.

"I am Jim Lieteau, your platoon evaluator, and my assistant platoon evaluator is SFC Varin." And he pointed to an NCO that had just walked in the room. "SFC Varin, is an active duty sergeant first class, and distinguished infantryman who wears the Combat Infantryman's Badge, which he earned in Vietnam. He knows his shit gentlemen, so you'd better listen to him."

"I'm an Armor officer, and my role is to evaluate all of you with the assistance of SFC Varin. The drill sergeants are responsible for your daily training and to make sure you get where you're supposed to be on time."

"My evaluation is designed to determine if you have the potential to become Army officers. During the next six weeks you will be placed in various leadership positions and subjected to various leadership-challenging exercises in the field to evaluate your leadership potential."

He looked around the room for any inquisitive looks. Finding none, he continued, "In addition to the leadership aspect of Camp, you will go through an approximation of what basic trainees go through to include: drill and ceremonies with the M-16; basic marksmanship also with the M-16; live-fire exercises, physical fitness every day, the AFPT twice during the cycle, confidence and obstacle courses, hand-to-hand combat, bivouacking, road marches, first aid, pugil stick training, and individual tactical training."

He consulted the papers in his hand, "You will also be trained in some things that basic trainees are not normally exposed to such as map reading, land navigation and orienteering; survival, escape, resistance and evasion or SERE training, the combat water survival test, familiarity with several weapons systems, tours of Fort Knox, and being assigned an officer mentor to give you an idea of what it might be like to be an active duty Army officer."

"As you may know, while you're here you can compete for a two-year ROTC scholarship. If you're interested, see me after the meeting and I'll give you the details on applying."

That caused some muted whispering.

As he reviewed his notes, he said, "Finally, in order to successfully complete Basic Camp you must pass the End of Cycle Proficiency Test or EOCT and the PT test." And then with a little twinkle in eye, "And, oh by the way, each of you will also get to experience that time-honored Army tradition called KP, better known as kitchen police." And all the NCOs laughed. He continued, "On the lighter side, you will have some leisure time on the weekends and some evenings when you're not involved in night training. The drill sergeants will give you more details on the Cadet Lounge and the PX facilities."

"Any questions?"

No one raised their hand.

"Okay gentlemen, good luck."

As he rose, DS Carroll again called the room to attention and we all popped up in a rigid posture as CPT Lieteau and SFC Varin left the platoon bay.

Whew! That sounded like a lot to be accomplished in just six weeks, but he seemed confident that all of us would succeed and march across that graduation parade field at the end of our cycle of Basic Camp. Of course, that wasn't the case, and as it turned out, we had several guys decide that this was not what they wanted in life and did the "duffel bag drag" to quit ROTC Basic Camp and not pursue a career as an Army officer. Not me. I was determined to make it through at any cost, regardless of the fact that I was the youngest cadet to ever go through Fort Knox ROTC Camp and the smallest in my platoon. As I found out, I was competing against both 18-year-old high school graduates who were to attend two-year military junior colleges like NMMI or Wentworth, and against guys as old as 22 who were juniors in college at four-year institutions, and much more physically and emotionally mature than me.

Yeah, a familiar tune for me.

CHAPTER 20

The Crucible

I stared up at the ceiling from my top bunk as Howard snored below me. Tucked under my tight sheets and blanket, like a second skin, my head resting on a thin pillow, I couldn't sleep as my mind roiled with almost equal parts dread and excitement at the unknown that would begin the next day.

At five the next morning they came for us. They startled us awake by the sounds of yelling and screaming from Drill Sergeants Thompson and Youngblood, who would lead us in our first session of physical training (PT). We leapt out of our beds and rushed around the bay to throw on our clothes, hit the bathroom, make our beds, and fall outside within the few minutes they gave us to get ready. The drill sergeants, or drills as we called them, constantly barraged us with their screaming, cursing and berating us as being pieces of shit. We couldn't do anything right, fast enough, or well enough to meet their standards.

Oh boy, here we go—six weeks of hell.

We did PT every weekday morning for the six weeks we lasted in Basic. That first morning as we fell out in fatigue pants, white t-shirts, and combat boots had me huffing and puffing. The morning was beautiful. As the sun began its ascent, we began our first PT session in near darkness. But it was cool, and the dew was still on the ground. Of course, it would get hot during the day, but at that point it was still nice.

The drills arranged us in an open-PT formation to give us room to go through the various calisthenics and exercises. We started off with some warm up and stretching exercises before getting to the more difficult stuff. We went through a progression of exercises starting with jumping jacks (the Army called it the side straddle hop), then stand-squat-extend to push up position then back to squat then stand, windmills, jump and reach into the air with arms extended, lunges, T-bones, scissor kicks, push-ups, and sit-ups. I hadn't exercised this hard in several years. I struggled, already out of breath, and exhausted just from this first session. At the end, I bent over at the knees gasping for air. My penalty for not having done P.E. for the past four years. Sigh…who knew?

Once we had finished the exercises, we formed up in four columns for a two-mile run. I had never run in formation before, so this would be a new experience. I was not looking forward to this. I could barely breathe as I looked around at the other guys. Like in marching, we had a drill sergeant giving commands to get us to the street so we could begin the run. His first command, "Forward March!" got us moving to the street. We would have different drill sergeants leading the runs on different days.

As soon as we got onto the street, the drill sergeant gave the command, "DOUBLE TIME, MARCH!" And we started to run.

The drill sergeant at the side of the platoon began to call "Jodies" or running cadences, where he would call something out in rhythm to our steps, and we would respond in kind—either repeating what he said or giving the required response—all on the left foot, to keep us in step with each other. We had to keep our eyes forward, but also keep aware of the distance between each of us so that we could maintain a tight formation. With our arms pumping at our sides, and boots hitting the pavement in rhythm, I calculated our initial pace at about a 9-minute mile pace. That wasn't too bad for me from my previous training, but I was much more tired than I normally was when I trained. I had just gone through a fairly difficult exercise regimen, and now this run—this was kind of tough. Plus, singing the cadences with the other cadets used up what little breath I had, and so about halfway through the run I stopped singing the cadences and focused on just breathing and finishing.

By the time we got to the end of the run, and the drill sergeant called out "QUICK TIME, MARCH!" I was breathing hard and my tongue felt glued to the top of my mouth. But I had survived my first run at Basic, and I felt pretty good about myself.

Each day the exercises got a little harder—they kept adding more of them and we did more repetitions of each—and the runs got a little longer and faster, but we were getting in better shape.

At the beginning of the second week, we took our initial APFT to determine where we stood physically. I was extremely nervous as we fell out of the barracks that morning dressed in white t-shirts, green fatigue pants and combat boots. Although it was another beautiful morning, I dreaded this test because I still didn't have much confidence in my physical fitness and ability to perform on a physical fitness test. While I was getting stronger, and running faster, I'd never seen the Run-Dodge & Jump event and didn't know how to navigate it very well. I also had little experience with the inverted crawl and the horizontal ladder, except what little we had done during PT. I didn't have much confidence in my ability to do very well on those events. I looked around as we were marched to the PT field to take the test and saw the confident smiles on many of my classmates' faces. I didn't feel confident and hoped I could just get through the test without embarrassing myself.

Well, that didn't happen. The drill sergeants lined us up in front of the horizontal ladder, the RD&J and inverted crawl area to give us a demonstration before we had to perform those same events to the "best" of our ability.

"Awright gentlemen, this is the Run Dodge and Jump event of the Army Physical Fitness Test. You are required to navigate this 26-yard course as quickly as you can by moving quickly in and out of each of these obstacles." The African-American drill sergeant pointed to the obstacles that were made out of iron pipes two inches in diameter in the shape of a squared off horseshoe, about two and half feet tall and two feet wide.

"Each obstacle has a red arrow painted on it to aid you as you navigate this event," he continued. "Sgt Smith will demonstrate how to navigate this event."

The drill sergeant pointed to another NCO who was lined up at the beginning of the course. "On your mark! Get Set! Go!"

We watched as the second sergeant navigated the RD&J like a seasoned pro. He smoothly moved between the obstacles and rows and deftly jumped over the trench located right between the rows of obstacles. The finish line was a few yards to the left of the start line. The sergeant, also African-American, ran it like he was on a football practice field.

The drill sergeant finished his speech, "As you can see, this event combines your ability to move quickly between obstacles. The best way to navigate this event is by being able to laterally move and jump, as well as running. Think of it as broken-filed running in football. This is a timed event, so do your best gentlemen." *Great.*

Youngblood and Thompson marched us over to the horizontal ladder area. The horizontal ladder stood ten feet off the ground, 20 feet in distance with 14 rungs. They gave us a demonstration on the horizontal ladder. The monkey-like movements to swing from rung to rung looked easy enough, but the intricate turn at each end looked a little difficult, but it looked doable. The objective was to do as many rungs as possible in one minute.

Finally, we marched over to the inverted crawl lanes to watch a demonstration of that event. Youngblood himself demonstrated this event.

"Look alive cadets, this is how you do the inverted crawl." Thompson said. "First, you line up at the start line with your feet toward the far end of the course. The course is 20 yards long. You will navigate the course in the inverted crawl position which is also called the 'crab walk' with your hands on the ground and your bellies up. Drill Sergeant Youngblood will demonstrate this event. On your mark…get set…go!"

Youngblood took off like a huge white crab scuttling down the course. At the end of the course, instead of turning around, he touched his foot on the line and then crawled back with his hands leading instead of his feet. *Damn, that looked hard, but he made it look easy. Well, if he can do it, I can do it.*

As Youngblood jumped up, Thompson asked, "Any questions on any of the events?"

No one raised their hands.

"Awright cadets, each of you will begin at one of the four events, horizontal ladder, inverted crawl, run dodge and jump, and situps, and will rotate through all the events until everyone has completed those events, then everyone will complete the two-mile run together. Any questions?" Thompson looked expectantly.

Again, no one raised their hand.

"Good luck gentlemen." He grinned wolfishly.

The drills divided us into four groups with three columns for each group. Howard lined up in my group as did another cadet going to NMMI, Gary Davis. He was 18, but about my height and weight. He had been struggling with PT like me, and he looked as apprehensive as I felt. Well, at least I thought I could beat him, so maybe I wouldn't have the worst score today.

Our first event was the RD&J. I was about four people deep which gave me the opportunity to watch as other cadets navigated this event. They ran three through each time, so I got to watch nine cadets run it before it was my turn. Most seemed like they knew what they were doing, but it still seemed like a mystery to me. As my row of three stepped up, I looked to my left and saw Howard looking confident. This was something right up his alley since he used to play high school football. Gary, to my right just looked scared. I wanted to look determined, but I know that didn't come off well.

The NCO at that event, the same African-American sergeant who gave the demonstration looked at me, "You okay cadet? It's nothin' but a thing." He smiled.

"Yes, drill sergeant!" I gave a sickly smile back. *Let's just get this shit over with.*

"On your mark…get set…GO!"

Off we went, well except me, I ran in the wrong direction. *Shit!*

"Wrong way cadet, that's going to cost you time!" The drill sergeant yelled.

I quickly reversed myself, but too late. I lagged several seconds behind even Gary and totally failed that event by going the wrong direction. I had seen Howard briefly and he looked like a pro going through the event. In contrast, I couldn't even run, dodge or jump worth a shit. And yeah, several of my classmates made sure I knew I had gone the wrong way. *What a great start to the PT test, damn.*

For the next event, we had to do the gut-busting sit-up. I was again fourth in line. I didn't anticipate any problems with this event, but you never know. The object was to do as many sit-ups as possible within a minute. When my turn came around, I laid down on my back with my knees bent and my hands interlaced behind my head. To perform the prescribed sit-up, required me to raise my head up so that my back was straight and then drop back to the original start position. Another cadet aided me in doing the sit-ups, in this case Howard, by holding my ankles for the entire minute.

At the word, "GO!" I started pumping out my sit-ups, slamming my chest against my knees and slamming my head against the ground to get the benefit of the bounce to get up for the next sit-up. I knocked out 50 sit-ups in that minute and easily passed that event. I actually felt pretty good about that event. Next up, the horizontal ladder.

You know, it seemed a little unfair not have had an opportunity to train on this apparatus and the RD&J before it and then be tested on your ability to navigate the damn thing. But here I stood, never having done the horizontal ladder and expected to imitate an ape and do well on this thing. This would probably be another embarrassing event. I mounted the horizontal ladder when it was my turn and looked down the length of the thing and wondered how I was going to turn around and come back. I was supposed to go down and back as many times as I could in one minute. I had done monkey bars as a kid and even a horizontal ladder like this, but I wasn't timed, and I didn't have to turn around.

The drill sergeant shouted, "Go!" And we all started to swing.

I grasped each rung with the opposite hand and swung with an easy rhythm until I got to the end. I had seen other cadets do a turn around that required me to twist my wrist around and change directions and grasp the rung behind me all in the same motion. Well, at least I didn't let go and fall to the ground, but it was awkward, and I lost several seconds trying to figure it out. I wasn't fast enough on my turns and didn't get enough rungs to qualify. I failed this event too. I no longer found this to be fun, and I was tired of failing.

My last event before the two-mile run was the inverted crawl. We had done the inverted crawl during our daily PT sessions, but not timed. We had done them as part of a relay race, where you raced down one end and back and touched the guy behind you and then he took off. That had been fun, but now it was an opportunity to fail…again. When it came to me, I got down in the proper position and when the drill said, "Go!" I took off.

I was surprisingly good at this event, and learned when going back to push off with my feet rather than pull with my hands and I surprised everyone by having one of the faster times in the inverted crawl for my platoon. Well alrighty then!

After we dusted ourselves off, we were marched to the starting line for the two-mile run. I knew this would be somewhat difficult. I had never been timed on a run and didn't have any kind of strategy on how to run the race. I guess I would figure it out during the run. It would be conducted on a half-mile track, so the first mile would take two turns around the track, and the full two miles would take four turns.

As we lined up for the run, we were amassed near the start line. The drill sergeants told us to stay near the back if we were slower runners. Of course that meant me and some other younger or shorter cadets. I was still winded from doing the four previous events. The morning was becoming warmer and more humid. A bright blue sky with few clouds stared down at me. *These next several minutes would not be fun.*

"On your mark…get set…GO!" The drill sergeant bellowed.

Off we went. The guys who were "runners" took off at a faster pace, and set the pace for the rest of us. I looked for Gary and decided to run with him. That was my strategy—if I could keep up with him, I had a chance to pass this thing.

He and I started off with a pretty slow pace, but not the slowest. By unspoken agreement, we stayed with each other and ahead of all the fat boys and the guys *really* out of shape. After the first mile, marked by someone holding up a sign, I started to feel the effects of the first four events. I was getting tired. Gary kept encouraging me, but he was getting tired too. I was encouraged by the fact that more people had fallen behind us, but discouraged by the fact we had been lapped by several of the faster runners. Damn, I did not want to fail the run.

After the third lap, I knew I was in trouble. My legs felt like lead and the combat boots got heavier. I could see Gary struggling as well, but our determination would not allow us to stop as we had seen others do. With a quarter-mile to go, I could see the finish line and I got my "second wind."

I yelled, "Let's go," and took off on as fast a sprint as I could manage. Gary took off with me and we finished the run together—gasping and trying to bring in huge amounts of air as we stood off to the side with our hands on our knees, bent over and sweating like horses that had been ridden too hard.

But we passed! Barely, but we passed the run! Not everyone did, and we both felt pretty good about that.

Unfortunately, I did not pass the initial APFT. I flunked the RD&J and the horizontal ladder. I still had some work to do, but those were technique-driven events, and I felt confident I would eventually master those techniques and pass the final end-of-cycle APFT.

CHAPTER 21

Enduring Hell

Over the weeks we endured inverted crawls, push-ups, guerilla exercises, two-man fireman's carry, log drills, rifle drills, road marches up to five miles with full packs, rifles and helmets; and of course the Obstacle and Confidence courses, and the Combat Water Survival Test (CWST).

We went through the CWST in the third week because if a cadet were to fail, he would be pulled aside for swimming lessons over and above our normal PT to train him to pass the CWST. Strangely, most of the persons pulled aside were from our fairly significant Puerto Rican contingent. I guess I stereotypically thought they could swim. I mean really, they come from an island; but, apparently, like many urban youth, they couldn't swim, so they ended up going through the remedial swimming lessons. Included in the remedial swimming were cadets who knew they couldn't swim and made sure everyone knew it. Howard happened to be one of those, and on the weekends, he spent his Saturday mornings learning how to swim.

I actually enjoyed the challenge of swimming 25 yards with a rifle in the air; jumping into the water with full gear and taking it off before coming to the surface; and jumping blindfolded from a three-meter board into the water… it reminded me of jumping off the high dive at RGAFB. The Obstacle and Confidence courses were another matter entirely.

The Obstacle Course was daunting as they walked us through it. They made the obstacles out of wood beams or logs and there were obstacles for jumping, for dodging, for vertical climbing, for horizontal traversing, for crawling and vaulting, and finally for balancing. The course was several hundred yards long and was a timed event. They allowed us one practice run to familiarize ourselves with the course and develop any strategies for overcoming the obstacles in as short a time as possible. I went through the course slowly the first time and found that I could negotiate almost all the obstacles except those that required me to climb over them and use upper body strength. My upper body strength wasn't well developed at that point and I found it difficult to pull my own weight over these obstacles. So, when my time came to run the Obstacle Course for time, I didn't do very well—couldn't get past the Climbing Rope—I gave it the old college try, but I wasn't able to negotiate that obstacle. The course monitors told me to move on, I held everybody else up; so I didn't really pass the Obstacle Course, although I got credit for the attempt.

The Confidence Course was the Obstacle Course on steroids.

The apparatus were significantly larger and more difficult to negotiate than the obstacles on the Obstacle Course, and many of them required a team effort to overcome. They didn't time the Confidence Course; the objective was to complete all the apparatus, if possible. The only deterrence from completing these apparatuses was the cadet's fear. In my case, I had a fear of heights, so the Skyscraper and Confidence Climb were going to be my "Waterloos" because each of them had platforms or boards that were approximately six feet apart and would require someone to help me get over them. The Confidence Climb was basically a vertical ladder with the rungs about five feet apart and there were six rungs. You had to climb up one side, go over the top, and then climb back down. I was able to negotiate the Confidence Climb with some difficulty, particularly coming down; but not the Skyscraper, not the first time. The second time I tried the Skyscraper I was able to go up, but coming down was a problem. I was able to climb the poles between floors to negotiate the climb up, but once I got to the top, the difficulty was getting back down. I made it, but it wasn't easy.

The physical fitness training was difficult, but at the end it imbued me with the confidence to accomplish more than I thought possible. Several times I thought I would give up and quit, but I willed myself to "drive on." Especially during the road marches.

I had never walked any significant distances before Fort Knox. I always had the advantage of motorized transportation. Even our forays out to the desert and to the woods growing up were typically by bicycle, not significant walking. Well, soldiers do it differently. Soldiers walk or run everywhere, and ROTC cadets in Basic training were no exception. The first time we were told we were going to "road march" somewhere it sounded like we were going to take a little hike around the corner. Uh uh, nope, that's not what it was at all. This was my first really grueling experience at Fort Knox.

This particular morning—thank God it was morning—we lined up outside our barracks appropriately outfitted for our first road march. Each of us had our M-16 in a port arms carry position, a rucksack on our back filled with various items weighing up to 35 lbs., our load-carrying equipment (LCE) harness and webbed belt festooned with flashlight, ammo pouches, lensatic compass, and two one-quart canteens. On our heads rested the helmet liner and steel helmet attached with a chin strap. My chin strap never fit properly and my helmet was always flopping around on my head. I looked like a green Q-tip. On top of the rucksack was the sleeping bag pad, tightly rolled up and resting comfortably through the LCE. I don't know what the actual weight of all that equipment was, but I felt like Atlas with the weight of the world on my narrow shoulders.

We lined up in two columns, and the drills told us we would be at a "route step" pace without cadences to keep us in step. Drill Sergeant Thompson was leading the road march with Youngblood assisting. Thompson informed us we would be going on a six-mile road march and we would be gone for two hours.

Thompson gave the command, "Forward March," and we started off down the road in the two columns in step.

Once we moved away from the barracks area he gave us the command, "Route step, March," and we began to walk without cadence.

The pace was set by Thompson who had the benefit of a walking stick and, of course, no rucksack or anything else except his canteens. The pace wasn't so bad to start off, but as we continued to walk, the weight on my back began to get heavier and heavier. There is a gait that people who road march get into that takes some practice and years of experience. It's not as fast as a jog, but it's faster than casual walking. This was a means of travel, so the object is to get there fairly quickly. At the time I wasn't very tall, and my legs were shorter than almost everyone in the platoon except Gary. We had a hard time keeping up with the pace, but we hung in there, keeping our heads down and focusing on putting one foot in front of the other. That is, until Agony.

We moved along a gradual incline after the first few miles when before us loomed a really big-assed hill.

As I looked up I saw a sign, "This is Agony," *yeah, no shit*. This was the infamous Agony Hill and along with its sister hill, Misery, were two of the most notorious hills at Fort Knox. These hills had broken many a soldier, and I did not want to be next. At this point, I felt the pain of exertion in my hamstrings and calves, and now my quads were getting into it. I just looked up at this ridiculously tall hill and thought, *How the hell am I going to make this?* I looked over at Gary and could read the same thought in his mind, but I also saw determination on his face. Well, if he could do it, I could do it. So, I put my head down and started climbing up Agony.

One foot in front of the other, the morning was heating up and I began to sweat profusely. All I could see was the asphalt and rocks on the roadway and the feet of the guy in front of me. Nothing else in the world mattered at that point except making it up that damn hill. The feet in front of me began to get farther and farther away.

Drill Sergeant Youngblood came up to me and said, "Pittard if you can't keep up, fall to the back of the formation."

"Yes, Drill Sergeant!" I gasped. I began to drift towards the back of the formation and let the other guys move past me as I fell back. This gave me a chance to get my breath. Youngblood had given Gary the same command and he was falling to the back of the formation too.

I finally noticed there was a deuce and half truck that had been following the formation, and there were some cadets already in the truck.

"If you fall back to the truck you will have to get on it Pittard." Youngblood bellowed.

Hell, that sounded like a good idea.

"Like a little pussy!" He added with a wicked grin.

Oh hell no! I was not going to quit now under any circumstance. They were going to have to drag my ass before I fell back to the truck.

As Gary and I fell back to the end of the formation, the truck was like… right there. So close I could smell the diesel and hear the voices from the back of the truck. There wasn't much room to fall back, we would have to make it or be humiliated by the drill sergeants.

The platoon had only marched about halfway up the hill. Gary and I began to jog, because our walking pace just wasn't fast enough. Every step echoed the jingle jangle of noise from all the equipment bouncing around on our LCE, my head banged against the inside of my helmet liner, and the sound of the M16 banging against everything else. We would run several yards, then walk to catch our breath, then run some more until we caught up and stayed ahead of that damn truck. Finally, after several minutes of this I saw the crest of the hill. The front part of the platoon had reached the crest, now it was our turn.

Gary and I just started to run to make sure we stayed ahead of the truck. We ran and ran until we finally got to the top of the hill. At that point I didn't care, and I just stopped because I couldn't go any further.

Gary looked like he was about to drop, but he encouraged me, "C'mon Chris, don't stop now, we're almost there," and pointed off to our right.

"Okay," I panted with some effort. I raised my head and saw where he pointed. Our platoon had gathered in the shade under some trees as the cadets began filling up their canteens with a cold green fluid of some kind from a bunch of tall, sweating 10-gallon silver bullets. They had removed their helmets and were drinking out of their canteen cups as they watched us approach.

That got me motivated, and I kept walking to keep up with Gary as he ambled over to where the rest of the platoon rested. By this time the truck had pulled off to the side of the road and the driver was pulling the wayward cadets out of the back. We stumbled up to the rest of the platoon and I heard DS Thompson, "Well you made it…barely. Congratulations."

"Get out your canteen cups and get some cold Gatorade." He continued.

That sounded good. I got my canteen cup and marched over to the nearest silver bullet and filled it up with this funny looking green fluid. It was ice cold and delicious. I'd never had Gatorade before, but nothing ever tasted as good as that Gatorade on that hot summer day in Fort Knox following the six-mile road march. I was hooked on Gatorade.

As I drank my fill of Gatorade, I looked around and saw the grinning faces of the rest of the platoon. Later I heard there were bets I wouldn't make it up Agony. The smiles were from those that thought I would make it. The other guys seemed okay with that. Everybody was happy…well, except for the guys who didn't make it. They were not able to partake of the Gatorade and were made to sit separately from the rest of us. The mark of shame for not making it through the first road march. I'm just glad I made it.

After that the road marches got easier, even the one up and down Misery Hill. We also had runs up and down the lesser-named hills of Fort Knox like "Widow Maker," "Oh Shit," and "Stairway to Heaven," but I survived them even though they were some of the toughest runs in my life. I prevailed and became the stronger for it. And although, I felt I was being subjected to some sort of Army hell in the hot, humid, sub-tropical climate of Fort Knox, Kentucky, I was being forged into a stronger, more confident person and cadet. I felt I could succeed at almost anything and overcome almost any obstacle. I'm sure that was the objective of the tough physical training, and for me, it worked.

Conventional wisdom states that, "If your body is strong, that will, in turn, strengthen your mind and fortify your will. Your body is a holistic unit where the body, mind, and will come together and allow the person to become stronger in all areas." At least that's the theory. In my case, as I got physically stronger and more confident, it did translate into more confidence in other areas. The physical training was concurrent with the rest of the basic training, and as the body became stronger, the mind was also being trained, as was the will to succeed and win.

The other factor that contributed to my will to succeed becoming stronger was the behavior of Drill Sergeants Thompson and Youngblood. They homed in on me from the very beginning with insults, push-ups, and just being in my face all the time. Youngblood, in particular, was a real asshole. I complained to DS Carroll about their treatment, but that just seemed to goad them on.

The second Saturday, between lunch and dinner, I was walking by myself returning from the cadet PX. I had just spoken to Mom and she had told me my Aunt Ginny Dews had just died, completely unexpected. That news really upset me, and I went to the PX to pick up some toiletries and some books to try to relax. As I entered the barracks I had to pass by the drill sergeants' office. I saw Thompson and Youngblood sitting inside in deep discussion.

Damn, I thought, *I do not want to deal with them today, not now.* But there was no avoiding passing by their office.

As I passed by their office Youngblood called out to me, "Hold on there Pittard, we need to talk to you!" *Shit.*

"Yes, Drill Sergeant!" And I stopped where I was, in front of the wall facing their office in the corridor. The wall to my back was covered with various notices and bulletins stapled to a bulletin board and flapping in the wind coming in from the open barracks doors. There was no one else around. Everybody was out enjoying their Saturday.

They rushed out of their office and stood in front of me, one to each side, so if I looked at them individually I would have to turn my head from side-to-side.

"Stand at attention shithead!" Youngblood bellowed.

I was already standing as straight as I could, but I stiffened up even more, and stared straight ahead, waiting for the verbal onslaught sure to come.

"We heard you complained to Drill Sergeant Carroll about us!" Thompson hissed. "We don't like that shit. We're just trying to make you into a soldier Pittard."

"You're a pussy Pittard, you're never going to be shit, and you're never going to be a soldier." Youngblood whispered into my ear. "And you'll never be an officer you weak piece of shit. I'll never salute the likes of you."

"You need to shut the fuck up and act right." Thompson said, "And quit complaining. Or else we're going to make your sniveling life holy hell."

I stayed silent and continued staring straight ahead, my thoughts racing a mile a minute. *Be quiet, don't say anything that'll piss them off even more. Be cool, be cool…don't let them see they've gotten to you. Don't cry, don't cry…*

"You understand that shit Pittard?" Youngblood, could barely contain himself. "Don't fuck with us anymore!" I could smell his bad breath in my nostrils.

"Yes, Drill Sergeant!" What else could I say. I didn't turn my head, I didn't want to look at them in the eyes. I'm sure that would have made it worse.

"We ain't gonna hear this from Drill Sergeant Carroll, are we?" Thompson said.

"No Drill Sergeant!"

"As long as we understand each other." Youngblood said.

"Yes, Drill Sergeant!"

They just glared at me for several seconds and then turned and stalked back into their office, apparently their vitriol against me spent.

I stayed braced against the wall until they slammed their door shut. When I was sure they were done and not coming back out I shuffled back to my bunk with my head down. Several minutes later, Howard found me crying by my bunk.

"Did they fuck with you again?" He asked with some sympathy.

"Yeah, but that's not why I'm crying." I said. "My mom just called and told me my favorite aunt died unexpectedly yesterday." I sniffled.

"Oh man, I'm sorry to hear that." Howard said, and put his arm around my shoulder. "Don't let these assholes get you down."

"Yeah, fuck them," I said through my tears, "I'll be alright, I just didn't want them to think they'd beaten me."

"You'll be fine." Howard said as he left me to my misery.

I finished my grieving and steeled my resolve. I would not quit and give these white motherfucking asshole drill sergeants that satisfaction. *Fuck them!*

⟡   ⟡   ⟡

Basic rifle marksmanship (BRM) proceeded normally. The BRM instructors introduced us to the M16A1, 5.56mm rifle, with a maximum effective range of 460 meters, and selector switch that allowed the shooter to fire the weapon on single shot, 3-shot, or on full automatic. They trained us on the basic characteristics of the weapon; taught us how to disassemble and assemble the weapon in the standard times; how to clean and take care of the weapon; how to drill with the weapon; and of course, how to fire the weapon. We had to "zero in" the assigned weapon, then learn to fire it from the "prone," "kneeling," and "prone supported" positions shooting at half-man and man-sized targets at 50 meters, 100 meters and out to three hundred meters.

Eventually, I qualified as a marksman, the lowest possible, but that was okay, I didn't need to be a sharpshooter or an expert to get through basic training, all I needed was to pass. Mission accomplished.

Along with BRM we trained on first aid—working on mannequins with simulated wounds; learning cardiopulmonary resuscitation (CPR) techniques, practicing on each other; and learning techniques for carrying wounded soldiers off the battlefield. During the third and fourth week we went through some of the more interesting, and in turn, more difficult training. This was when our instructors introduced us to land navigation, map reading, and orienteering. They taught us Individual Training Techniques (ITT) including low crawling, crawling under barbed wire on your back with a weapon on your chest; negotiating a live-fire course at Easy Gap firing range; learning to use cover and moving from one covered position to another; and throwing hand grenades.

Other instructors gave us familiarization training with other types of weapons, including the M79 grenade launcher, the M2 (Ma Deuce) .50 cal machine gun, and the M60 7.62mm machine gun. One day we watched a demonstration of such monstrous weapons as the M60A1 tank firing the 105mm sabot round; the MGM-51 Shillelagh anti-tank missile being fired—maybe the loudest sound I'd ever heard; and artillery barrages from the towed 105mm Howitzer and self-propelled 155mm Howitzers and 8-inch guns. Now this was fun! This is what I thought of as the combat arms and heavy weaponry of the U.S. Army!

Along with that training was Leadership, and Small Unit Tactics, both designed to teach us how to be leaders at the small unit level—squad and platoon level tactics. During these exercises the leadership instructors gave us arm-brassards with simulated rank from corporal to staff sergeant, to identify what position we would occupy during the exercise, from assistant squad leader to squad leader. We performed one platoon-level exercise led by an Army 2nd lieutenant assigned to us as squad leaders. The platoon evaluators graded us on how well we performed during the tactical exercises as well as how we performed daily in leadership positions within the platoon.

Interestingly, when CPT Lieteau evaluated me on my performances I received great evaluations for my tactical exercises, but not so high for my daily performance with my platoon mates. He was at a loss to explain the differences. I had an idea because my platoon mates discussed me *ad nauseum* because of my age and lack of size. I didn't have much respect within the platoon, except from Howard, who was just amazed at the fact I was 16 years old competing against such older guys. Some of the other, more enlightened guys felt the same way, but they were in the minority. However, when I was out in the field I tended to assert myself, and pushed people to do their jobs and perform, and as a result, I did well in the tactical evaluations.

Those particular evaluations were done by NCO's, the platoon evaluations by Lieteau and Varin, and the peer evaluations by my platoon mates. I was at the mercy of the guys who were either jealous or incredulous of me competing against them. Of course, I didn't help matters by making sure that each and every one of them knew I was better than them. I had little tact in that area, and could be an obnoxious little prick sometimes. Well, most of the times. I was cocky about my military knowledge. Unfortunately, the daily platoon evaluations and peer evaluations were two of the areas of consideration for the two-year scholarship, and as a result, I didn't get selected for the two-year scholarship. Sabatini did, of course.

Some of our training took place at night. We bivouacked at night, and learned how to set up individual defensive positions at night, digging foxholes, and learned about "fields of fire," and setting up squad defensive positions, and night patrols and tactics. Very cool stuff. In addition, we also did a night land navigation course, where we used a lensatic compass to find points on the map at night, write down the numbers and letters at those locations, and then go on to the next location until we completed the course.

On a dark, rainy night we negotiated the night land nav course. The lane graders sent us out with maps marked in grease pencil with the notations of the location of the various points we were to locate. This might have been more fun had it not been raining. Unfortunately, the water tended to obscure the notations made on the map and the score sheet made by the waxy marker we were given. This made finding your points a little dicey out there in the wilds of Fort Knox, and created one of the more depressing moments of my time during Basic.

I was out there, by myself, couldn't detect anyone nearby, didn't know where I was because I couldn't read the soggy map, and had no clue where to go. Dressed in my wet fatigues, a dark green poncho around my body, with rain dripping through and running down my neck made me miserable.

I could feel the rivulets of water streaming down my back. I felt water seeping into my boots, my socks and feet beginning to get soggy. My helmet liner and helmet, wobbling with uncertainty on my head, felt heavy with dripping water on my shoulders and face. My thin neck could barely keep them level. My rifle strapped across my back felt awkward and slapped me on every step. My glasses fogged up in the rain and I couldn't see anything. No lights in the sky, and completely alone.

I just wanted to cry, but, this is where the physical training and additional will to succeed kicked in. I gathered myself up and decided I'd figure out where to go. I could see lights in the distance, so I started in that direction and eventually ran into a well-used dirt road turning to mud, and saw some other cadets walking alongside the road. I recognized them as being from my company and on the same exercise. They were on their way in and after I caught up with them, they allowed me to use their numbers and letters as my own to show I had completed the course. Yeah, I cheated, sort of, but I didn't know what else to do and these guys helped me out a lot. When I got in, the instructor didn't even look at the cards, just marked me off the list of cadets to make sure they had a record of my getting back. Apparently, the objective of the exercise wasn't necessarily to find all the navigation points on the map, but instead, to build confidence in our ability to navigate at night. Yeah, right—it didn't work out so well that first time, and I pledged I would master the art of land navigation and orienteering.

Finally, in the fifth week of training, the most interesting night exercise was the SERE training. Earlier that day, the instructors took us through the preparatory training as a part of SERE. As an example, they told us how to trap and kill small animals in the woods. The instructors taught us how to silently kill sentries if we escaped from an enemy POW camp, including how to kill a man in several unusual ways using just a wool sock. Amazing!

The trainers then explained the SERE training exercise and its objective which was simply not to get caught, period. They would put our company in pairs and take us out to the woods and drop us off at various points within the exercise area. They gave us one map and compass per team to evade capture by the enemy forces patrolling the area. The goal was to get to the "safe" area on the far side of the exercise area, the area of operations (AO), within a three-hour period. If we didn't make it within that time, they considered us captured.

As they continued to explain, at the end of the exercise they would sound a loud horn and we would have to make our way to the closest road and wait until elements of the enemy forces picked us up. Under those circumstances, we would spend the night in the enemy encampment as prisoners until they released us the next day. As I sat there, I thought, *this is really cool. I can do this.*

This is where the night land navigation skills would come in handy, as well as the night tactical exercises, the individual tactical training and our conditioning through running and long road marches. Now was the time to put all that together and use our heads to be stealthy and quick. We spent the day at the SERE site, we ate our dinner meal in the woods, and the trainers assigned us our partners. Those of us that still had bunkmates, they became our partners. Howard was mine.

Poor Howard—having him as my partner was like having a disoriented duck on the team. He wasn't that good at anything, although he could run in short spurts. But he didn't know land nav that well, nor did he really understand stealth techniques. Obviously, my recent experience with night land nav proved unsuccessful, but I continued to improve my land nav skills in daylight exercises and felt more confident to tackle this exercise. Pluses that night, were a clear sky and warm weather. I anticipated no adverse conditions to interfere with my vision and confidence. Only the enemy on the ground.

The trucks dropped us off at our start point, and the trainer in the truck gave us our location, and the location of the safe area. We fled into the nearby woods, and sat down to look at the provided map. I pulled out my tactical flashlight with red lenses which reduced their signature in the woods. I did a map recon and determined the best route to take, figured out the proper azimuth and oriented myself with both the map and the lensatic compass. Howard watched in awe. He didn't have a clue on how to do what I had just done.

"Okay, we need to move east along an azimuth of about 92 degrees." I explained.

"Why?" Howard asked.

"Well, this is our location," I pointed to a coordinate on the map. And this is where we have to end up." I pointed to the marked safe area.

"Okay."

"It's on an almost straight azimuth of 92." I said.

"Okay."

"We've got a few roads to cross along the way, I'm sure the enemy will be patrolling them."

"Okay. What do we do when we get to the roads?" Howard asked.

"They showed us how to do that." I was exasperated with Howard's ignorance. "We cross one at a time. We make sure no one is around, one of us goes first, listens and if no one is coming, then signal the other guy to cross. The first guy provides overwatch until the second guy gets across. Before the second guy crosses, he makes sure no one is coming before he crosses. We do that before crossing any man-made or natural obstacle." I sounded just like the instructor.

"You remember all that shit?" Howard asked wide-eyed.

"Yeah, you ready to move out?" I asked.

"Yeah, you lead." Howard said.

"Okay." I reoriented myself and took off at a slow trot on a 92-degree route, checking the compass as we moved out.

I fell back on my experiences at night at Richards-Gebaur and at night in Oregon, making my way through those woods as silently as possible. That was the key here, being quiet and then moving quickly when necessary.

About thirty minutes into the exercise we got caught trying to cross a road. We got to the road, our second, so we had developed a system to get across. I would get close to the edge of the road to make sure the coast was clear, and if it was, I signaled Howard to run across and establish an overwatch on the far side. It worked the first time, not so much the second time.

"Hold up Howard, I hear something on the far side," I whispered as we peered across the road. Both of us in a prone position looking across the road, I couldn't see anything, but could hear rustling.

"It could be an animal." Howard said.

"Dude, I can hear voices, animals don't talk."

"I think I can make it. They won't see me." Howard insisted.

"Well, hold on, maybe they'll move on."

"Nah, I'm going now, we'll be good." Howard rose up into a low crouch and ran across the road.

As soon as Howard reached the other side, flashlights lit up and voices began shouting, "Got one! Got one!" I heard bolts charging on M16s. Damn.

"Where's your partner?" An authoritative voice demanded.

I saw Howard gesture in my direction, and another voice ordered, "Come out, we know you're over there."

I rose from my hidden position with my hands up and slowly walked across the road, thinking about how to get out of this one.

When I reached the other side, one of the enemy soldiers told us to wait in a ditch while his partner radioed for a truck to come pick us up. I looked around and saw it was just the two of them. One had his weapon on us and the other was on the radio, looking in a different direction. They had us in the ditch facing the road, in the opposite direction we had to go to get to safety.

As we lay in the ditch, I felt in my pocket and got an idea. I whispered to Howard, "I have my camera in my pocket, it's got a flash. I'm going to pull it out and take their picture. When the flash goes off run like hell into the woods behind us."

I always carried my 110 Instamatic camera with me, to take pictures of the interesting stuff we saw during training. I thought I could blind these two guys long enough for us to run in the direction we had been going.

"Okay, sounds good." Howard agreed since he didn't have a better plan and didn't want to spend the night in a POW camp.

I waited for the enemy soldier to turn away and then I signaled to Howard to get ready.

I pulled the camera out of my pocket, powered up the flash, looked directly at the soldier and said, "Cheese!" As soon as he turned his face towards us I hit the flash. It exploded like a sun gone nova in those dark woods.

The soldier yelled, "Oh shit! I can't see!"

Howard and I took off climbing out of the ditch and then running in the opposite direction from the soldiers. Unfortunately, I caught part of the flash since I only closed one eye, and Howard had to drag me out of the ditch and pulled me as we started running.

"Come on Chris, we got to get out of here!" he yelled, and kept pulling me behind him.

We could hear the soldiers yelling for us to stop and firing their weapons—blanks of course—but we didn't stop. Thank God there were no obstacles, because it took me a few minutes to get my full night vision back, but by then we were several hundred yards away.

Once I got my night vision back I was able to see the compass and map and determine where we were and where we needed to go. As it turned out, there was only one line of resistance for us, so once we got past those guys it was smooth sailing to the rendezvous point. As one of the first teams in from our platoon, we had a hell of a story to tell!

The sixth week was made up of preparations for graduation, taking the final APFT, and the EOCT. We also received our final evaluations from CPT Lieteau. Mine was okay. He told me I had a lot of potential, but I needed to be more assertive when placed in leadership positions and use the knowledge I had to take charge, particularly with my peers in the garrison environment. He said he had been impressed with my knowledge, my ability to perform under pressure and my will to succeed. I never forgot him or his words of encouragement. What I remember most was his saying, when asked about Ranger School and becoming a Ranger, that he was Armor and didn't believe in that "Ranger danger shit." Oh well, no one's perfect.

I passed the EOCT with flying colors, and finally passed the APFT. I was so happy that I actually went to the Cadet Club and had a beer; my very first beer. I didn't drink alcohol at that time, but as a cadet, I had a special ID card that allowed me to buy alcohol at the Cadet Club. I finally got around to buying my first beer.

During that last week I also met my "officer mentor" a white first lieutenant from The Citadel, a very racist white military institution in South Carolina, the subject of the book and movie *Lords of Discipline*. He met me for the obligatory drink at the Officer's Club, and then he left. Not like the other officer mentors who actually did something with their cadets, like inviting them to their homes, or out to unit functions, or something else interesting.

That last weekend at Fort Knox I finally got to the bowling alley and bowled a few games. Shot a 581, which wasn't too bad for me at the time.

Interestingly, when I was on my way back from the bowling alley, dragging my one-ball bowling bag, an African-American lieutenant colonel stopped his car and asked me if I was a ROTC cadet.

"Yes sir." I said.

And he asked me if I would like to attend a unit picnic with him and his family. I quickly agreed and off we went. I met his attractive wife and two little boys. And when they found out I was the son of a recently retired LTC, they treated me like family. He talked to me about a career and gave me encouragement. He and his family were astounded that I was 16 going through the Basic ROTC Camp, and chalked it up to my being both smart and ambitious. This was exactly the sort of mentoring and encouragement I needed at a critical time during basic. After the picnic, LTC Anthony Brown took me back to the barracks and said goodbye. I never heard from him again, but that one day was well worth it, and was deeply appreciated.

Graduation day was finally here. We marched in formation and "passed in review" in front of the reviewing stand where the guest speaker, a Lieutenant General, stood at attention. We were dressed in our khakis with helmet liners, and boots. We had turned all our equipment in earlier, except the helmet liner, which we were to leave on the end of our bunks. We came back to the barracks and changed into our civilian clothes for the trip back home. Charter buses took us to the airport—a lot different than how I arrived at Fort Knox. I said my goodbyes to Howard at the airport, and never heard from him again.

I was happy to put Fort Knox in my rearview mirror, but I left with a feeling of real accomplishment and an anticipation of my future at New Mexico Military Institute and beyond.

CHAPTER 22

RAT Year

RAT—a word I would learn to hate. This was my RAT year at NMMI and it was not going to be fun. My parents drove me the four hours to Roswell on the day I would report for New Cadet Training, a week of training and orientation for those of us starting our first year at NMMI. RATs could be as young as freshmen in high school, and as old as freshmen in college, and all of us would have to go through the New Cadet Training. Unfortunately for the high school new cadets, their RAT status lasted the entire school year; unlike the college new cadets whose RAT year was only a semester. Regardless, we all shared like experiences, particularly during the New Cadet Training.

The cadet cadre assigned to put us through the ordeal of New Cadet Training was hand-selected the previous year for higher rank and responsibility, although many of them were not yet promoted to their final cadet ranks. The cadet cadre was made up of the platoon sergeants, the platoon leaders, first sergeants, and troop commanders. The squadron commanders and regimental commander were also in attendance, but more for administrative purposes rather than for the actual training.

Like at Fort Knox that first day was primarily in-processing. I was assigned to Mike Troop, and had a mini-reunion with some of the cadets I had met the year before who were RATs, and now in charge. The cadre showed us our barracks room, which consisted of two-man dorm rooms with bunk beds, one sink, a double closet where we kept our M14 rifles, and two desks for studying. The rules allowed us to have one device for playing music or watching TV. Luckily, my new roommate, a nice white guy from Prescott, Arizona, Tom Pratt, whose father was mayor of his town, had a stereo system. I had a combination FM/AM radio with a pop-up 7-inch, black and white TV, so we were set. The cadre didn't allow us to have a refrigerator in our rooms, nor any other types of devices. We lived on the third floor, and hated going up and down the stairs when it came time to fall in for formation. Yep, I was back on the Slab.

The supply guys issued our NMMI uniforms which included several short-sleeved and long-sleeved poplin shirts, khaki pants, olive green pants and blouse, saucer cap, overseas cap, and black shoes. Those of us who were contract ROTC students received additional uniforms and equipment at a later time. They also issued a laundry bag, a student number, and a charge card for the cadet store. The cadre gave us an orientation similar to the ones I had previously attended, so this part was old hat to me. By the end of the day, we had eaten two meals in the mess hall and had been holed up in our rooms putting them together in the approved NMMI manner. Our platoon leader was a nice looking white guy who seemed genuinely interested in whether we succeeded or failed. Of course, if we looked good, he looked good, so it was in his best interest to train us well.

That evening he had a platoon meeting to introduce ourselves and get to know each other. Several of us had been together at Fort Knox, and had some familiarity with each other. We established ourselves as an interesting mix of new cadets. I was the only Black New Cadet in the troop, although as I found out later, we did have a Black freshman football player. Apparently, they were too busy and too good to be with the rest of us. I had absolutely no respect for any of the football players and their supercilious, arrogant attitude towards the rest of us.

As usual, I was on my own again. I didn't realize at the time, how racist and bigoted many of my new cadet peers were in their attitudes towards Blacks, particularly Raun Watson ("If black is beautiful, I just shit a masterpiece.") and Rick Megahan (I challenged him to a fight when he kept using the "N" word. We didn't fight, but he stopped using it in my presence. He never called me a nigger to my face.). I also learned how much of a redneck school NMMI really was; and yeah, Kaleho had been right.

Cadets hailed from various parts of the country—Texas, New Mexico, Pennsylvania, Hawaii, Arizona, and California—and from varying ethnic groups, Hispanic, Black, whites, Asian-Americans, and Hawaiians. Initially, we all tried to mesh together as a team, and when it came to drill and ceremonies and various military-related activities, we did function well as a team. In fact, our platoon won Best Platoon both semesters my first year, and one of our squads won Best Squad twice as well. Our troop, Mike Troop, had the reputation of being a little on the wild side, and our troop commander, Captain Amos White, a Bostonian, was an Airborne Ranger and strutted around like he owned the campus.

He was definitely the epitome of what most of us wanted to be, an Airborne Ranger, and had that cocky attitude of someone who has done something very few of us would ever accomplish in life. That attitude permeated throughout the troop and we all felt that we could do anything, that we were better than everyone else; and we tried to show it at every opportunity. Our troop motto was "When the going gets tough, the tough get going, Mike Troop leads the way!" We had the Ranger Tab and silver jump wings on our troop flag.

Yeah, Mike Troop led the way.

We strutted when we marched; we were the best of the best and regularly won Best Troop competitions on a monthly and quarterly basis. For better or worse, we had a hell of a reputation as rabble rousers, but we were also very good at whatever we did—intramurals, inspections, marching, Best Cadet competitions, Best Squad, and Best Platoon. Even when I made the varsity bowling team, it added points to our totals for Best Troop, and of course we won Best Troop our first semester.

My physical transformation was little short of amazing. When my high school classmates had begun to mature physically, I was still a little runt. I didn't begin to mature physically until I began college at NMMI. For the first time, I shaved because the hair on my face was actually becoming visible, a sure sign of physical maturation. I began a regimen of running longer distances. Tom was a long-distance runner as was Ric Kuhlbars, another Fort Knox graduate from my company, and they taught me how to run long distances. We had the oval running track right in front of the Slab, so we could get out and run at any time of the day or night. I took advantage of that opportunity whenever I could.

I ran and ran, sometimes from two to three miles, up to five miles, at least three times a week. I worked on speed and endurance, and my crowning achievement that year was running a mile in 5:45. I was confident in my ability to do well on the PT test and to keep up with my peers when it came to running. The next step was building my scrawny little body.

I grew six inches that year and gained over forty pounds, most of it lean muscle. I wasn't fat, and still looked fairly slender, okay skinny, but it was mostly muscle. I drank protein shakes, got on a weightlifting regimen, and did thousands of push-ups and sit-ups to develop my upper body and core strength. And yeah, I finally learned how to properly execute inspection arms. I finally had the strength to perform the maneuver properly and was able to successfully stand inspection.

As contract ROTC cadets we were Military Science (MS)-III students based on having attended Fort Knox Basic Camp or having completed at least three years of Junior ROTC, and signing up for the two-year Sr. ROTC program. Not everyone in the junior college was a contract or MS-III. Some were MS-Is attending NMMI just for the academics and did not plan on making the Army a career.

During the RAT orientation, the MS-IVs marched those of us who were MS-IIIs over to the ROTC department and introduced us to the cadre of NCO's and officers who ran that program. One of the officers was a Cavalry captain who sported a bushy, British-style mustache, the Ranger Tab, jump wings, and attitude. On his desk was a sign that proclaimed, **"If You Ain't Ranger, You Ain't Shit."** I loved it, and knew that these guys were serious about our training. In addition to meeting the ROTC cadre, we were issued our green fatigues, boots, and TA-50 equipment which we were required to keep in our rooms.

Both Tom and I were MS-IIIs, so that made it convenient. Most of the MS-IIIs were so matched, but some were not, and at times that created a little friction. MS-IIIs had different priorities, and sometimes we couldn't be bothered with some of the more mundane RAT tasks with which the non-MS-IIIs were stuck.

Our ROTC commitments always took precedent over NMMI requirements. Our cadet cadre was almost all contract cadets, so they understood and, in most cases, facilitated our commitments.

The new cadet orientation went without much drama, and after a week we were ready to meet the rest of the first year cadets. Once the rest of the troop showed up, we new cadets were integrated into the rest of the troop. I had a new squad leader, a cadet staff sergeant who was kind of a slow-witted guy, who never really seemed interested in being a squad leader. He was a MS-IV who had just returned from ROTC Advanced Camp at Fort Riley, Kansas. He didn't talk to us much about that experience, and seemed more interested in tripping us up rather than training us into a good squad.

Despite him, we turned out to be a good squad, and were part of the Best Platoon both semesters of our new cadet year, a very difficult accomplishment. Our platoon had many former high school and current NMMI drill team members, so we were very good at drill and ceremonies, and took extreme pride in our ability to march and look sharp. We had that Mike Troop swagger about us and we liked to win.

Our official designation was Second Class cadets, the second year cadets in the junior college were the First Class cadets. The lowest level in the hierarchy of class designations was the freshmen in high school who were Sixth Class cadets and each higher classification of students received a lower Class number until you got to the top of the food chain, the junior college sophomores, the First Class. Some guys spent six years at NMMI and were pretty institutionalized.

They viewed us with suspicion and looked down on us as interlopers. We got hazed by everybody who was a First Class cadet or "Firsty" and technically anyone else who had been at NMMI for at least a year; but we didn't take much shit from anyone in high school.

The RAT ("Recruit at Training") semester proceeded as expected—we ran everywhere; we marched to all our meals; we had study time every night; and limited access off campus. This was a structured environment and as RATs we were on the bottom of the hierarchal pyramid. Our privileges were limited, but that was expected—we were RATs. However, our ROTC training was different, and while we attended classes at the Military Science building, we were MS-IIIs, not RATs or new cadets.

The ROTC training was intense. Different from high school, this would train us as future officers in the U.S. Army. The goal would be a Distinguished Military Student or Distinguished Military Graduate, and get a regular Army commission rather than a reserve commission. Being a DMS or DMG also qualified you for jump school or Airborne training at Fort Benning, and Ranger School, also at Fort Benning.

We executed simulated squad-level tactics on campus, as well as additional drill and ceremonies. We learned military history, weapons, radios, radio communication, leadership and command, squad and platoon level tactics in the offense and defense—how to integrate squad and platoons with company and battalion-level tactics and operations. The ROTC instructors taught us how to write five-part operations orders and we simulated being staff officers at the battalion level, responsible for each part of the operations order. This was all the theoretical side of the training, and in the spring, we went out to the field and conducted field training exercises (FTXs) to put it all in perspective and to actually perform the tasks on which we had been training.

During the FTX we all had an opportunity to lead at the squad and platoon level during offensive and defensive operations. We stayed out in the field from Friday to Monday, and got very little sleep during that four-day FTX. We established bivouac areas where we set up two-man tents as a part of the squad, and larger eight-man tents for cadre, similar to training at Fort Knox. This wasn't new to us, but the requirement of acting in leadership positions was different and separated the good leaders from the poor leaders.

I scored in the middle of the pack in leadership evaluations; but excelled in the technical aspects of the training—land navigation and orienteering, BRM, radio commo, map reading, weapons training, and knowing and understanding squad and platoon-level tactics. As the youngest guy in the program, I still had a hard time getting my "peers" to follow me, even when they were supposed to. At least it wasn't as bad as Fort Knox had been. These guys were also relatively young—just not as young as me, and they understood the challenges of being young in a leadership position.

The year-long training prepared us for Fort Riley. The NMMI ROTC cadre actually considered not sending me to Advanced Camp because of my age. No one had ever been to Advanced Camp at the tender age of 17, and they didn't think I would be successful. Unfortunately for them, I had been successful during every aspect of training at NMMI and they couldn't find any other excuses for not sending me to Riley. I was tops in the class in testing and other technical aspects of military training, but again, their concern was more along the lines of how I would do in leadership positions and competing against my much older "peers" at Advanced Camp. Most of those guys would be 21 years or older, many of whom were prior service and much older than me. I believed I was up to the challenge and asked to be allowed to go. Reluctantly, they agreed, and that summer, 1974, saw me going to ROTC Advanced Camp at Fort Riley, Kansas.

CHAPTER 23

Fort Riley

The NMMI ROTC cadre gave extensive briefings to those of us going to Riley on what to expect at Advanced Camp. One of our goals as cadets was to come back RECONDO-qualified, which meant expertise in various military skills including land nav, the APFT, BRM, leadership, military stakes and successfully negotiating the obstacle and confidence courses. Our training at NMMI prepared us for those challenges, and I felt well prepared to succeed at Fort Riley.

To further prepare, I continued my regimen of physical fitness: running, lifting weights, doing push-ups and sit-ups to get me ready for Riley. My goal was to maximize my score on the record APFT at Advanced Camp and show that I could compete with these older guys. I didn't go to Riley until mid-June, so I continued working out at home; going down to the high school and running along Yarbrough up to five miles every other day. I also swam in our backyard pool daily, to keep in shape and prepare for any swimming tests or water-borne requirements while at Riley.

The trip to Fort Riley was more direct and less fraught with the unknown than the previous summer's trip to Fort Knox. This time I traveled with several people going to Fort Riley once I made the connection in Dallas and flew to Kansas City. From Kansas City we flew a "puddle jumper" regional propeller plane to Junction City, Kansas. I had never flown in such a plane and almost threw up several times because of the turbulence and constant adjustments in altitude. Not a very good flight for me, but I kept my cookies to myself.

Military escorts met us at the airport and loaded us on buses that took us out to Fort Riley. The ROTC Camp was located some distance from the post proper, unlike Fort Knox where they integrated the cadets onto the main post. Our escorts inprocessed us and took us to our company training area and platoon barracks. That's when our platoon evaluator, CPT John Sorensen, a white guy from the Midwest, introduced himself. He was an Infantry captain, big and shaped like a pear. He was a joke physically and I couldn't believe this guy was an officer, much less an Infantry officer. He didn't have jump wings or a Ranger Tab, so how could I take him seriously?

Maybe my disdain for him showed because almost immediately he made it known that he disapproved of junior college cadets, who were significantly younger than the general population of cadets, and me in particular. He rode me the entire time I was there, and tried his best to embarrass and ridicule me during my six weeks at Advanced Camp.

His attitude towards me encouraged a like attitude amongst my peers in the platoon, and made it difficult to succeed in platoon leadership positions. He made my age an issue and controversial amongst my peers. We slept in a two-squad bay, about 20 men; with the other two squads in the platoon in the adjacent bay. Many of the guys in my bay supported me and some were astounded that a 17 year old could actually compete against them on equal footing. Others felt somehow insulted and were outright angry about my age. Many were married with children, and you would have thought I was taking food out of their families' mouths. The oldest guy in our platoon was 28, a Vietnam prior service vet going through the 2-year program. He was probably the most vociferous about my age, and coincidentally, or not so coincidentally, a favorite of our platoon evaluator. Most of the guys' age ranged between 21 and 24 years old. There were a couple of other guys in the platoon from Wentworth, another military college, but none from NMMI. Those guys were either 19 or 20, so a little older than me.

My two friends in the platoon were the two other Black guys, one from Lincoln University, and the other from Alabama A&M, both Historically Black College and Universities (HBCUs). I hung out with them when I could, but they both had cars, so they normally took off on the weekends. This was also my first opportunity to interact with cadets from other HBCUs, including Alcorn State, and Prairie View A&M. I also met guys from Texas A&M and the Corps. I found them to be both impressive and weird.

ROTC Advanced Camp served two purposes—first, to weed out weak leaders or persons with little leadership potential; and second, to test cadets in various military skills. We underwent the Combat Water Survival Test, the Confidence Course, and the Obstacle Course. They introduced us to hand-to-hand combat and pugil stick training, as well as bayonet training. We had live fire exercises and training on various weapons used by the infantry, artillery, armor and engineer branches, to include: the M2 .50 cal machine gun, the M60

7.62 machine gun, hand grenades, the M203, firing 105mm Howitzers, driving M60A1 tanks, and using explosives. Some of the same things we had done at Knox. We also watched artillery barrages from a "danger close" position in a glass-encased bunker to give us the feel of being subjected to an artillery barrage.

The cadre tested our leadership potential using both garrison leadership and tactical leadership scenarios. Garrison leadership consisted of leadership positions within our platoon for administrative purposes while in a non-tactical setting. Tactical leadership involved us performing in leadership positions during field training exercises at the squad, platoon and even company level. Again, similar to Knox.

And again, like Knox, I performed well in the tactical leadership positions, particularly when the trainers threw me in with cadets not in my platoon or company. However, when the cadre placed me in a garrison squad leader or platoon sergeant position and I had to deal with my own platoon members, that seemed to pose problems. Of course, I didn't always help my situation, because not only was I the youngest, I may have been one of the cockiest guys in the platoon. I had more ROTC experience than most of the guys and excelled in the technical areas of military science. Only the Vietnam vet had more military experience than me. This didn't endear me to many of my peers, and that reared its ugly head when I was put in garrison leadership positions. On one occasion I was in charge as a squad leader and gave tasks for various squad members to perform. One white cadet flat out refused to perform the assigned tasks until the African-American cadet from Alabama A&M, who was bigger and older than the white cadet, stepped up and told him to do what I ordered. This pattern persisted throughout Advanced Camp, and significantly affected my peer ratings and evaluations. These experiences also showed me that maybe my age wasn't the only issue with these white cadets.

Ironically, CPT Sorenson, the person who helped cause the problem, took no responsibility for my issues of leadership in the platoon, and severely criticized and downgraded me on my evaluations for my leadership of my "peers." These evaluations also had a deleterious effect on my ability to assume greater rank at NMMI and kept me from being promoted to an officer position until right before graduation. Of course, I didn't know that at the time, and these same evaluations would also have an effect on my eventual commissioning. I'm sure Sorenson knew the consequences of his actions and was trying his level best to keep me from being commissioned eventually as a U.S. Army officer. Well, *fuck* him, I was going to be a U.S. Army officer despite his best efforts.

Unfortunately, during my six weeks at Fort Riley, I was prone to getting sick. As it turned out, I got sick most of the time I lived in either Kansas or Missouri, but at the time I wasn't aware I was allergic to something in the Midwest. I suffered from chronic bronchitis, and while playing flag football with my company, I suffered a "trauma" to my neck when an opponent struck me in the neck, paralyzing my neck for a few days, keeping me from turning my head without turning my entire body.

I had gone on sick call during my second week at Riley. They conducted sick call every morning for cadets that had injured themselves or felt ill. The process included informing the platoon evaluator that you needed to go on sick call, then all the cadets going on sick call marched over to the Troop Medical clinic (TMC) to get checked out by a physician's assistant. On this particular day, I reported to Sorenson that I continued to have problems breathing and had injured myself playing football the night before. Reluctantly, he authorized me to go on sick call. I saw the PA and described my symptoms, he listened to my chest and discovered my lungs were full of fluid and congested. He also checked my neck and range of motion without pain. He diagnosed me with bronchitis and neck trauma; and prescribed various antibiotics and cough syrup and pain meds for my neck. I returned to the platoon within an hour after going on sick call. The platoon stood in formation preparing to go to that day's training.

Sorenson stood in front of the platoon with his little ammo belt around his bulging waist, a canteen on each hip. He motioned for me to report to him.

"Sir, Cadet Pittard reporting back from sick call." I stood at attention in front of him and saluted as I reported.

He returned the salute, "What did the doc say Pittard?"

I looked around, thinking it wasn't anybody else's business what the PA had told me.

"Go on Pittard, tell us." Sorenson ordered.

"I have bronchitis and neck trauma," I said, "I'm not to do any physical activity for the next few days." I handed him my doctor's excuse.

He just looked at me for a few seconds and ordered, "Turn around Pittard."

I turned around and faced the platoon.

In a loud voice he said, "This is what a pussy looks like gentlemen. Someone always looking for a way out of training and someone you can never depend on. Cadet Pittard will never be an Army officer."

I just stood there, staring at nothing, enraged at this white racist motherfucker. I didn't change my expression. I refused to give him the satisfaction of reacting to this bullshit.

"You may get your equipment and fall in at the back of the formation," Sorenson ordered.

I turned back around to face him, with hatred in my eyes, saluted, and ran to the barracks to get my LCE. I almost cried in angry frustration as I put on my equipment, but again, I did not want him to know how I felt. I ran back out and took my place at the end of my squad. I could hear members of the platoon snickering. The next couple of days were not pleasant as I was restricted from participating in any physically taxing training. After just two days, against medical advice, I went back to full training. But the damage had been done.

This story circulated amongst the entire company, including the other guys in the company from NMMI. That story made its way back to NMMI. Is there any wonder that the platoon thought me unworthy of any respect from them, particularly in any leadership position? And, is it any wonder that Sorenson made it more difficult for me to succeed, regardless of his motives?

Again, *fuck him*.

I knew however, Sorenson could not take away my expertise in every other area except the garrison leadership evaluations. I excelled in every aspect of military stakes, land nav, orienteering, BRM, the confidence and obstacle courses, the record APFT, and the tactical leadership courses; and as proof, I earned the coveted RECONDO badge.

Yeah, *fuck* him—he had to pin it on me the day we graduated—I know that bothered the hell out of him when he had to congratulate me on earning that unique qualification badge. Yeah, well…*kiss my 17 year-old ass.*

Fort Riley taught me a lot about leadership of my peers and how to make myself fit in. I vowed that if I ever encountered a similar training situation I would make myself indispensable and would be a better leader of men. In this instance I was handicapped by my age and inexperience as a leader; but I learned a lot and knew—whether they knew it or not—I had great leadership potential and would show it if ever given the chance again. I would show everyone.

Now it was time to return to NMMI and my First-Class year. I looked forward to being on top of the pyramid this time as I put Fort Riley and Sorenson in my rearview mirror.

CHAPTER 24

Firsty

My semester began the week after RAT orientation. I had not been designated as one of the cadet training cadre the previous year, and therefore, was not destined for high rank or position. In fact, I was a squad leader, with Frank Sickles as my assistant squad leader, and roommate, this time on the second floor. Frank was a good guy, just really fat. He was a non-contract cadet and the subject of much ridicule during the previous year. I got along fine with Frank, but his assignment as my roommate and assistant squad leader was a slap in the face and told me what the troop leadership thought of me.

The Mike Troop leadership consisted mainly of Rick Megahan, the troop commander, who had gone to Ranger School, but didn't graduate, and Raun Watson, the executive officer. I knew I had to get out of the troop as soon as possible. I had no chance to be promoted or to ascend to any positions above squad leader, with those two racist bastards in command of the troop.

Luckily, a good friend of mine, Greg Robison, a fellow varsity bowling team member, was the troop commander of Echo Troop, and requested I come over and be his field first sergeant, a cadet Master Sergeant. So, I became Cadet MSG Pittard instead of cadet SSG Pittard, and wore three stripes up and three stripes down, one position below the First Sergeant, but above the platoon sergeants.

Greg, a six-year cadet, had grown up at NMMI. He and I were friends from the bowling team, and I enjoyed working for him. He didn't care about Fort Riley, only that I did a good job for him. I took on the duties of a field first sergeant with gusto and tried to mold the young cadets the best way I knew. Echo Troop was one of the high school troops in The Box and that made it a different experience because now I dealt with younger kids, not men, between the ages of 14 and 18, not up to 21 years old. This took a completely different mindset for leadership and motivation. I had fun and enjoyed the job.

Unfortunately, NMMI relieved Greg of his position because of an incident that happened on a bowling trip to Las Vegas, that, ironically, my mother didn't allow me to go on. When he came back he was demoted and relieved of command. His replacement was Dan McElroy, and I hated him.

McElroy had been in my company at Fort Riley and was aware of all the issues I had at Riley, so he came with his preconceived opinions of me and treated me accordingly. I stopped enjoying the job and tried to get transferred out or promoted out of the troop. But the Commandant's secretary, Ms. Croix, told me they had received complaints about there being too many Black cadet officers and that the Commandant decided to leave it at two, Chester Pettis, and Lionel Pittman, the third "P," me, would not get promoted any time soon. So, I had to endure the abuse heaped on me by McElroy. Most of the time the abuse occurred in front of the subordinate cadets, which undermined my authority in the troop. I hated being in the troop, but I had to make the best of it, so I became more abusive of the high school new cadets. Their RAT year lasted an entire year, so they had to endure a much longer period of hazing than I had on the college side.

Unfortunately, the more abusive I became, the more respect I seemed to gain. This wasn't leadership; just bullying, and eventually had its own price to pay.

The ROTC side went fairly smoothly. I was initially counseled on my return from Fort Riley and told that my leadership evaluations put me in the bottom quarter of my class. I was determined to change that, and did.

First, I was a RECONDO recipient. Strangely, there weren't a whole lot of those at NMMI. In the hierarchy of qualification badges, it ranked behind the Ranger Tab, jump wings and Air Assault wings, but still pretty special. So, I had proven myself in the military skills and physical fitness realm. I continued that progression and became even more expert on those skills. Second, I volunteered for every leadership position I could within the ROTC department, and tried to show that I had been given an erroneous rating at Advanced Camp. Apparently, I succeeded, because by the end of the first semester I was praised on my performance both in and out of the classroom. The ROTC cadre allowed me to be an instructor in map reading, land nav, orienteering, and other military skills, and they asked me to assist in the planning of the spring FTX.

The garrison side of the house was different. As the only Black guy in my troop, I could feel the racism cascading from many of these white cadets, both the new cadets and old cadets subordinate to me. I ranked as the second-highest NCO in the troop, and a Firsty. That made me an equal, although outranked by the other four officers. One of my jobs was to discipline new cadets. The cadet first sergeant, a second-class cadet, delegated that to me, so I engaged in various forms of discipline, some of them consisted of hazing in form and execution.

On one such occasion, I had three new cadets in a "stress" position called "hanging around" where they hung from the back of their door, facing the door, with their legs bent to support their rifle in the crook of their knees. These guys were particularly contemptuous of me and that's why I had them up there, for insubordination. However, one of them challenged me to a "no rank" fight. They were all varsity wrestlers and thought they could take me in a one-on-one fight.

This was a challenge, and if I didn't accept it would be all over the troop and maybe the school that I chickened out, so, reluctantly, I accepted.

Shit, now I've got to fight three guys in a row. We set it up for that same night out near the stables, away from everything and everybody. I hadn't fought anyone for real in a while and not since Fort Riley had I engaged in any kind of pugilistic endeavor. I still dabbled in tae kwon do, not really sparring, but that's all I had to fall back on. So, with an air of resignation, I went out there. Naïve me, I thought it would only be a handful of us, but most of the troop materialized out there, minus the officers and the first sergeant.

All those guys formed a circle around me and the three combatants. We were in a field where the wild grass wasn't too high. The four of us were dressed in white tee shirts and khaki pants, with tennis shoes. Out there behind the stables, I could smell the horse shit and hay, almost a prophetic background to this clear, moonlit night.

By agreement, I would fight them one at a time. So again, with an air of resignation in the midst of an air of expectation from the crowd, we got started. I'm sure they wanted to see me go down, but they were to be disappointed, at least for the first two fights. The first two were the smaller guys, in good shape. The first one, I guess the braver of the two sauntered out to the middle of the circle.

When I got into a fighting stance, somebody from the crowd said, "Watch out, he knows that 'Kung Fu Joe' shit." Yeah, I did.

The first one tried to bull rush me to get the fight over quickly, but I stepped aside to my left, pivoted on my left foot, and executed a pretty good roundhouse to his stomach with my right foot. He wasn't expecting that and folded at the waist. I didn't press the attack but waited to see if he was still in the fight. Apparently not, and he walked a little unsteadily back to the circle.

The second guy, now a little more nervous, was also more cautious. He got in a classic wrestling stance and we circled each other for a few moments. He feinted towards me to see my reaction. I stood my ground and waited for something more significant. I was not going to be the aggressor but would defend myself. Egged on by his white classmates, he launched himself at me from about three or four feet away. I took him with a straight fist to the chest and sat him down. Although not a wrestler, I did have the benefit of some training in tae kwon do and the Army methods of unarmed combat, so I had a clue how to defend myself. He got up and walked back to the circle. That left the biggest and oldest of the three.

I didn't hit anyone in the face, so I left no black eyes or obvious bruises. I aimed all my blows to the midsection of the body. I didn't let them get close enough to get me to the ground.

And yeah, a roundhouse kick and punch ended the first two, but I got tired, and the third guy, the largest of the three bull-rushed me so fast that I wasn't able to throw a kick or an effective punch. He got in close and threw me to the ground and pinned me. Once he pinned me, and pushed my face in the ground, he let me up and it was over, but not before someone in the back muttered, "Nigger" under his breath. I guess they finally got what they came to see, my comeuppance as an "uppity nigger."

I trudged back to my room as they all ran back to the troop area. I hated having lost at all, but at least I could hold my head up because I met the challenge head on and at least took two out of three.

I got cleaned up and vowed I would never be in that situation again, and if I ever had to fight I wouldn't hold back. I think I held back because I was fighting high school guys and didn't want to injure anyone. No more. If I ever got into another fight, it would have to be "no holds barred."

As an interesting aside, my stock in the troop seemed to rise because I didn't fall back on my rank, and I got out there and mixed it up with those white boys. Go figure.

A couple of weeks later, the week before graduation, they finally promoted me to cadet second lieutenant and I crossed the graduation stage with my Sam Brown belt on and the single pips of an officer on each shoulder. I was the last cadet promoted to second lieutenant. I guess the school could afford to have the third Black officer promoted at the end of the school year when it would not offend anyone's white sensibilities, and I wouldn't be in charge of anyone's precious white sons.

I learned a lot from my experiences at Fort Knox, NMMI, and Fort Riley. Valuable lessons I would take with me for the rest of my life. But I was glad to put NMMI behind me.

I looked forward to the University of Texas, finishing my education and finally beginning my career as a commissioned officer.

CHAPTER 25

The Interim

My introduction to the University of Texas at Austin, home of the Longhorns, occurred in the Fall of 1975. The NMMI ROTC cadre had instructed me to introduce myself to the UT ROTC department and make them aware I would graduate within a two-year period and be commissioned. Once classes began, I trooped over to the ROTC department and introduced myself to the professor of military science (PMS) at UT, LTC Jonathan Sain, and offered my services to him and his ROTC program. He told me he didn't believe in cadets like me from NMMI going through the program so young. He also indicated he didn't need to see me again until my commissioning two years away and didn't need my services. Well, I guess I just have that effect on people. Okay, my obligation in that regard was over, and I proceeded to learn all about being a student at one of the largest, most prestigious universities in the country.

Although I was no longer in ROTC, I continued to exercise my leadership skills in various forums and venues. Almost from the first day on campus, I became involved in African-American related activities that showcased my greater awareness of being Black in America. I was a writer for the short-lived Black student newspaper, *Blackprint*. I participated in protests on campus and sit-ins having to do with the stance of the administration towards Black students, and the views of certain professors concerning the intelligence of Blacks and how it related to physiology and genealogy. The militant side of me finally came out having been given a forum to express itself. As a history major, I crafted my own Afrocentric history curriculum. If there was a requirement for English or sociology, I took Black Literature, or Black sociology and so on. I became much more informed and educated about the Black experience in America. I also got involved in dorm politics.

I stayed at Jester Dorm, was elected vice-president of the dorm council and I created the Multi-Cultural Committee to serve the minority community of dorm residents in the largest dorm in the country, over 3,000 co-ed residents.

UT could only claim about one percent African-Americans in its undergrad population, and we were definitely an underserved minority.

I continued my workout regimen from NMMI, and ran 3-5 miles three times a week and continued to lift weights, do sit-ups and push-ups, and stay in shape. I also helped to establish a chapter of Kappa Alpha Psi Fraternity, Inc. at Texas.

We started pledging on or about February 5, 1976, and "crossed the burning sands" on April 22, 1976, eleven weeks later. My fellow pledges voted me president of the pledge line, known as the "Premiers of Destiny," and we guided the establishment of my fraternity at UT on December 3, 1977. I was also a resident assistant during my senior year at Texas and I received my commission on May 21, 1977, as a second lieutenant in the air defense artillery branch of the U.S. Army. I deferred going on active duty because of my admission to law school at UT.

While at UT my dream of becoming an Airborne Ranger was somewhat sidetracked. No longer in that ultra-military environment of NMMI, the urgency of becoming an Airborne Ranger lost some of its immediacy. In fact, I was commissioned a second lieutenant in air defense artillery, probably the least aggressive of the combat arms branches. I learned from my father, who didn't like going to the field and doing all that "infantry shit," that ADA was the way to go, and probably the safest way to go.

In addition, with law school looming in my future, I might not serve a day as an ADA officer, and instead fulfill my military obligation as a Judge Advocate General (JAG) officer—one of the Army's lawyers—and they certainly didn't go to jump school or Ranger School. So my dreams of becoming an Airborne Ranger were pretty much dead in 1977, and into the foreseeable future. But of course, life has a habit of changing....

❖ ❖ ❖

After a pretty adventurous summer in 1977, which included a road trip in my new Trans-Am, my arrest in California, and seeing Mom and Dana head off to the United States Military Academy at West Point, I started law school at Texas in the fall, at the tender and immature age of 20.

My first year of law school turned out to be an academic disaster. There were only six Black law students in my class and that made being there somewhat of a challenge because you knew many of your professors and classmates didn't think you belonged. Unfortunately, I played into that belief because I didn't take it seriously. I fell in love with the idea of being a law student, rather than applying myself to be a successful law student. I was in a fraternity, living in an apartment for the first time, driving that fabulous special edition, black and gold, Trans-Am, and trying my best to mesmerize all the ladies. Hell, who had time for law school?

Being in the prime of life, I enjoyed myself, and going to class and serious studying ranked way down on the list of priorities. At least I stayed in shape by keeping up my running, and doing push-ups and sit-ups.

In the back of my mind, unlike most of the other law students, I knew I had a career as an Army officer, so being a lawyer was icing on the cake. Regardless of whether I graduated law school, I would go into the Army as an officer, and that was a comforting thought. I excelled in the brief writing and advocacy components of my first year of law school but didn't do very well in most of my classes. Unfortunately, I spent an extreme amount of time involved in getting my fraternity established on campus and reveled in just being me. That did not bode well for my grades.

In the spring of my first year in law school, four of us drove in my car to Atlanta for Spring Break. I had met a girl during a New Year's Eve party at my cousin's house in Aberdeen, MD, and we hit if off pretty well. Coincidentally, her father was also a Kappa, so that didn't hurt my chances of dating her. I had let her know I wanted to visit her during my spring break, which didn't match up with hers, which meant she would still be in school while I visited. She was a student at Spelman College in Atlanta. I'd never been to Atlanta and wanted to visit. She said it was no problem, so, Cornell, C. Victor, George, and I piled into my car for the long haul to Atlanta. Victor, a second-year law student, and George, a grad student, were both graduates of Morehouse College, also in Atlanta, and wanted to go back to visit.

We arrived in Atlanta at about three or four in the morning on a Friday. George and Victor gave me directions to the Spelman campus, and with the name of the girl's dorm, they told me its location on campus. I dropped off George and Victor where they wanted to go, and Cornell and I went to the Spelman campus. Unfortunately, an iron fence surrounded the campus, and each dorm was locked down tight with a resident mother assigned to keep unwanted males from unannounced visits and staying over with her virtuous wards.

Undaunted by the specter of the fence, and having learned certain lessons from my California trip, I parked the car in a nice surreptitious spot so as not to arouse the suspicion of any roving campus police. I scaled the fence closest to where I thought the dorm might be and used all my training in evasion techniques from years of ROTC to make my way unseen to the locked doors of the women's dorm where my friend stayed. Again, undaunted, I found a way into the dorm without being seen by campus police or the dorm mother. There are always methods to get around locked doors.

I located the directory downstairs with the names of the girls and their room numbers. I made my way to the second floor and softly knocked on Linda's door. After the second knock, she came to the door dressed in a light blue robe, matching slippers, and her hair in rollers. I thought she might faint.

She rushed me into the room and whispered, "How did you get here?"

"Over the fence and through the woods," I smirked.

"You could get in big trouble being here, and I could get kicked out!"

"Okay, I just wanted to let you know I was here. When can I see you?"

"Uh, I'll be at the basketball courts at Washington Park around noon, I can see you there. Now you have to leave." She insisted, fear writ large on her face. "Okay, I'll see you then." I turned back to the door, and then I looked out into the hallway to make sure the coast was clear.

"Now get out!" She whispered, but she had to smile as she pushed me out the door.

Luckily her roommate had spent the night elsewhere, so there was no one there to see me go in or come out of her room. As surreptitiously as I came in to the dorm I went back out. As I left the dorm I checked for campus police, and when I saw no one out and about, I made a beeline for where I'd left Cornell and the car.

"Everything go okay?" Cornell asked.

"Yep, no problem, I'll see her later today at Washington Park." I said as I started the car.

"Boy, you got some balls, I'll give you that. Damn. Breaking and entering into Spelman and one of the women's dorms, that's wild."

"Yeah, well, it's all that Army training. You should know, you've been through SERE too."

Cornell had gone through the two-year program at UT and was going to be commissioned as an ADA second lieutenant in a couple of months. He had gone to Knox and Riley as I had and I had given him the benefit of my experiences before he attended those camps. Unlike me, he excelled in his peer evaluations, and like me, he also earned the coveted RECONDO badge.

"Yeah, yeah, but they never taught us that!" He laughed.

"Sure they did," I laughed, "You just got to apply your training to the appropriate situation. This was definitely survival, escape and evasion." We both laughed at that.

Then we drove to his cousin's house where we were to stay during our time in Atlanta. After a short nap, Cornell and I made it to Washington Park where unexpectedly I met Linda's boyfriend. Uh huh, she had a boyfriend she forgot to tell me about. That's the reason she appeared so flustered when I showed up at her dorm, other than the fact she could have been tossed out of Spelman, she had a boyfriend and she really didn't expect me to show up in Atlanta. Well that was a revelation. She invited us to a party that night, and Cornell and I hung out with Linda and her boyfriend. A very enlightening experience. I never let on to the other guy I had come all the way from Texas to steal his girl. Not worth the trouble.

The next morning when Cornell and I went downstairs for breakfast, his cousin announced she was going out of town and we could no longer stay in her house. We had to leave after breakfast. Terrific.

Cornell had a back-up plan, he caught a bus to visit his parents in North Carolina. That left me stuck in Atlanta for the rest of the week. The girl I came to see had a boyfriend, so I no longer had a reason for being in Atlanta, and now I didn't have anywhere to stay.

Well, I was in a frat, so I went to the Kappa house at Morehouse to find somewhere to stay. I got over there, introduced myself, proved my fraternal credentials and was introduced to all the Brothers and their Diamonds, the little sister organization.

That proved to be fortuitous for me because there was one Diamond whose nickname was R2D2 after the Star Wars droid character. She was pretty, light-skinned, with long brown hair, not very tall, and had a bubbly personality, hence her nickname. She and I took an immediate shine to each other and after staying one night in the frat house, I moved into her apartment for the rest of my spring break. By the time Cornell came back from NC, I was pretty much entrenched in the Atlanta night life. I even got us invitations to the Atlanta Alumni Chapter Black and White Ball through my Uncle Donald Hollowell, a Laurel Wreath Awardee—the highest award my Fraternity confers on an individual Brother for lifetime and important achievements. Cornell took R2D2's cousin, Janet, and I took R2D2.

When we drove back to Austin, I obviously had the more exciting adventures compared to the more mundane spring break the other three guys had experienced. They were pretty amazed at some of my stories, but even more amazed at my audacity in getting some things accomplished in such a short period of time.

This whole episode and the road trip the summer before demonstrated to me that I probably wasn't well suited to be an ADA officer, and probably not well suited to be a JAG officer either. I had too much piss and vinegar, and way too much audacity to sit behind some desk in the Army.

I started thinking again about whether I really wanted to be a JAG officer or anything other than Infantry.

CHAPTER 26

Going Infantry

In the fall of 1978, I moved onto the graduate floor of Jester Dorm. This was sort of my last-ditch effort to focus on law school, complete my legal education and go into the Army as a JAG officer. That fall I met Karen, an incoming freshman at UT, and eventually married her, but that's a different story for a different time.

More importantly, I quit law school in the spring of 1979. In February of that year, a congenital physical defect decided to rear its ugly head and caused me to miss a month of law school. The condition caused excruciating pain and required emergency surgery to correct it. Once it was over, I couldn't sit down without significant pain and certainly couldn't concentrate on studying the law because I stayed high on pain killers for two weeks.

So, disillusioned with the whole law school experience, this seemed like a sign from God to move on and put law school in the rear view mirror. I had never quit anything in my life, but this seemed like the right decision. I made an appointment with the Dean of Students, Dean Thomas Gibson, and informed him I wanted to withdraw from law school. He accepted my letter of withdrawal, and just like that, I was no longer a law student at the University of Texas School of Law. I vowed I would eventually go back, but I felt such a feeling of freedom that I had never felt before and was ready to take my commission in the Army and go out into the world.

I informed the ROTC department that I had withdrawn from law school, much to the surprise of LTC Sain, and they began the process to reactivate my commission and put me on active duty. Within a few weeks I received my paperwork placing me on active duty and reactivating my commission. But to my great surprise the Army changed my branch from air defense artillery to Infantry. I called Personnel at Army HQ to find out why that had happened. They told me they had a greater need for Infantry officers than ADA officers. Huh. Ok.

My frat Brother and good friend Cornell had been commissioned ADA the previous year, and was newly assigned to Fort Hood, about 60 miles north of Austin. I called him and told him I was no longer ADA, but Infantry. He amusingly gave me his regrets and let me know Infantry was for "hard core" guys and wished me luck. I called Mom to let her know I would be going Infantry and she cried and said she would call my Uncle Ed, a retired Major General and former Deputy Commander of PERSCOM, the Army's Personnel Command, and get his opinion. He told her Infantry would be good for my career and he also wished me luck.

Now, all of a sudden, becoming an Airborne Ranger became a real possibility again.

❖   ❖   ❖

I received my orders to report to Fort Benning, GA, with a report date of September 30, 1979, and then to report to Infantry Officer Basic Course (IOBC) on October 14, 1979, for my initial six-month training as a young Infantry officer. During the summer I began getting into the mind set of potentially going to jump school and Ranger School.

Mom was a Department of the Army civilian stationed at West Point, so that's where I stayed that summer prior to going to Fort Benning. I worked that summer in a manufacturing plant, manning the production line producing florescent light fixtures. That experience gave me some insight of how low-wage, less-educated persons viewed management and gave me invaluable insight on interacting with a variety of persons, of varying age groups, genders, and education levels.

My brother, Dana, had just entered his "Cow" or third year at West Point. He had attended jump school that summer and gave me some pointers about what to expect. He told me I needed to work on my upper body strength and running. He suggested a lot of pull-ups, chin-ups, sit-ups, weight training and running distances up to five miles. In furtherance of those suggestions I bought a set of free weights and began lifting weights at home, and went to the Stewart AFB gym three times a week religiously. I wanted to be ready for IOBC and possibly jump school and Ranger School.

In addition, I was reunited with my high school protégé, Andy Bland, entering his Firsty year at the Academy. Andy, now over six feet and in great shape, along with many of his classmates, anticipated going to Ranger School, and once again I was surrounded by cadets in an ultra-military environment. That got me excited all over again about the prospect of going to Ranger School.

By the time September rolled around, it was time for me to make that long drive to Fort Benning. I weighed 165 lbs., and in good shape. I had gained about 10 lbs. over the summer, almost all of it hard muscle. I had forged myself into what I hoped was an Infantry officer well prepared to become an Airborne Ranger. Yep, it was time to see what I was made of at the Home of the Infantry—Fort Benning, Georgia.

CHAPTER 27

Fort Benning

I arrived in Columbus, GA, the city adjacent to Fort Benning at about 9 p.m. on the night of September 29, 1979. I decided to go to the post to report in and get a room at the bachelor officers' quarters (BOQ), before officially reporting in the following day.

It was dark and I didn't get a good look at the post as I found my way to Olsen Hall, where the second lieutenants attending IOBC were quartered. As I drove up to Olsen Hall it reminded me a lot of the Box at NMMI—it had three levels and was shaped like a horseshoe. I went to the office and presented my orders to the young specialist on duty. I guess, because I arrived early, he gave me a single room with a bathroom on the first floor. It was a choice room with a single twin bed, 19-inch color TV, study desk and chair, private bathroom, and it was in a great location.

I rolled my Trans Am around to my room, unloaded the car, and settled in to my new home. I was finally here, the Home of the Infantry, and it felt right.

The next day I officially reported in for IOBC and found out that I was going to "snowbird" for two weeks until my class actually started. "Snow birding" is the Army's name for soldiers that arrive early for a course and are put to work doing details and other menial work until their class begins.

In my case, the First Sergeant of the IOBC Company assigned me to various other IOBC classes to work tedious tasks on rifle ranges, live fire courses, and machine gun ranges. I was a warm body that could perform manual tasks, but I took it as an opportunity to learn about these courses and what it took to be successful in navigating them. I also took the opportunity to quiz other lieutenants going through the courses ahead of mine to get the "411" on IOBC and ways of getting ahead of the game. There had to be some advantage to being here early and I set out to take advantage of the opportunity.

I listened to guys talk about the land nav course, squad and platoon level FTXs, and I watched them maneuver through the live fire exercises on a few occasions. I talked to guys who had been through Ranger School and jump school and heard what they thought it took to succeed in those two courses. One of whom was 2LT Leo Brooks, a West Point grad, and the first Black officer I had seen wearing the Ranger Tab. The more I heard and saw, the more motivated I became to succeed in IOBC and make it through jump school and Ranger School.

When IOBC Class 1-80 started, I was ready.

✦ ✦ ✦

We started the second week of October. The IOBC cadre divided us into four platoons, two mechanized and two "light" infantry. Those divisions were based on the units to which we would be eventually assigned. In my case I wore the patch of the First Cavalry Division at Fort Hood, Texas, the largest mechanized post in the world. Within each platoon we were divided into four squads in alphabetical order. My squad was consisted of lieutenants whose names began with M through P—John Moriarity, Chuck Minnicks, Don Nelson, Manuel Quispe, Earl Morgan, and oddly, Wesley Spears, an African-American lawyer from Florida. He and I hit it off pretty well. I was one of the few who understood him. Our class, being so late in the year, only had one West Point grad, the rest of us were either ROTC or Officer Candidate School (OCS) graduates.

To my surprise, my "old friend" from NMMI, Rick Megahan was in this class. Yeah, he seemed pretty surprised too, but because he was going to the 82nd Airborne Division, they placed him in one of the two light platoons, so we didn't have much interaction. The mech and light platoons took PT tests together, did our 12-mile road marches together and prepared for and took the EIB (Expert Infantryman's Badge) test together. Certain other generic classes for mech and light infantry we did together, such as land nav, map reading, and BRM, but when it came to mechanized versus light infantry tactics and FTXs, we did those separately.

The mech training consisted of: familiarization with the mech infantry's work horse, the M-113 Armored Personnel Carrier (APC), the TOW (Tactical Optically Guided Weapon) missile, the Dragon Anti-tank missile, the LAW (Light Anti-tank Weapon), moving as a platoon with the APCs; field training with the APCs; digging foxholes; training in offensive and defensive tactics at squad and platoon level; leadership techniques; proficiency with all Infantry weapons systems including the M2 50 cal machine gun, M62 7.62 mm machine gun, hand grenades, M203 40 mm grenade launcher combo with M16 5.56 mm rifle; and live fire exercises at squad level and with the APCs.

My learning curve remained quite high because it had been four years since I'd had anything to do with the tactical and field training side of Army training. I had to relearn everything and do it in a hurry. I spent innumerable hours in the manuals when my peers went off to enjoy the pursuits of women and fun in Columbus, and nearby Panama City, Florida, and even Tuskegee University, Alabama. I had to catch up and then get ahead of my classmates academically, and in that I succeeded.

We spent a lot of time in classrooms, learning about the enemy that we anticipated seeing on the battlefield, namely the U.S.S.R, and its Warsaw Pact allies. Instructors taught us how to recognize various types of military hardware, such as T-64, T-72, and the newest addition to the Soviet inventory, the T-80, main battle tanks. Various cadre taught us how to recognize OPFOR mechanized and motorized vehicles, self-propelled air defense weapons and artillery pieces, as well as various types of enemy aircraft. Our trainers showed us the types of infantry weapons the Soviet and Warsaw Pact soldiers used, and the fact they used a 7.62 mm round compared to our M16's 5.56mm round. More importantly, they taught us how the enemy operated in combat, potential battle formations, their concepts of combined forces, and the methods we would use to counter their operational strategies. Artillery NCO's taught us how to plot artillery targets in the offense and defense, and how to call in air support. I found all this training to be eye opening, because it showed us that there was a reason for our training and a real enemy did exist out there.

The training was designed to prepare us to take over a mech infantry platoon at our first duty station. Cadres of NCO's conducted our classroom training, but the leadership portions and our evaluations were done by our platoon trainer. I'd been down that road before.

CPT Richard Baines, a senior Infantry captain, and a big ol' white guy, commanded the IOBC Company. He was kind of an asshole, and not Ranger-qualified. We nicknamed him "Ayatollah Baines," in recognition of the furor going on in Iran and the taking of the American embassy and the hostages. We felt we were being held hostage by Baines.

Each platoon had a platoon trainer at the rank of captain. In our case, it was CPT John "Moon" Mullins, a balding white guy, who stuttered, wore horned-rimmed glasses, had a stocky build, but was also Airborne and Ranger qualified. He did not fit my image of the Airborne Ranger Infantry officer, but somehow, he was just that.

One look at him, and I thought, *If he can make it through Ranger School, I'll bet I can.* I began to seriously think about Ranger School and becoming an Airborne Ranger.

Another factor that contributed to my belief that I might be successful in becoming an Army Ranger was the performance of my classmates. Within a couple of weeks of starting, the company first sergeant gave out applications for both jump school and Ranger School. I filled out the one for jump school and held back the application for Ranger School. I still wasn't sure I would measure up to making it through Ranger School. I thought I had a little time and I wanted to see how I stacked up with all the guys who talked incessantly about going to Ranger School. I didn't tell anyone I wanted to go to Ranger School, that was my little secret.

Since Ranger School focused on light infantry tactics and patrolling, the light infantry guys applied for Ranger School at a much higher rate than the mech guys. In fact, most of the light guys applied and most of the mech guys didn't apply. The light platoon trainers encouraged their guys to apply, and it appeared as if the mech platoon trainers almost discouraged us from applying. The rationale was that we wouldn't need the skills as much as the light guys would, and for them it could be a career-ender if they didn't go to Ranger School. I observed both the mech guys who wanted to go and the light guys who were going to go to see if I measured up to them…and I did.

It didn't take long for me to figure out that not only did I measure up, but I outperformed almost all the mech guys and many of the light guys that wanted to go to Ranger School. Again, when competing against my peers, I became extremely competitive. After a few more weeks I put in my application. The first sergeant told me that my application was late, and I had missed certain requirements. Most importantly, all the other guys had gone through the CWST and they did not plan to administer it again.

"Can you swim?" He asked as he looked over my application.

"Like a fish." I said.

"You know you have to pass the CWST right?" He asked.

"I've passed it before. At Knox." I said.

"Okay," he said, "I'm going to mark you as passed on your CWST, just don't drown." Then he laughed and handed me the completed form.

I laughed with him, because I knew I was really going to Ranger School!

I still needed the recommendation of my platoon evaluator, and even though he and Baines didn't like me they couldn't stop me from going to Ranger School. I had outperformed just about everybody in every testable event and was in the running for Distinguished Graduate for my class. Yep, although I had a disdain for both Mullins and Baines and didn't hide it very well, they both recommended me for Ranger School. They both called me in to "counsel" me on my attitude towards "authority" figures, particularly them, but they couldn't stop me from going to Ranger School. They told me I would attend Ranger School right after I graduated from jump school. I was going to pursue my dream of becoming a fabled U.S. Army Airborne Ranger, and prove wrong each and every motherfucker along the way, who tried to stop me and keep me from attaining my goal. Fuck all of them. Yeah, I had a big-assed chip on my shoulder.

Now, knowing I would be going to Ranger School, I intensified my physical training and focused more on honing my leadership and tactical skills. I read all the manuals on tactics at squad and platoon level, continued my weight lifting regimen to increase my upper body strength, and increased my running distances and speed to build up my endurance. I was going to be ready. I refused to fail after all this time. I had gone through too much to fail now.

One of the main differences in going through IOBC and the two ROTC summer camps was that the cadre at Fort Benning wanted us to succeed. They wanted us to come out of IOBC as trained infantry platoon leaders, so the emphasis was different. They weren't here to embarrass us or weed us out as leaders. We were already leaders, now they had to forge us into Infantry officers and leaders of Infantry soldiers—a different breed of men. We had to become masters of all weapons used by the Infantry, understand platoon and company level tactics, and be able to show our mastery of all aspects of being Infantry. One way to do that was by earning the EIB…sigh.

✦   ✦   ✦

My only low point in IOBC was not earning my EIB. The Expert Infantryman's Badge was the next best thing to earning the CIB. In order to be eligible for the EIB, the soldier had to be Infantry; and to earn the EIB, the Infantry soldier had to pass a series of tests showing mastery of Infantry-related skills. The EIB required: shooting at least Sharpshooter in BRM; to complete the 12-mile road march in less than three hours; to be proficient in radio commo techniques, how to set up and use the ANGR-77 field radio (commonly known as the "Angry-77"); how to disassemble and assemble the .45 cal pistol and the M16A1; targeting the TOW; setting up the Dragon and LAW anti-tank weapons; calling for and adjusting indirect fire; showing expertise with the M60 7.62mm machine gun and M2 .50 cal machine gun; plotting points on a map; day and night land nav techniques; using hand grenades; employing an M18A1 Claymore anti-personnel mine; moving under direct fire, and indirect fire; and other Infantry-related skills.

We practiced for several weeks on the various skills required by EIB testing, and came in on weekends to practice. Certain skills could only be accomplished in more official environments, such as BRM, where I qualified "Expert" with the M16. The 12-mile road march was not easy to practice for either. The mech guys did not road march as much as the light guys. We rode in APCs much of our time in the field, and road marched when we had to walk, but not to the same extent as the light guys.

I ran in boots to help prepare for the road march, and ran with weights on my back. The 12-mile road march was conducted with full equipment, including an M16, steel helmet, full rucksack with 50 lbs., and LBE (Load Bearing Equipment) harness, with two-quart canteen, and all the other accoutrements found on the LBE.

We took the actual EIB in early January. Although we didn't have to earn the EIB to graduate IOBC, it was a big deal, and earning your EIB would help upon arrival at your new duty station and give you instant credibility with your soldiers. However, even if we didn't pass the skills events the first time on the designated EIB test day, we still had to pass them to graduate IOBC. Prior to taking the EIB I had passed all the stations, so I knew that I had shown mastery in all these events. It was just a matter of putting it all together for the EIB test.

In addition, we had to pass the 12-mile road march to graduate IOBC. There were various strategies to pass the road march. I figured I would start out fast, get ahead of the 15-minute per mile standard to pass, and then gut out the last few miles. Sounded good in theory, but since I had never actually done 12 miles, I was about to find out if it worked in reality.

The platoon trainers conducted the 12-mile road march in the early evening, when it became cool, and in January, it could get downright cold, even in Georgia. We lined up by platoons, with the two light platoons first and second, my platoon third, and the second mech platoon bringing up the rear in fourth.

The platoons took off in five-minute intervals. The route was six miles out to a turnaround point, and six miles back—simple. We had our flashlights and our "Ranger Eyes" on the back of our helmets, rectangular pieces of luminescent tape so we could be seen from behind, when the road march extended into the night. There would be some light along the way to mark the route, but other areas along the route would be shrouded in darkness, and we did not want to get lost wandering around in the Georgia wilds.

Our platoon lined up to go during still daylight, at about 5:15 pm, but it would soon be getting dark and everyone wanted to get underway.

Captain Baines stood on the start/finish line with a whistle and when the second hand showed 5:15, he said, "Go!" and blew his whistle. And we started out. I noted the time on my watch so I could keep track of my pace. I had until 8:15 to finish the road march.

I positioned myself near the front of the platoon, and started out at a nice jog, which I planned to maintain as long as I could. Within a few hundred meters of the line, I shifted the rifle over my back, so it lay across the rucksack. It put more pressure on my shoulders, but made it easier to run without it in my arms or hanging off one shoulder. Soon after heading out, I stopped with another platoon mate, Spears, as we took off our helmets and put them in our rucksacks, under the top flap and put on our fatigue hats. The rules said we had to have the helmets with us, but not necessarily wear them, so we took them off. It made running so much more comfortable without the steel helmet and helmet liner bouncing on our heads.

Once we made the necessary changes, I took off again at a slow jog, again trying to push myself up front as much as possible. After the first few miles, I checked my time and saw that I was moving at a 12-minute pace, ahead of the minimum 15-minute pace. Each mile was well-marked on the route so I could check my times as I progressed through the road march. I slowed my pace down by running for a half mile, then walking a half mile, still keeping ahead of the 15-minute minimum. After five miles, near the halfway mark, I didn't see many of my platoon mates, but I had been passed by someone in the platoon behind me. To my credit, however, I had caught several people in the platoon ahead of me, some of the light guys. That felt pretty good.

The six-mile point and turn around was marked by several vehicles with their headlights on, and a sign that unnecessarily said, "Turn around—6 miles."

By this time, sweat poured profusely down my face. I tried to conserve my water to keep hydrated and keep moving at the same time. As I made the turn, my time was 80 minutes, instead of the minimum of 90 minutes—I was 10 minutes ahead of the minimum pace. Okay, alright, I'm going to make it in time.

After I made the turn, I began to jog again, but got tired fairly soon and had to resort to the "road march stride" which is a longer stride than normal, but that didn't last long. I then resorted to a faster mode of walking until I could rest enough to start jogging again.

At the eight-mile marker, I was at 110 minutes, which meant I did the last two miles at the minimum pace, but I was still ten minutes ahead of the overall minimum pace. Okay. It was time to try to pick up the pace. I gathered up my energy and began a slow jog, slower than before, but faster than the fast walk I had been doing the past two miles. I maintained the slow jog for about a half mile, then had to resort to an even slower walk to rest from the jog. After walking for a few minutes, I began to jog again, and continued this pattern until I hit mile nine. There were a lot of guys from the various platoons walking, then running in spurts, and I joined some of them that I thought I could keep up with.

We jogged for about three hundred meters, then walked for about the same, then started running again. Some of these guys had more endurance than me and after a few iterations of running and walking, began to pull away from me. At mile ten, I felt really tired, and knew that this was the portion of the road march that required me to "gut it out." I had 37 minutes to finish the last two miles, and now only seven minutes ahead of the minimum pace. These last two miles were definitely going to be the most difficult.

The cold night air helped to keep the sweat to a minimum, but I still sweated profusely and tried to drink as much water as I could. My legs felt like lead, and made it difficult to move much faster than a really slow jog, and that's the mode I went into—head down, and moving in a slow jog for as long as I could stand. That eleventh mile was the hardest, but I kept at it until I could jog no more, and resorted to a slow walk, as purposeful as I could manage.

A few hundred meters ahead of me I could see the 11-mile marker and that galvanized me to get back into my slow jog. I almost tripped as I made it to the 11-mile marker, where several cadre stood encouraging us on. Even Moon Mullins was there to encourage his platoon members to finish the road march on time. Mullins was the proud wearer of the EIB and wanted as many of his LTs to earn the coveted Infantry badge, and this was one of the prerequisites. I'm sure it also made him look good if he could get most of his LTs to earn the EIB.

"Alright Lieutenant Pittard, not too far to go, one more mile and you've got it!" He encouraged.

I smiled wearily. I actually liked him at that point, as I gathered myself for this last mile and the completion of the 12-mile road march in less than three hours. When I hit the 11-mile mark I had twenty-one minutes to do the last mile, but I didn't want to take any chances, so I began to push myself as hard as I could stand. I felt my hamstrings on both legs begin to tighten. I gave an internal order, *don't cramp up, only one more mile to go!* They held on.

That last mile seemed to extend into eternity. I just put my head down and walked and jogged as much as I could. I was not going to fail this event. I caught up with Wayne Christian, an attorney from Texas, and in the light platoon ahead of mine. We had developed a friendship because I had gone to law school at UT and understood what he had endured to be a lawyer. As I caught up with him, we both gave a little grin at each other and continued to gut it out to the finish line. I got my second wind, and was able to drive on. Within a few minutes we espied the finish line, brightly lit up with headlights and flares. We had about three hundred meters to go and decided to run it in.

"You ready to run?" Wayne said.

I just nodded, I was too tired to speak.

"Okay," he said, "let's pick up the pace."

We started to jog that last three hundred meters and as we got closer we began to run, crossing the finish line at a dead run. He made it with two minutes to spare, and I made it with seven minutes to spare. We did it—completed the grueling 12-mile road march in less than three hours. Unfortunately, not everyone was as lucky, particularly amongst the mech guys, who had to retake it later on their own time on a Saturday. I was happy I passed the first time; I did not want to do that again.

It's interesting how we get conditioned to the way things are in practice, and when they aren't that way in reality or on a test, we don't know how to adapt. At least that applied to me during the EIB testing, on the TOW portion of the test.

I failed it…stupidly. The test involved preparing the weapon for firing, then locking it on its locking ring. In every practice, the weapon locked toward the front and at the eventual target. On the day of testing, it locked towards the rear, away from the target. I only had to rotate the weapon completely on its 360 horizontal axis and I would have passed. Unfortunately, I tried to get it locked towards the front, and when it didn't I got frustrated and time ran out. The testing cadre used one finger to rotate it to the rear and it locked. Damn, it was something simple, as it usually is, and I felt really stupid. I passed all the other events, but fell short of earning the EIB by that one event. That was okay, it just motivated me even more to succeed in jump school and Ranger School.

I graduated IOBC on February 8, 1980, and began the grueling odyssey to becoming an Airborne Ranger.

CHAPTER 28

Jumpin'

On February 8, 1980, I left IOBC graduation and reported to 42nd Company, 4th Airborne Training Battalion, The School Brigade. The Basic Airborne Course (BAC) would begin on Monday, February 11, 1980. Two things happened when I reported that Friday—first, the duty sergeant informed me I could remain in my BOQ room, and not have to move into the barracks; and second, I was assigned as a platoon leader for one of the four platoons going through the course. *Terrific.*

Not only did I have to learn how to jump out of a perfectly functioning airplane, now I had to set an example for the rest of the soldiers in my platoon. Well, maybe that would be a good thing; it would force me to jump out when I might not necessarily want to. Regardless, it would be an interesting experience.

On Monday morning I reported to the United States Army Airborne School. The Airborne instructors, known as "Black Hats" organized the 42nd Airborne company into four platoons. I was already identified as a platoon leader for the First Platoon. The Black Hats divided the platoon into "sticks" or squads and each stick had a "stick leader" usually an NCO. I had four sticks of ten men in my platoon. Each of the four platoons had a second lieutenant out front.

The training consisted of the three phases divided into three weeks. Ground Week included the basics of how to land and fall from an aircraft. In Tower Week the Black Hats taught us techniques of jumping from an aircraft by simulating jumping with a zip line from the 40-foot towers and then dropping with a parachute from the 250-foot tower. And finally Jump Week, which required us to make five jumps including a jump from a propeller plane, normally a C-130 or C-123; a jump from a jet aircraft, normally a C-141; three "Hollywood" jumps with no equipment; two "equipment" jumps with rucksack and weapon; and lastly, a night jump. Three weeks of fun, fun, fun! I looked forward to the challenge.

❖   ❖   ❖

The initial challenge that first day required us to pass the Airborne physical fitness test. This APFT incorporated sit-ups, push-ups, pull-ups and a two-mile run. I passed easily, but we lost some students who couldn't get past either the pull-ups or the run. We also had classes and a test on the history of the Airborne concept of vertical envelopment from WWII to the present. Once we passed the PT test and got through the classes, the next items on the training agenda were the techniques on how to fall and land from an aircraft. Welcome to Ground Week.

Each day in Ground Week began with PT—with a run of some distance up to three miles, push-ups, sit-ups, pull-ups, and various other calisthenics. There was a method to the madness because an airborne student had to be able to run off the drop zone with his equipment, control the parachute with the risers which required upper body strength, and needed all around fitness to complete the training. The Black Hats also used push-ups as punishment for any poor performance or other transgression in their eyes. Push-ups universally served in all Army training as punishment or "positive" reinforcement of a particular point of emphasis by the instructor.

The various apparatus we trained on during Ground Week included the Mock Door, which is what it sounds like, a mock aircraft door to teach us how to properly exit the aircraft using a static line and our parachute pack. The Black Hats also trained us on the Lateral Drift Apparatus (LDA) to teach Parachute Landing Falls (PLFs). The five-point PLF was a fundamental that we had to master—hitting the ground first with the balls of your feet, falling to the side with your calf, then the side of your thigh, buttocks, and finally, the side of your body on your lats. The Black Hats taught us to keep our bodies slightly bent, with elbows in front of our face throughout the PLF. The jumper may fall in one of six directions based on the wind direction, drift, speed, terrain, and oscillation of the jumper. They taught us to execute a smooth PLF after many repetitions jumping from a platform into a sawdust pit. We did it so many times it became second nature. But when we made a mistake we'd hear it from the Black Hats.

So, when you heard a Black Hat say, "Get your head out of your fourth point of contact!" What he really meant was, "Pull your head out of your ass!"

The final apparatus of Ground Week carried into Tower Week and was probably the most difficult apparatus to master. The difficulty was due to the contortionist L-shaped body posture we had to execute after exiting the aircraft. We practiced this maneuver on the 40-foot tower. Just climbing up the stairs to the top was scary, but when they strapped you into the zip line across the 50-foot space between the two 40-foot towers that's when you really felt like you were training for jumping out of an aircraft. I don't know why, but this scared me more than any other phase of training during jump school. The Black Hats would sit on the ground with their clipboards and make colorful comments about how badly we performed the L-shaped exit from the aircraft. We would hear it from the Black Hats at the exiting tower and at the receiving tower—you just couldn't win.

In order to pass each apparatus you had to demonstrate you could perform the maneuver twice in a row correctly, and then you earned your "GO" on that apparatus. It took me a few times to go up the 40-foot tower before I passed, but I did pass, even though I was told on a few occasions I looked like a really large limp dick coming out of the tower. Hardy, har, har. The Black Hats thought they were such comedians. Well, on to Tower Week.

✧　✧　✧

In Tower Week we increased our expertise in simulated jumps by our simulating mass tactical jumps from the 40-foot tower, which involved several jumpers coming out of a single aircraft. In addition to the mass tac simulations, the Black Hats introduced us to three new apparatus.

The Swing Landing Trainer (SLT) was an apparatus that simulated landing and executing a PLF from about 10 to 15 feet off the ground. We would stand on a long platform with a parachute attached to a free-hanging set of risers. We would then leap off the platform to simulate falling from an aircraft, and execute a PLF in the saw dust pit below.

Another new apparatus was the Suspended Harness; a device which consisted of another set of risers attached to the roof of the building and also attached to each student with a parachute pack on a long platform about five feet off the ground. We would hop off the platform, pulling down on the risers to simulate directing the chute using the risers.

And, finally, there stood the 250-foot tower.

I once wrote a poem describing the three 250-foot towers as "prehistoric beasts of prey rising above the jungles surrounding Fort Benning, raising their heads to scream their defiance against the impending doom of the twilight of their existence." Metaphorically speaking.

In reality, the 250-foot towers were the last step, a final test where we had to put all our training together to show we could make a simulated jump and fall from an aircraft and execute a perfect PLF. The 250-foot tower resembled an amusement park ride from Six Flags Over Texas. They were tall metal towers with four anchoring legs wider at the base than at the apex. At the top, the towers had three arms reaching out with the parachute attached. We were hooked into an already deployed parachute attached to one of the arms by a cable. Hoisted up in the air 250 feet, you got an eagle's eye view of Fort Benning. Once you got to the top of the tower, you lurched to a stop. After a moment of hesitation, it unceremoniously dropped you 250 feet back to the ground. At this point, if you dreaded heights, and you hadn't lost your nerve with the 40-foot tower, this would put you over the edge!

It was actually fun, and I enjoyed the sensation of floating to the ground. Almost as soon as they let you go at the top you had to get into a proper positioning for a PLF. Then once you got within 50 feet of the ground, you made sure your feet were together, knees slightly bent, and prepared to hit the ground with the balls of your feet. I executed a perfect PLF, and didn't have to do it again. Unfortunately, the former student company commander was not so lucky and broke his leg on his first attempt. Now, by virtue of being the First Platoon leader, I became the new student company commander as we headed into Jump Week.

Although I had a fear of heights, I made it through Tower Week and moved on to Jump Week. Jump Week would be the real test of my ability to get over my fear of heights, and the unknown.

⋄　⋄　⋄

The first day of Jump Week did not begin with PT as did all the other days of jump school. Instead, we reported to the normal company area and the Black Hats placed us into a running formation. Once in formation, we ran the two miles down to Lawson Army Airfield for our first jump.

At LAAF we found several rows of parachutes and reserve chutes waiting for us on the ground near a C-130 aircraft, our winged Pegasus for our initial "Hollywood jump." The C-130, the workhorse of the Air Force when it came to transporting Army parachutists, was a four-prop, gray-painted aircraft with a side door for individual exit in flight, and a large garage-style rear door that lifted up to allow us to board in two rows.

As the student company commander, the jumpmaster told me I had the honor of jumping with the first aircraft. I would be the last one on the aircraft, and I would be the first one "out the door." So, for every jump, I jumped first. Great.

We donned our equipment for that first jump. My equipment was out front by itself and I put it on and sat down waiting for instructions. They organized us according to sticks, and I jumped with the first stick, followed by the First Platoon leader and the stick leader. The jumpmasters got us up and led the student jumpers in two long rows onto the aircraft through the back cargo door. I was the last one on the aircraft and closest to the door from which we would jump.

We sat in the canvass seats on the C-130 as it prepared to take off. We sat in two rows facing each other on both sides of the aircraft. Olive green netting covered the walls inside the aircraft. The stink of fear and dread permeated the cavernous interior as we raced towards our very first jump. The jumpmaster sat near the door when the aircraft took off. Until then, maybe it hadn't become real, but as the plane climbed into the air I experienced a stab of fear and dread, and surprisingly, an indescribable thrill. I was really going to do it! I was really going to jump out of an airplane on my way to becoming an Airborne Ranger! Whoa! I could hardly believe it.

I looked around the aircraft and saw reflections of my own feelings in the faces of other students. Some looked ready to vomit, others bored, most with an expression of fear and excitement. I needed to keep a calm demeanor if I was going to set the example and tried to keep my face expressionless, but on the inside, I churned with excitement and fear.

The jodies, or running cadences, from long ago ran through my mind, *"C-130 rolling down the strip, Airborne daddies gonna take a little trip."*

The Black Hats had taught us, and the jumpmaster reiterated, as a part of our pre-jump instruction, the sequence of events while on the aircraft prior to the jump. I turned my head towards the exit door and watched and waited for the first commands.

The jumpmaster stood near the exit door, and above him the light bulb remained dark.

As the aircraft neared the drop zone, the jumpmaster yelled, "Six minutes!" and held up six fingers.

That was our first indication of how far out we were from Fryar Drop Zone (DZ). I felt the anticipation grow inside the aircraft. Students stared expectantly at the jumpmaster.

The jump became real when the jumpmaster yelled the first jump command of "Get ready!"

That told us to be alert, the DZ was fast approaching. Everyone's attention was riveted on the jumpmaster.

When the aircraft leveled off at 1250 feet, the jumpmaster looked down the aircraft and pointed at the row of jumpers furthest from him, "Inboard personnel Stand up!" Alright, here we go.

Once that row stood, he issued his third command, "Outboard personnel Stand up!"

"Stand up hook up, shuffle to the door," the jodie continued.

I was on the "outboard" side, and stood up with my stick. I had to believe this was really about to happen.

The jumpmaster then commanded, "Hook up!"

We all hooked our parachutes to the static lines stringing down each side of the aircraft. We looked like parachutist preparing to assault Normandy.

"Check Equipment!" The jumpmaster commanded.

At that command, each of us checked the jumper in front of us to make sure his parachute, reserve and static line were properly secure. Once we checked each other's equipment, we responded with "Number one equipment okay!" and so on.

As we accomplished that we continued to near the DZ. The rumbling of the engines seemed even louder in my ears.

The jumpmaster yelled, "One minute!" with one finger held up. The light above the jump door turned red. Tension began to build. Oh, shit.

"Thirty seconds," and the jumpmaster held up a crooked index finger to indicate half a minute. He then opened the door, and I could hear the wind howling outside as the aircraft flew at speed. My eyes squinted against the howling wind as I tried to get a peek out the door.

Then came the most dreaded command, *"Stand* in the door!" The jumpmaster looked at me and pointed.

Shit! Here we go!

So, I did the "Airborne Shuffle" to the door, a modified way of moving in the aircraft, kind of a shuffling and stomping of the feet. I stood in the door with my "knees to the breeze" and my hands on either side of the door waiting for the light bulb to go green. The green light meant we were in position above the drop zone. The wind was howling by me, and the engines louder than before. I could hardly hear the jumpmaster as I waited on his final command.

I could see the drop zone down below to the right, and the smoke pots giving us the wind direction on the ground. That was scary.

"Jump right out and count to four." This was it, just like the song.

When the light turned green, the jumpmaster said, "Go!" smacked me on the butt, and I launched myself out the door using my hands and feet to give me maximum separation from the aircraft door and the jumpers behind me.

"One-thousand one, two-thousand two, three-thousand three, four-thousand." I repeated waiting for the chute to deploy as I was whipped by the prop blast towards the rear and below the plane.

"Erk!" The chute pulled by the static line, deployed and jerked me upward. Whew! A successful deployment! My training kicked in and I looked up and checked the chute for holes. All I saw was a beautiful T-10 in full bloom above me and the edges flapping in the wind. Thank God!

"If my main don't open wide, I got another one by my side." At least I didn't have to worry about that this time..

I diverted my attention down at the DZ and saw the smoke pots at the end of the drop zone to determine wind direction. I started to manipulate the risers of my T-10 chute to move me towards a hopefully soft landing.

The feeling of floating was indescribable! It was so quiet up here. No sounds except the rushing of the wind in my ears. I could see for miles around, and never wanted that feeling to end, but end it must. As I floated closer to the ground, the ground started to rush towards me. At about 100 feet up I began to prepare for my PLF. The Black Hats had told us, "a good PLF was one you walked away from." My objective was to execute a good enough PLF, so I could run off the DZ without injury.

"If that one should fail me too, tell the ground I'm coming through." I didn't want to contemplate my own death on this jump; and I did not want to hit that hard, just walk off the drop zone.

I continued to guide my parachute towards the ground. As the ground rushed up at me, I kept my eyes open the entire time, although the urge to close them was strong. I prepared myself for the imminent contact with the ground and put my elbows up, bent my knees and put them together, and I hit the ground with the balls of my feet, then my ass, and then my back. Well, not a perfect PLF, but I appeared to be all there, all parts accounted for, and no broken bones or bruises. I got up quickly as I had been taught, hit the release on my now depleted parachute bag, gathered my chute before it could blow away from me, and ran off the drop zone towards the trucks standing by to receive the used chutes.

Damn! My first jump! Wow! Four more to go and I couldn't wait for the next one. I was hooked!

The next two Hollywood jumps were unremarkable except one of them we jumped out of a C-123 cargo plane—a smaller plane than the C-130, painted in a woodland camouflage pattern, and held fewer students—so there were more flights of jumpers. We made the second Hollywood jump that same day. The second jump was almost identical to the first jump except there were fewer jumpers on the aircraft. My PLF was a little better, but more importantly I ran off the DZ without serious injury ready for the next jump. That was a hell of a first day in Jump Week. Three more jumps to go!

The next day we made our third Hollywood jump, from a C-130 again. Again, no problem, and my PLFs improved with practice on a real drop zone.

That night we made a fourth Hollywood jump, this one was from a jet aircraft, the C-141, and we were to jump at 1,500 feet instead of 1,250 feet. Although at night, the airfield was lit up by arc lights to give an almost daylight like brightness. We donned our parachutes and approached this squatting monstrosity from the rear. The C-141 was enormous with wings drooping from the weight of the huge turbofan jet engines. and the experience of coming out of the door was quite different. Painted a glossy silver we knew the jet jump was going to be significantly different than the previous three jumps. The speed of the C-141 was faster than that of the C-130, and as a result, when you came out of the aircraft you came out faster. However, you had to avoid getting caught up in the jets so your position coming out of the aircraft was even more important. The chute deployed at about the same time, but you moved much faster and had to start looking for the smoke a little sooner. That's one reason they dropped us at 1,500 to give us additional time to get our bearings as we neared the drop zone. As before, I was first out the door and watched as the terrain sped by even faster than before. When the light turned green and the jumpmaster yelled, "Go!" I jumped out as far as I could, pushing out with my hands and legs. That was a rush coming out of the C-141, and feeling the wind that fast in my face, especially at night.

Yep, we made our night jump out of the jet. At night I couldn't see the ground like during the day and had to rely more on training and instinct to get to the ground safely. At night they had white smoke so it could be seen easier, and flares and lights around the DZ to better mark it for our landing. Another important difference was the ground coming up closer and faster than during the day. Luckily, because we were a little higher when we came out we had an opportunity to have a few more seconds to read the situation and to determine the location of the ground before impact. Unfortunately, more students suffered injuries to some degree during the night jump because of the miscalculation of when they would hit the ground. I felt elated to walk away from that one uninjured. Overall, I liked the jet jump better than the prop jumps and wished we could have done more of them, even at night.

⟡　⟡　⟡

Our last jump was the combat equipment jump. The combat equipment jump, made with 35 lbs. of equipment and a rubber M16, was more difficult. The equipment jumps were unique and required a slightly different skill set than the Hollywood jumps. They hooked the rucksack and weapon to us from the front with a nylon line and a quick release that we could pop at any time. The Black Hats trained us to drop our rucksack and weapon after chute deployment as we neared the ground, otherwise the weight of the equipment on our bodies might cause us to be unbalanced upon landing and not be able to execute a proper PLF. Even though you dropped your equipment and weapon and they hung from you by the nylon rope, you had to avoid them as you neared the ground and not hit them on impact with the ground. Luckily, we didn't have to do the equipment jump at night. That would have really made it exciting. Imagine, a jet jump at night with equipment. Whew! That might have been a bit much for rookie jumpers like us. I survived my combat equipment jump, out of a C-141, and was ready to have my United States Basic Parachutist Wings pinned upon my chest at graduation on the airfield the day after our last jump.

Airborne all the way!

⟡　⟡　⟡

On Friday, February 29, 1980, yeah, a leap year, they pinned my silver jump wings on my chest. The Black Hats had challenged us to get "blood wings" which were new jump wings with two sharp points on the underside punched into your chest through your fatigues without the benefit of the holders to protect your skin. Okay, like duh! Of course, I wanted blood wings, I was the student company commander.

So, when they came down the line and the conferring Black Hat asked if I wanted blood wings, I said, "Airborne All the Way!" which meant "yes" in

Airborne-speak. The Black Hat conferring the wings positioned the wings in their proper position on my chest and punched me to drive the points into my chest so the wings would stay in place. Damn that hurt! But I was proud to have done that and set the example for anyone else who wanted to experience their own blood wings. I was now a member of the international brotherhood of jump-qualified airborne soldiers, an Army parachutist, and now ready for the challenge of Ranger School.

Airborne! All the way and then some, sir!

CHAPTER 29

Class 7-80

Later that same day, on February 29, 1980, I drove out to the Ranger Department, located at Camp Rogers, on Fort Benning, for the initial phase of Ranger School—as a newly minted Airborne-qualified Infantry officer, the blood still staining my fatigues, like a badge of honor. The Ranger Department was located in a more isolated part of Fort Benning. I drove through the woods on a lonely two-lane road following the signs to Ranger School. As each mile passed, my anticipation grew. I knew I wasn't going to start Ranger School that day, but the experience of Ranger School grew closer with each passing minute and mile.

My first indication I had arrived was the sign proclaiming this was the Home of Ranger Department, Camp Rogers. I saw weathered buildings surrounded by gravel paths, with the accoutrements of Ranger School right there in the open. There was the infamous Worm Pit, a field that had the Ranger Tab displayed in all its glory above it, all tucked into a vast wooded area. The signs pointed me towards a larger wooden building "Ranger Department Headquarters." I pulled up and parked in the gravel parking lot near the front door, got a set of my orders assigning me to the 3rd Ranger Company and walked in. A sergeant in fatigues sat at a desk near the door.

As I walked in he stood up, "May I help you sir?"

"Yes sergeant, I wanted to report in for Class 7-80."

"Can I see your orders sir?" He reached for the orders I held in my hand.

I handed him my orders and looked around. The unit insignia of Ranger units, plaques, pictures of Rangers on the walls, and pictures apparently from various combat zones impressed me. I was in the right place.

He reviewed the orders, "You need to report to the 3rd Ranger Company, the next building over. Just go back out the door and it's to your right."

"Ok," I said as he handed back my orders, "thank you." I turned around and walked out and saw to my right another sign that indicated the 3rd Ranger

Company. A plainer building than the headquarters building, a guidon with the black and gold Ranger Tab embroidered and 3rd Ranger Company proudly displayed, stood guard next to the front door.

I climbed the steps and opened the door into a small reception area where a corporal stood up at his desk upon my entry. I handed him my orders and told him I wanted to report in. He told me I could report the next morning at 0800. However, as before when I reported to IOBC, since my class didn't start for almost three weeks, I would be snow birding again.

The next day I reported back along with several other new Ranger candidates. A sergeant asked us if anyone knew how to type. I raised my hand, and he assigned me to the Ranger Department, right next to the sergeant I'd met the day before. As an officer, and typist, I avoided the more menial details other officers and enlisted were stuck with, like painting rocks and otherwise cleaning up the Ranger Department grounds. My work as a clerk and administrative assistant in the Ranger Department HQ gave me a chance to see how they did things in the Ranger Department and interact with some of the leadership. Not a bad way to spend the next few weeks.

There were some colorful characters walking around the Ranger Department, one being COL Bud Sydnor. I asked some of the clerks and NCO's about the colonel walking his little black and white dog around the Department.

"You don't know who he is?" Whispered the same young sergeant.

Obviously not or I wouldn't be asking. "No," I said. "Who is he?'

Another young corporal chimed in, "That's Colonel Elliott "Bud" Sydnor. He trained and led the ground forces in the Son Tay raid on November 21, 1970, to rescue the POWs held by the gooks at the Son Tay prison, outside Hanoi."

Shit, that was impressive! I had no clue what the Son Tay raid was, or its significance in the special operations community, but it sounded impressive.

"That's a bad muthafucka right there," another clerk added in awe. "He's a legend in the spec ops community."

I looked at Sydnor a little differently after that. I guess he could walk his little rat dog anywhere he chose, even if the privates had to clean up the dog shit.

I learned later the Son Tay raid ultimately failed because of poor intelligence. We didn't know the prisoners had been moved before the raid, but that did not diminish the bravery of the Rangers and Special Forces soldiers that participated in the raid. Colonel Sydnor was one of those legendary soldiers and now Commandant of the Ranger Department. It impressed me that someone with those real-world credentials was in charge of the Department. That boded well for the level of realism of the training at Ranger School.

The class I would start with was Class 7-80, technically the last winter class of the year. The distinction of a designated winter class was that you were allowed to "unofficially" use white thread to sew on your Ranger patch to denote you had graduated from a winter class at Ranger School. Another distinction of winter classes was the attrition rate was much higher than the summer classes… as was the death rate. More students died in winter classes than other classes, from hypothermia and other exposure illnesses; falling in the mountains of Dahlonega; or drowning in the swamps of Florida. I hadn't planned on being in a winter class, but that's how the dice rolled, and I felt ready for the additional challenge. And yes, it can get cold in Fort Benning. In fact, it snowed the night before I reported to the Ranger Department to begin Class 7-80, and that did not portend well for the class. I had suffered from hypothermia one miserable night during IOBC, and it had been painful. I did not want to experience that again.

Over the next three weeks I doubled my efforts to prepare myself physically for the rigors of Ranger School. I ran two to three miles every day, and up to five miles on Saturdays. I continued to do my weightlifting regimen, and did push-ups and situps until my abs, pecs and triceps screamed at me. I wanted to be in the best shape of my life when I started Class 7-80.

On March 18, 1980, I reported to Class 7-80, 3rd Ranger Company. This time for real. In the best shape of my life, I felt prepared to tackle the challenge of becoming an Army Ranger.

That first day, the cadre assigned our barracks, which were platoon bays, and issued our equipment for the course. Our equipment consisted of the normal TA-50, the same as I had been issued as far back as Fort Knox, but also included some Ranger-specific items such as a mountain rucksack that could hold more than a regular rucksack; poncho liner, two-quart canteen, and tent half.

Prior to our arrival, the Ranger Department sent us a list of equipment to bring to Camp Rogers. They allowed us personal knives in addition to the normal equipment. My first knife was a 4-inch Buck folding knife that I believed would serve me well in Ranger School. However, when I started the class I saw the type of knives the guys from the Ranger battalions brought with them, I immediately suffered from "knife envy." At my first opportunity I acquired a proper knife—an old WWII-era bayonet with a wooden handle that I lovingly sharpened to a sharp edge, and called "Snake Sticker." I carried that sucker through most of Ranger School, and beyond, and yeah, it came in handy.

The Ranger Department directed us to buy a dozen shoe strings and condoms. We used the shoe strings to connect all our equipment to our LBE, and the condoms were to protect the end of the weapon during water-borne operations. Although we could probably buy everything at several different locations, the best place proved to be Ranger Joe's, a local retail store that specialized in providing Ranger-related gear and equipment. They had the same list we had and made sure they had a variety of non-issue items available. I reported to Ranger School with all the proper equipment. Ready to go.

The class consisted of a combination of officers, NCO's, and younger enlisted soldiers. The officers were primarily Infantry, along with smattering of other combat arms branches. The NCO's came from either the Ranger battalions, the 1st/75th Ranger Battalion at Fort Stewart, GA, or the 2nd/75th Ranger Battalion at Fort Lewis, WA, otherwise known as the "Bats," or from Special Forces units. All the younger enlisted, usually E-4s or E-3s came from one of the two Bats. The officers were called "O's" by the guys from the Ranger Bats, and they were the "E's." Even in this environment where we would to have to work together as a tightly-bound group there still existed a division between the O's and E's. That was going to have to change if we were all going to work together over the next eight weeks.

This class had a lot more E's than O's, and not very many NCO's, and that made it a somewhat interesting mix when it came to assigning tasks and duties for patrols, planning for patrols, and planning the airborne and air assault missions. My squad consisted of mostly E's. Many of them were suspicious of the O's, and from conversation it was mostly because of how the officers at the Bats dealt with the junior enlisted guys. Well, this was a different environment and we had to work together, so I did my best to ensure that I got along with everyone. I was not going to make the same mistakes I had made in the past at Fort Knox and Riley.

The Ranger Department assigned our class a TAC or tactical officer and platoon evaluator and an NCOIC platoon evaluator. The TAC was a white captain who didn't seem like he had much use for African-American Ranger students. There weren't many of us in that Class. The NCOIC was also white and he seemed like he had the same attitude. They led the class, but did not conduct training. All the training was conducted by Ranger Instructors (RI's) or specific committee cadre on a specific type of training. Primarily though, our training was conducted by the RI's. The RI's prided themselves on their physical conditioning and made sure we knew that the time we spent at Camp Rogers for City Week would be pure hell—starting the next day.

◇ ◇ ◇

The next day began at 4 a.m. with the loud cacophony of RI's coming through the barracks waking us up. This was it, our Ranger training would begin for real.

We fell out in the dark and the cold, our breath visible in clouds around our heads. The Ranger School uniform consisted of green fatigues with shirts out, combat boots, and no rank or insignia, only our name tags. As Ranger students, we had no rank or identity.

They marched us over to the sawdust pit area to take the Ranger Physical Fitness Test (RPFT). But first they put us through a regimen of calisthenics, to wear us out a little before taking the RPFT. We had to perform side straddle hops, windmills, lunges, T-bones, and scissor kicks. Once properly warmed up, we had to line up to take the RPFT which entailed four events we had to pass at the standard for the youngest age level—sit-ups, push-ups, pull-ups, and the two-mile run.

In excellent condition, the warm up exercises didn't bother me too much. I passed the RPFT without a problem and when we completed the RPFT we marched into the sawdust pit in preparation for a little more PT.

The sawdust pit, or the "Worm Pit," was circular and about 30 feet wide and 50 meters in diameter, with an inner circle with the Ranger Tab and platform for the RI's to direct the activities in the Pit. The RI's lined up the class by platoon in columns with a four-man front. They thoroughly wet the sawdust to enhance the activities.

The RI's ordered us to get down in the "high crawl" position and once accomplished, ordered us to begin crawling. As I crawled, the sharper pieces of sawdust pierced my knees and elbows right through the thin fatigue material. We high crawled for a half turn around the Pit, then changed to the "low crawl." As I low crawled with my face and body dragging along the ground, I constantly spit out sawdust that gathered around my mouth and on my face. My uniform, covered in a mixture of mud and sawdust, made me feel as though I hadn't bathed in a week. The smell of sweat permeated the air as much as the yelling of the RI's. We did another half turn around the Pit in that position. The RI's then ordered us into the "crab walk" or inverted crawl which we did for another half turn around the Pit. For the next half turn we "duck walked" with our hands clasped behind our heads to increase the pressure on our quadriceps. My quads burned with the exertion. They ordered us to stop and get on our backs for scissor kicks, and we kicked for several minutes, my abs churning with the effort. This was getting to be kind of difficult.

With no time to rest, the RI's ordered us onto our stomachs for push-ups, and with our triceps and pectorals screaming for some relief we went into the position for more high crawling, then low crawling, and on and on it went for about another half an hour. Even though I was in pretty good shape, this little exercise took its toll on me. My body yelled at me to stop this nonsense, but I couldn't stop. Certainly not on the first day, and during the first PT session.

When they finally allowed us to stand, I bent over at the waist to get my breath and recover my strength. Some students threw up. Our bodies were spent by the time they called a stop to our suffering. This was the first hour of Ranger School.

During this whole ordeal the RI's had been yelling at everyone, "KEEP GOING RANGER OR QUIT!" Over and over again they repeated their mantra, "YOU'RE NOT GOOD ENOUGH TO BE A RANGER—SO QUIT!"

And we would answer, "HELL NO WE WON'T QUIT!"

But damn, on that very first day the thought of quitting seemed inviting. Apparently it was inviting to some, because we lost a few on that first day with just that little bit of physical exertion and intimidation. Obviously, they had no mental or physical fortitude. It would be a very long eight and half weeks.

Following our initiation into the rigors of the Pit, the RI's introduced us poor students to the outside shower facility, which consisted of a metal shell with a line of shower heads under which we had to run once they turned on the water. Each of our four columns had a showerhead. Once they turned the water on, we ran through the water long enough to rinse the sawdust off our bodies, not necessarily to get clean, just with less stuff on our uniforms. The water was cold, *very* cold, and the air outside was still cold. This was March, with snow still on the ground. I just hoped I didn't catch cold, or worse.

Welcome to Ranger School.

Every day of City Week we had a routine of PT, then classroom work, lunch, more classroom work, dinner, then more classroom work, then some sort of night activity, followed by bed around midnight.

PT consisted of the normal regimen of sit-ups, push-ups, pull-ups, side straddle hops, T-bones, scissor kicks, guerilla exercises, lunges, and whatever other exercises the RI's could think of in their evil little minds to try to break us down. The calisthenics were normally followed by a run between a mile and three miles. I would come out of the PT with muscles burning and near exhaustion, and that was just the beginning of the day.

The RI's instructed us in various forms of unarmed lethal combat without a hand gun or rifle. They taught us rudimentary hand-to-hand fighting skills. Probably just enough to get us killed. They paired us with someone of the same approximate size and weight, and taught us how to throw an opponent, how to defend ourselves in a knife fight, to attack with a knife, techniques of the silent kill, and how to fall. Initially, they paired me with a young Marine, slightly smaller than me. Having had some instruction in the martial arts off and on for eight years, I jumped into this training with enthusiasm. Maybe too much enthusiasm. Unfortunately, the Marine wasn't very good, and didn't learn how to fall correctly; or maybe I threw him too hard. Anyway, he hurt his knee in a throw early in City Week and was eliminated from the program. I felt kind of bad about that, but shit happens. After that I paired up with a much bigger opponent and I became more cautious when practicing my hand-to-hand techniques.

Our classroom work focused on principles of patrolling, map reading, including recognizing terrain features, airborne operations, air assault operations, and how to plan for all those types of operations. In order to move forward out of City Week, we had to pass various classroom written exams, and the day and night land navigation tests.

I maxed the written exams and maxed the day and night land navigation courses. When it came to written exams and land nav, whether day or night, they were in my wheelhouse, and I excelled at that stuff. Yeah, I had no more frightful nights of being lost like in the rainforests of Fort Knox.

In order to assimilate us into the survival aspects of being a Ranger and get us used to being out in the field, we spent a lot of time at night in the forests around Fort Benning. They issued us a shelter half and bed roll with sleeping bag, along with a mountain ruck sack so we could carry more equipment. At night, my Ranger buddy and I would set up in our assigned position, either tactically or more administratively in either a pup tent with our two shelter halves or use them to make up field shelters against the elements.

The other aspect of our tactical training involved how we moved from point A to point B. We road marched or ran everywhere we went. Part of our daily routine was road marching with 50 lb. rucks on our backs with M16s, M203s, or M60s, depending on your role in the squad. We rotated leadership positions tactically and in garrison, the same as all my other training environments. The M16A1 was fairly lightweight and fired a 5.56mm tumbler round in either semi or auto mode. Almost everyone carried the M16A1, including whoever occupied a tactical leadership role. The M203 was the squad's indirect fire weapon; it's a combination M16 and M79 40mm grenade launcher and can fire a variety of 40mm grenades up to 400 meters. The M60 is the heavy weapon of the Ranger squad and fires 7.62mm rounds at a cyclic rate of 500-600 per minute with an effective range of 1,100 meters. We affectionately called the M60 "the Pig" and it was usually carried by the bigger guys in the squad. I carried either the M16 or the M203. The one time I carried the M60 it weighed me down so much I could barely keep up, and the squad determined I wouldn't carry that heavy sonofabitch anymore. Thank God.

Of course, since we spent a majority of the time out in the field we were exposed to the elements. In March the nights could still get pretty cold. Whenever the RI's gave us field showers or ran us through any type of water, the water was invariably cold, extremely cold. Within five days after starting Ranger School, as I feared, I had to visit the medic with a burgeoning cold, and a deep cough, trying to keep it from getting worse. I already had a history of chronic and acute bronchitis from my youth and I didn't want that to interfere with my training like it did at Fort Riley. I didn't want that indignation in front of my peers again. I mean, damn, I was trying to become an U.S. Army Ranger, the epitome of Army manhood. I did not need this shit.

As I stepped into the small first aid station, I saw the medic reading a comic book. He was a white soldier, lounging behind his desk.

"Can I help you Ranger?" He asked as he put down his comic book. Heavy reading for the young man.

"Yeah, I've got this cough that I can't get rid of, and I'm hoping you have something for it." At that time, I gave out one of my deep, wracking cough.

"It sounds like you've got a URI," the medic said.

"What's a URI?" I asked.

"An upper respiratory infection. That requires antibiotics, and I don't have those here and I'm not allowed to dispense them." He still hadn't gotten out of his chair.

"Okay, what do you have that can help me?"

"I've got cough syrup and Tylenol," he said looking at his shelves.

"Okay, give me that," I said, "maybe that will help."

He finally got his lazy ass out of his chair to get the medicine from his storage cabinets. He stood there for a few moments peering into the cabinet before making his decision.

He reached in and pulled out a bottle of Robitussin cough syrup, and a bottle of Tylenol pain relief medicine, also known as "Ranger Candy," because we all used it for the pains and aches of Ranger School.

"Here you go," he said as he handed me the medicine, "I hope it helps."

"Yeah, me too," I said, as I took the bottles and turned towards the entrance to the first aid station. My last vision of the medic was him settling back into his chair.

"Good luck Ranger," I heard behind me.

I waved back at him as I walked back to my platoon area.

An integral part of my education in Ranger School was learning more about the Ranger community and especially the Ranger Battalions—the 1/75th located at Fort Stewart, Georgia; and the 2/75th located at Fort Lewis, Washington. Our platoon was loaded with enlisted guys from both Bats, and there was always good natured woofing going on about the better and tougher Bat.

I learned the Ranger companies were organized into platoons, and how they consisted of squads where the squad members, all trained in the basic skills of being Rangers, also had additional skill sets like HALO (high altitude low opening) airborne operations; SCUBA (self-contained underwater breathing apparatus) for underwater operations; mountaineering, Arctic operations, and jungle operations. The Rangers could operate from as small as four man teams, to squads and platoons, and occasionally as companies. Different from Special Forces/Green Berets, Ranger missions were primarily to kill the enemy, or to secure tactical or operational targets, or be the tip of the bayonet in various assaults—from helicopters, airborne operations, and waterborne operations. We would learn all of those basic techniques while in Ranger School.

I also learned some of the culture from a 2nd Bat E, Dennis Dunn. He told me about the process for the E's to get to Ranger School; how he had to go through RIP (Ranger Indoctrination Program) which taught the young enlisted soldiers about the basic Ranger techniques, so they could succeed in Ranger School. In addition to RIP, they were exposed to training with their platoons which helped prepare them for Ranger School. They were also put through a vigorous physical fitness regimen. RIP probably better prepared these young guys for the physical aspects of Ranger School and the patrolling techniques than most of the officers. But they were not as proficient in the art of tactical and operational planning as the officers. When the duties were divided up, the officers normally ended up doing the planning and executing; and the younger enlisted did most of the executing as far as patrolling. The more seasoned NCO's were involved in the planning to a lesser extent than the officers and did more of the executing than the officers. Officers still led patrols, but the young enlisted Rangers were given the assistant patrol and team leader positions, to make up for not having participated in the planning of the operations. This worked in this Ranger School class because of the ratio of enlisted to officer.

During City Week, we practiced different formations in patrolling out in a field where we could see each other and get the spacing right. Then we took it into the woods to practice our patrolling techniques in more simulated situations. This was all a prelude to going to Camp Rogers, where we would begin the graded phase of patrolling at Fort Benning.

Ranger School was also the great equalizer. It denigrated all of us equally, and it was up to the individual to survive his own RI-created degradation. One of the ways we were equalized was at meals.

On the second day of Ranger School, as we lined up for lunch outside the mess hall, one of the RI's bellowed, "One time around Rangers and that's it!"

We looked at each other, what did that mean? I'm sure our faces displayed confusion over his order.

"Rangers, you got one time around the inside of the mess hall to eat your meal. When you go in, get your food, walk around the mess hall, then dump whatever you have left in the garbage. So, you better eat fast Rangers!" Then he laughed.

And that's what happened. When I entered the mess hall I picked up a tray, the cooks behind the counter slopped a plate of food on the tray. I got a glass of juice and kept walking around the outer perimeter inside the mess hall. I could see the guys who had entered in front of me and saw them dumping all their uneaten food in the garbage near the front door. I tried to scarf as much food as I could and gulp as much juice as I could before reaching the front door. This couldn't be healthy for the digestive system, but I'm sure our comfort was the last thing on the RI's mind.

When I got to the front, I dumped everything left on my tray in the garbage and went out the door. That's how we ate the rest of our hot meals, while we were at Darby. Other meals consisted of either C-Rats (Combat Rations from WWII or Korea or Vietnam) or LRRPs (Long-Range Reconnaissance Patrol meals in pouches that we filled with hot water). This got us in the mind frame of not eating as much, and beginning to understand that we could do 20-hour days on a lot fewer calories. That's how I ultimately lost 35 lbs. in Ranger School.

Once we finished City Week, and passed all the required tests, we set out for Camp Rogers. Not by bus or truck, but by a 15-mile road march with full mountain rucks that allowed us to carry twice as much as regular rucks. We carried up to 50 lbs. in those rucks, which made the 15-mile road march that much more fun. All our other stuff was put into a duffel bag and transported by truck. Camp Rogers would make or break us for the Fort Benning phase, because now we would go out on graded patrols; and plan and execute airborne missions out of UH-1 "Hueys" as a part of our graded exercises. It was for real now.

Our entire time at Camp Rogers we stayed in tactical mode. We did not stay in any fixed structures, like the platoon barracks back at the main Ranger Department area. We stayed in our two-man tents and lived in the field. We took our meals tactically, where squads would eat one at a time, and the rest of the platoon would stay in our positions until it was our turn to eat. When we did eat, we ate at our positions with one man on guard and the other eating. We would only eat one item at a time, so that if we had to get up and leave, we didn't have a lot of stuff to dispose. We learned to eat quickly and efficiently, wolfing our food. After we ate, we would take our trash back to the trucks, and return back to our positions. This got us in the mindset of being tactical at all times.

The mission of our first patrol was to recon an enemy position. This would give us experience planning and executing a simpler patrol before we got to more complex operations to include airborne, or air assault components. We did our planning in the fixed bay areas designed for that purpose. The RI's gave us the regular five-paragraph mission order to set our mission and operational parameters. They gave us a certain amount of time to complete and execute the plan. Our planning involved using light infantry tactics and various operational and map aids, such as lines of departure (LDs), check points (CPs), objective rally points (ORPs), release points (RPs), and phase lines (PL). We relied on distances and directions from the maps, intelligence on the enemy units with strength and probable deployment around the objective. The mission order provided us the mission objectives, radio call signs and frequencies, maps of the area of operations (AO); artillery targeting, procedures for calling in air support; primary/secondary and tertiary approach routes to the objective and routes of return from the objective.

All these variables, along with many others, went into the planning of a simple patrol. This took several hours, with tasks delegated to those persons who had some expertise in that area. The more we worked through the planning, the better we got to know each other's strengths and weaknesses.

For my part, I tried to make myself indispensable by providing as much leadership and knowledge from my limited experience in IOBC and ROTC, as well as the principles of patrolling we had just learned. Based on the responses of my squad and platoon members, and the requests for my involvement in every aspect of planning except artillery targeting, I achieved my goal. This was much different than my previous experiences at Fort Riley and Fort Knox. I had learned my lessons and applied them to the ultimate in leadership and team building—Ranger School. And yeah, you could be eliminated from Ranger School through peer evaluations.

The first patrol went pretty well and the first patrol leader and assistant patrol leader received a "Go" for their efforts. The next patrol involved a daylight airborne operation, with an insertion by "vertical envelopment," from a helicopter over a postage-stamp sized drop zone in order to conduct a night raid on an enemy position, and finally, airlifted back out by helicopter.

Jumping from a UH-1 is a lot different than jumping from a C-130, C-123, or C-141, where you jump from 1,250 feet and the wind carries you past the aircraft, and the static line deploys your main chute which should open at the count of "four." In contrast, when you jump from a helicopter, you jump at 1,500 feet; you count to "seven" instead of four before your chute opens because there is less airflow and speed. Then you find yourself dropping straight down from the helicopter to this really small-assed DZ, instead of the mass tactical DZs at jump school. During planning I had a good look at the DZ and saw it was on top of a hill, surrounded by a lot of trees…a lot of Georgia pines surrounded the drop zone and made hitting the DZ even more of an adventure.

The RI's took us through a little airborne refresher for those who had not jumped in a while, and also for those of us who had never dropped from a helicopter. We were jumping with full rucks and weapons and that was significantly different than the "schoolhouse" jumps we had made in jump school. Hell, it was hard getting up once we had all our equipment and parachute strapped to our backs. I had to get someone to help me get off the tarmac, so I could waddle to the aircraft for the airborne operation.

Four helos lifted off in order at 15 to 30 second intervals. Each chopper had eight Rangers with four hanging on each side with feet on the skids. As we climbed into the Huey, we hooked our chutes onto the static line so when it was our turn to jump, we merely stepped off the side of the helicopter and dropped towards the drop zone.

The helicopter ride to the DZ was fun. It was exciting hanging out the side of the Huey and watching the Georgia countryside passing underneath us. We flew nap of the earth (NOE) until we got closer to the DZ, then we rose to the proper elevation. Then it was time to jump. This was only my sixth jump and the first one from a helicopter. At that point we went through an abbreviated version of the jump commands—"Stand up!" "Check Equipment!" "Stand in the door!" then "Go!" "Go!" "Go!" "Go!" And out we went.

That was the longest seven seconds of my life, as I waited for that main chute to deploy. It took forever…damn! And when it finally snapped open it didn't seem like it really slowed me down all that much. Shit! My equipment was so heavy that I was not slowing down like I was used to, and of course we jumped from 1,500 feet and didn't have that extra cushion of time and distance to slow down that we had from a faster moving aircraft. I was coming in fast and hard! The ground rushed at me way too fast! I put my legs together and bent my knees in preparation of hitting the ground.

I started yelling as I came in, "Ohhhhhhhhhhh shit!"

I could see other Rangers coming in as I geared up for my less than stellar landing. I did not look like the steely-eyed Rangers from the Bats. Not a fucking sound from those guys. They looked like what they were supposed to be—Airborne fucking Rangers.

I felt like a real dumb shit as I hit the ground. Fortunately, I didn't get hurt.After I executed my less than perfect PLF, I checked all my body parts, determined I was okay, gathered up my chute, and moved out to my designated RP off the DZ to establish a defensive position to prepare for our mission. Unfortunately, Dennis got hurt from the jump because he went into the trees. Like I said, the DZ was surrounded by trees—really big trees—and he went in without a sound. Me, I would have been yelling like a little girl…but that's me.

The mission went well—we completed the raid and were extracted at the designated extraction point without a hitch. When we got back, my name was on the board as the next patrol leader. Oh shit, here we go…

✧   ✧   ✧

I didn't get much sleep that night knowing I would be the next patrol leader. My patrol was relatively simple compared to the one we just executed. Mine was a simple recon—out and then back. It was a night mission, so we had all day to plan. One lesson I learned, rehearsal was the key to a successful mission, if you had the time. As patrol leaders we tried to put rehearsal time in as part of the planning. In the last exercise, we practiced getting in and out of aircraft, setting up a perimeter on a DZ and extraction point, and how we would execute the raid itself. This time, because it was a recon, we didn't need to practice as much, but we continued to work on our movement in formations, so we could do it at night without much thought. Operations like crossing water obstacles, open fields, and roads had to be second nature. At night you needed to be able to react without much thought, because that split second of indecision might cost you or your patrol their lives.

The planning went well as did the rehearsals. My assistant patrol leader, one of the E's from the 1st Bat, was eager to follow my lead without resistance. The RI who had been watching us go through our routine—the planning, delegation of tasks, rehearsals, and preparation of equipment for the patrol gave me a "Go" for that portion of the patrol leader's duties. That was a positive sign as he signed me over to the RI that who would grade me on the execution of my plan, and leadership of the patrol on the actual mission. That would be the real test. Planning and rehearsals was one thing—doing it for real was another. Now it was time to perform on a graded patrol.

Our mission covered about ten kilometers or "clicks" over the duration of the patrol—from our leaving the tactical area to our eventual return. The objective was about five clicks away and would take a few hours to get there, conduct the required recon, then return to the assembly area. I had to know our exact location at all times. I had done an extensive map study and became familiar with the terrain and the terrain features and their approximate distances during the patrol. I had various methods to determine where we were at any time during the patrol, knowing the direction and azimuth that we needed to move, and the location of the objective—an enemy compound that may have been a weapons cache. We had the mission to determine what was there and enemy numbers at the location.

After darkness fell, we lined up in our patrol formation and prepared to move out into the darkness. I looked us over and everyone was in their black and green camo, all equipment tied down, and eager to go. Everyone looked at me with anticipation. I gave the orders to my assistant patrol leader and team leaders to move out. *This was it*, I thought, as we moved out in the proper formation, out of the assembly area and into the dark Georgia wood line.

The primary RI, an Asian-appearing SFC, stayed with me and the assistant RI stayed with the assistant patrol leader. One method for keeping track of how far we had gone, was to have a shoestring on my LBE for the sole purpose of tying a knot in it for every 100 meters traveled. One of the standards for getting a "Go" on your patrol was to be able to know your location within 50 meters at all times, and be able to point it out on a map. Not an easy assignment at night, particularly if you had to bypass large open areas or cross water obstacles or roads. But you could always tell where you were as long as you stayed on the right azimuth and understood the terrain. Once you got to 10 knots on your string, that represented one click, and you went to the second string. Once you travelled 1,100 meters, you should have one string completed, and one knot on the second string. If you had to go around an obstacle you had to ensure that you kept track of how far around you went, the direction, and where on the other side you needed to resume the patrol on the proper azimuth. This was all part of passing your patrol. The RI's could give you three grades on a patrol—"Go" which meant you passed enough of the tasks to get a grade of 70 or better; "Honor Grad Go" representing a nearly perfect patrol and qualified you for Honor Grad consideration; and of course, "No Go" which meant exactly as it sounded…you failed your patrol. So far, I had a "Go" and I wanted that "Honor Grad Go" as well.

As we moved through the woods, I stayed with the first team to better control our progress and keep track of our position. The point man, an E from

2nd Bat, kept a good pace as he moved through the woods. Equipped with a machete, the point man broke brush when necessary. Anytime he heard a sound or came to an obstacle he stopped the patrol which caused me to move forward to evaluate the situation. There weren't many obstacles on this patrol, and our movement through the woods went fairly quickly. Within an hour and a half, we got within a few hundred meters of the release point (RP) prior to setting up for the recon of the objective.

During our approach to the objective, the RI periodically asked me to point out our position on a map. I was correct each time. Unfortunately, my assistant was not as lucky, and they replaced him with one of the team leaders because he had no clue where he was during the patrol. As we approached the RP, the location we used to disperse the patrol into their final positions to conduct the recon, I began to cough uncontrollably. My cold had finally caught up to me, at the worst possible time.

"You alright Ranger?" The RI asked.

"Yes, sir, just a little cold," I answered, and then let loose with a long and loud wracking cough that hurt my chest.

This was at night within a few hundred meters of the objective. My coughs were long, and deep, wracking, painful coughs that I couldn't stop.

"Ranger, I don't think that's a little cough. I'm not a doctor, but that sounds pretty bad."

"I can make it sir," I said. I did not want to be taken out of this position, not again.

"I'm sorry Ranger, but I can't allow you to jeopardize the mission. I also think you're not well, so I'm going to have to medevac you to the rear."

He then got on his radio, "We're going to need a medivac for one of the students." He paused, "Yeah, he sounds pretty bad. Yeah, we're at the RP for night recon." He paused again, "Yeah, that's the location, we'll be waiting."

He turned to me, "Alright Ranger, take a seat, the medevac truck will be here in a few minutes."

And just like that, it was over. I just sat there and waited for the truck. In the meantime, the RI brought my new assistant patrol leader up front and I briefed him prior to my departure. The last I saw of my patrol was from the back of a deuce and a half as they continued the mission. And yeah, that was the last I saw of Class 7-80.

Damn.

On April 2, 1980, they admitted me to the hospital with a serious case of pneumonia; and I remained hospitalized from April 2nd through the 9th, spending a little over a week in the hospital flat on my back. Dennis came by to visit me while rehabbing his knee. Both of us stated we wanted to get back into Ranger School. Secretly I had my doubts. This was a reprieve from Ranger training and gave me a chance to evaluate whether I really wanted to go back and complete the last seven weeks of Ranger School, and go through all that shit to earn the coveted black and gold Ranger Tab.

I started that class on March 18th and within five days I had been complaining of symptoms of a bad cold, and now 10 days later I was hospitalized. I had a lot to think about over that week or so in the hospital.

During my stay Claude Boggs, whose wife, Rena, was Cornell McGhee's sister, paid me a visit. He brought reading material, *The Destroyer* series, and got me hooked on Remo Williams, Chiun, the Korean master, and the myth of Korean martial arts, something I had dabbled in over the past 10 years. I really appreciated Claude's visits. He and Rena helped me a lot during my convalescence.

I was discharged on April 9th, but I was still in bad shape. The worst of my pneumonia had passed, but I still needed to get my conditioning back. I reported back to Ranger School, since that was my place of duty and the NCOIC told me I was being given a 14-day convalescent leave. After my leave, I needed to report back and prepare for Class 8-80, as a medical recycle.

Damn.

CHAPTER 30

"In the Breech, Again"

I spent most of my time in Texas, visiting my fiancée, Karen, and doing a lot of rehabbing—running mostly, trying to get back in shape for Class 8-80. I knew what was in store, so I kept up with my push-ups, situps, pull-ups and other exercises the RI's used to torture Ranger students. I needed to get in the best shape possible because I was resigned to the fact that I was going back into the breech…again.

It's an interesting phenomenon amongst Ranger students—something we talked about at times, that no one wanted to quit, but wouldn't mind if they got hurt to get out of going through the entire course. At least that would be an honorable reason for leaving—that you didn't quit, but were hurt. Some of us were unlucky, we got hurt and then recycled, so we spent even more time in Ranger School. I had been assigned to the Ranger Department since the end of February, and it looked like I would be there a little while longer.

Class 8-80 started on April 21, 1980 and would graduate on June 19, 1980. Coincidentally, on April 24, 1980, the day before I started with Class 8-80, *Operation Eagle Claw*, the attempt to rescue the Iranian hostages failed. This was a big topic of discussion as we went through Ranger School since many of these guys had been part of the support operations, and had actually rehearsed part of the potential rescue that ultimately failed.

I joined the Class on April 25, 1980, after I reported back from convalescent leave, and during their first week of Ranger School. I avoided the first few days of bullshit, but arrived just in time for the other fun and games associated with City Week. Here we go again.

❖   ❖   ❖

I initially reported to the 3rd Ranger Company at 0700 that morning as directed. The sights and sounds of Ranger School were the same. It was so surreal, I felt like I was coming home, or to the Twilight Zone. Take your pick.

I walked into the building with my duffel bag and saw that same corporal sitting where he sat the entire time I snowbirded. He stood up with a smile on his face.

"Hey, welcome back Ranger Pittard," he said as he signed me in off leave. "You know where you're going?"

"No."

"Okay, you need to report to your new tac officer, Lt. Gary Powell," he said as he handed me my new orders.

"Okay, where's he located?"

"You know where the Tac Officer's hut is?"

"Yeah, I think so," I replied, "over beyond the far side of the barracks?"

"Yep, report to him there, I think he's expecting you."

"Okay, thanks."

"Good luck Ranger Pittard," he added with a flourish.

"Thank you," I said. *Okay, here we go again,* I thought.

I turned from him, grabbed my duffel bag and jogged over to the Tac Officer's small office. The hut was made of corrugated steel that looked like it had been there a while. I knocked on the weathered green metal door and requested permission to enter.

I heard, "Come in Ranger."

I walked into his office and gave him my best salute, and said, "Ranger Pittard reporting for duty sir!" in my best parade-ground voice. We were both lieutenants, but since Ranger students didn't have rank, I thought it best to salute.

As I looked down at him, I saw a tall, dark-skinned, first lieutenant, wearing a Ranger Tab, leisurely sitting in the vinyl executive chair behind his gray metal desk. He was the second Black officer I had ever seen with the Ranger Tab. He wore starched jungle fatigues stuffed in spit-shined jungle boots. The name plate on his desk, a brass plate on an elongated pyramid-shaped piece of wood with the name, rank and branch, said "Powell." He sternly appraised me as I stood at attention with my right hand still perched at my right eyebrow. There was a stillness in the air. I could see the dust motes floating in the sunlit rays coming from the single window. It seemed like forever before he returned my salute.

"Take a seat Ranger."

I quickly dropped my duffel bag and sat down on one of the two straight-backed metal chairs positioned in front of his desk. The morning light from the one window in the room shone brightly on the desk.

I noticed my meager file, highlighted by the sun, in the middle of his desk.

"Ranger Pittard, huh? Recycled because of pneumonia, right?" He said it like I'd had the bubonic plague or something and he might catch it.

"Yes sir." Nothing else I could say.

"Where you from Ranger?"

"Texas, sir."

"Where'd you go to school?"

"Texas, sir."

"What?"

"UT, sir. You know the Longhorns?" I smiled as I made the distinction. I mean, I didn't want him to think I'd gone to UTEP or some other branch of the UT system, but that I'd gone to *The* University of Texas. Yeah, that shit made me proud.

"You pledge anything at UT, Ranger Pittard?"

Huh? What kind of question was that? And in this environment? I wondered. "Uh, yes sir, Kappa Alpha Psi, sir."

"Well Scroller, don't you know when you're in the presence of a Nupe?" He gave me this huge shit-eating grin.

Damn, he'd been pulling my chain all along. He knew I was a Kappa coming in. I wonder how? .

"Yes, sir. Sorry sir." I gave him the secret signal.

He returned the signal and stood up and shook my hand as only a true Kappa man could—and I knew I was in good hands. This would be a different experience from my last class, when I had that corncob-stuck-up-the-ass white captain TAC, who didn't say two words to me the entire time I was in Class 7-80. *Hell, this might even be fun.*

"I'm Gary, Gary Powell, from Hardin-Simmons University," he introduced himself. He looked like Thomas "Hitman" Hearns in build and height, and almost as dangerous.

"Chris Pittard," I answered reflexively. "How'd you know I was a Kappa?"

"Oh, I don't know, a little birdie told me," he said mysteriously. "We got an Alpha in here too, Leon Price, and a Sigma. You'll meet them both pretty soon."

"Okay."

He was referring to members of rival fraternities, Alpha Phi Alpha, whose colors are black and gold, and Phi Beta Sigma, whose colors are blue and white. In contrast, my fraternity's colors are "Crimson and Cream."

"While we're out there I have to treat you like a Scroller, but behind closed doors we're frat, okay?"

"Okay." I grinned. Now I knew I was in good hands. Yeah, this would be fun…well, as fun as Ranger School could be, I guess.

"What happened in your last class?" Gary asked.

"Well, I was doing okay until I developed a cough. I maxed all my tests and had gotten a "go" on the initial planning stages of my first patrol when my cough got so bad the RI medevacked me to the rear."

"Did you ever see or talk to your Tac Officer?"

"Nope. He seemed to resent me and any other Black Ranger student. He was a real asshole. Didn't say two words to me the entire time I was in his class."

"Yeah, that tends to be a problem with the guys assigned from Dahlonega." Gary shook his head.

"What do you mean?"

"Every class has a tac from a different Ranger Camp. I'm from the Florida Ranger camp, and that guy is assigned to the Dahlonega camp."

"Dahlonega, the mountain phase in northern Georgia, right?"

"Yeah. They have the reputation of being racist. In fact, there are no Black RI's assigned to that camp. There are a bunch of us here at Benning, at Eglin AFB, in Florida, but not in Dahlonega. I'm the only Black officer at the Florida camp, and there're two assigned to Fort Benning." He kept his voice low, "There've been rumors of how Black RI's meet with unfortunate accidents in Dahlonega, so no one wants to be assigned there."

Damn, well that could explain the attitude of the two guys in charge of my last class. Yeah, a lot of things fell into place with that explanation.

"There are a lot more Black Ranger students in this class and a better mix of officers and enlisted, so this should be a better class for you." He said.

I just nodded my head, trying to soak it all in. I knew this was information the other Ranger students probably didn't have and I was only getting it because of the fraternity connection.

"Your record looks good so far," he said as he continued to review my file. "And because you're a medical recycle, and not performance recycle, you're still eligible for Honor Grad awards."

"What does that mean?" I asked.

"Do your best and you have a shot at honor grad. I'll let you know how you're doing, but I can't give you any more help than any other Ranger student. Understand?" He looked me in the eyes.

"Yeah, I got it, thanks." I said as I got up to leave his office. I grabbed my duffel bag and walked towards the door.

"Once we step outside, you're no different from any other Ranger," he said again.

"Got it." I said again with a smile.

Regardless, I knew he had my back, and I wouldn't get fucked over by him unlike some of my previous experiences with Army training. That was a good feeling. When I stepped out of his office with my duffel bag, I had a renewed confidence in my ability to succeed in Ranger School.

⟥ ⟥ ⟥

During the time I met with Gary in his office, the class had formed up outside. He walked me out in front of the class, introduced me to the class and assigned me to the 2nd platoon, first squad. About that time, an African-American Ranger student, with a really big nose ran up to me and yelled, "Aargh! I'm Ranger Ugly!" and made as ugly a face as he could muster.

I just looked at him and laughed. I had actually met him at one of the clubs on post before Ranger School and knew he was an Army sergeant, Carter, assigned to Benning. The last time I had seen him he was dancing with this nice-looking chick at the NCO Club. Now he was Ranger Ugly and part of the welcoming committee for Class 8-80.

I joined my platoon and squad and dropped my duffel bag at the end of the squad formation. Further down I spied a familiar face—Dennis was also in this squad. I knew this would be good.

Inside the platoon bay I met the rest of the squad and platoon. Like Gary had said there was a lot better mix of O's and E's. In my squad there was: Robert "Beast" Bestian, a lieutenant who looked like a college football linebacker; Richard Shorey, an E3 from one of the Bats; Luke Richards, a PV2 from one of the Bats; 2LT Bill Klimack, also going to Fort Hood; 2LT Paul Haveles; SFC Frank Chun, a Green Beret from 10th Special Forces Group, and another recycle, but from a previous year; SSG Marvin Cummings; PFC Charlie Gant; and PV2 Kevin Poirier. In our platoon we had some real interesting personalities—PV2 John Cherrybone III [first time I heard "hooah" which is a derivative of HUA—heard, understood, and acknowledged], PFC Ron "Elvis" Jewell, SGT Dallas "Ranger Ugly" Carter, 2LT Leon Price, the Alpha, and all the other guys that made up this cast of characters.

Over the course of the training through City Week, Rogers, Darby, Dahlonega and the Florida swamps we had to find ways to keep our spirits up and keep motivated. During the first few days of Class 8-80, Gary had "encouraged" his Ranger students to come up with ways to keep themselves entertained and motivated. This was vastly different than Class 7-80, where the Tac Officer didn't seem to give a shit about his students.

One example was Ranger Ugly. However, the Ranger students came up with other ideas as well. One of them was singing to while away the time, and to provide entertainment. Sgt Carter served as the ringleader for that form of entertainment. Six of us sang with Carter. He would be out front and the rest of us harmonizing. I got drawn in primarily because I was in the same platoon and probably because I'm Black. Anyway, we sung *Daddy's Home* an R&B classic by Shep and the Limelites, and *Papa's Got a Brand New Bag* by the incomparable James Brown. I don't sing very well, so I just kind of harmonized and stayed in the background when we had to perform in front of the rest of the class. Ron Jewell did his best Elvis impersonation on hits like *Heartbreak Hotel, Jailhouse Rock*, and *Hound Dog*.

In addition to the singing entertainment, we staged an evening newscast on the fate of the Ranger students being held hostage in Class 8-80, at our various locations with "Ayatollah Powellmeini" (like the Ayatollah Khomeini who led the radical Muslim revolution in Iran), and SSG Wilson Hunt, our tactical NCO, he became "President Huntisdhar," like President Bandisdar, the new Iranian president. Each day we counted off like the Iranian Hostage Crisis on the news, and we would give a daily report on the "Ranger hostage crisis" of Class 8-80. All this to keep up the spirits of us Ranger students as we went through a daily hell…much different than the dour Class 7-80.

Then there were the Marines.

There was a squad of Force Recon Marines with two lieutenants going through our class. They kept them together as a squad. Probably a good thing because those guys were insane. Better to keep them from the rest of us in case we became infected with whatever they had. They were in the next platoon. One thing I will say to their credit—none of them dropped out or had to be recycled. They all made it through Ranger School.

The mail served as the biggest morale booster. Not everyone got mail, but those who didn't lived vicariously through those few who did, like me. I received a lot of mail, thanks to my pretty fiancé Karen. She wrote me faithfully on most days and would send pictures with some of her letters. I couldn't let my Ranger buddies read some of those letters, since some of them got pretty salacious. I could read them portions that I deemed acceptable. They were also quite complimentary of her pictures. They seemed to enjoy my letters as much as I did, and the anticipation of getting those letters helped sustain me, and them, during much of the trials and tribulations of Ranger School.

I made it through the Camp Rogers phase with no problem. I didn't have to take any of the tests, but I retook them to keep up my skills in land nav and techniques of patrolling. I didn't want to give the wrong impression in this class—of someone privileged—and I wanted to show off my prowess in those areas. I again maxed the land nav and maxed all written tests. I was ready. Camp Darby here I come…again.

⋄   ⋄   ⋄

The experience at Camp Darby wasn't much different this time around, with one exception—I didn't suffer from pneumonia in this warmer weather, and wasn't a liability to my squad or to myself.

We again trained on the techniques of patrolling, field-craft techniques, using explosives like C-4 and detonation cord, various battle drills, such as reacting to ambushes, conducting raids and recons, and planning and patrolling operations. We conducted similar patrols to my previous class. This time my patrol was a raid, rather than a recon, as a part of an air assault mission. This time I completed my turn as a patrol leader and received an "Honor Grad Go." This meant I remained in the running for Honor Grad at the end of the Class.

Our patrols included another airborne mission from a helicopter, my seventh jump. No problem this time. Both Dennis and I survived the jumps and were ready to move on to the next phase in Dahlonega. The only things that stood in my way were the 15-mile road march back to Camp Darby, the "Darby Queen" obstacle course, the five-mile run, and the Water Confidence Test. These would be a problem. I still suffered from the vestiges of pneumonia, which seemed to manifest itself as shortness of breath when I exerted myself after several minutes. I only had to hang on, and I would make it to the next phase.

⋄   ⋄   ⋄

The first test for my endurance was the 15-mile road march back to Darby. I had made the initial 15-mile road march out to Rogers with little problem, but this one seemed arduous. Maybe because it seemed to be more uphill, than down. During Ranger School, whenever an RI wanted you to continue to do something or carry on, he would utter the phrase, "Drive on Ranger!" During this 15-mile road march, with full ruck and weapon, I kept my head down and that became my mantra, *"Drive on Ranger, Drive on Ranger, Drive on Ranger... you can do this. You didn't go through all this shit to fall back on a damn road march. Gut it out, like Fort Knox, c'mon, Drive on Ranger..."*

Again, my breathing became an issue, but again, I got through. I didn't fall back, and I kept up with my squad members.

Richards, from Massachusetts, uttered in his uninimitable Boston accent, "Get hahd Pittahd!" when it looked like I started to tire and fall back.

His encouragement, as it were, helped give me the resolve to keep my head down and just gut it out the last few miles of the road march. Yeah, that 50 lb. ruck does get heavy after 15 miles. But I survived that test of resolve thanks to my squad's encouragement and my internal fortitude—*"Drive on Ranger!"*

The second obstacle was the Darby Queen. I had been through obstacle courses before, but the Darby Queen was in a class by itself. It incorporated the worst of the normal obstacle courses and apparatus from previous confidence courses. These type of apparatus pushed Ranger students to their utmost when trying to negotiate these obstacles. My breathing became an issue again, but I was able to get through the Darby Queen.

Then came the five-mile run. One of the hallmarks of getting around Camps Rogers and Darby required that we run everywhere we went. Sometimes in formation, or by ourselves, but we ran everywhere. As a result, the RI's tasked us to call our own cadences while in formation. In our class we had a limited amount of NCO's, which meant that either they pulled all the weight for calling cadences or other ranks had to get involved.

In our class, I got involved in calling cadences, something I hadn't done since my days at NMMI. I still had it, so I called cadences for my platoon most of the time we ran in formation. All the cadences I'd learned from my drills at Fort Knox and at NMMI came back, and I also incorporated cadences learned while in jump school, thus increasing my repertoire. I tried to make them interesting, motivating and fun, because running can be drudgery, and the cadence caller has the responsibility to make it as interesting and fun as possible.

They conducted the five-mile run on the same day as the Water Confidence Test, and thankfully the day after the road march. You had to pass the five-mile run, and then pass the Water Confidence Test to move on to the Mountain phase.

This was a big day for me because of the breathing issues, but I was determined to get past these last two endurance and fear-based tests. The RI's told us the five miles would be run at an eight-minute pace, and would take approximately 40 minutes. The route was mostly level, but there would be some running uphill and downhill, but primarily it would be on level ground.

Okay, I thought, *I can do this.*

We lined up in formation outside our platoon barracks. Dressed in fatigues, shirts out, and boots, we marched out into the street to begin the run. The RI's asked for volunteers to call cadence while they set the pace. I didn't volunteer because I didn't want to use up my breath calling cadence. So, Chun, Carter, and some other guys got out there as the preeminent NCO's to call cadence. So when the RI's called "Double time—March" we were ready to hit the road for five miles in forty minutes.

The first mile went pretty well. I was in good shape and again, I didn't waste breath responding to the cadence caller. During the third mile, a white PFC or private got out there to call cadence, and the formation began to fall apart. His poor timing in his cadences put everybody off in their steps. Some were hitting on the left foot, others on the right foot, and some were just confused.

After about two or three minutes, Ranger students from all the platoons began calling for me.

"Get Pittard out there! We need Pittard out there!"

I felt pretty good about being called out by name by the entire class, but I didn't really want to get out there because of my breathing issues.

Unfortunately, one of the RI's, who knew exactly who I was, ran up to me and said, "Get these Rangers back in step!"

So, I had no choice.

"Yes sir!" I yelled and jumped out of the formation to be in the best position to call cadence for the entire class.

We had three platoons, and I positioned myself towards the end of the second platoon so the two platoons in front of me could hear me as I projected my voice forward and the platoon to my rear could also hear me. Of course, at times I would turn and run backwards to give the third platoon the full benefit of my voice.

Within a few steps after I got started, I had the whole class back in step, and clapping with the beat and rhythm of my cadences. Oh yeah, I was in my element, and unlike the guys before me, the RI's kept me out there for the rest of the third mile, and the fourth mile. Finally, during the fifth mile I began to tire and my breathing became more labored. I motioned to the nearest RI that I needed a break, and he took over. He didn't call any other Ranger students out. I fell back to the end of the third platoon, although I was in the second platoon, I needed to be at the very back in case I started to fall back.

That last half-mile was one of the hardest I had run since Fort Knox. I was out of breath and the oxygen failed to get to my brain or my legs. I felt dizzy and weak.

The truck lagged behind the formation, and the RI trailing the formation said, "Ranger, if you fall back to the truck you will fail the five-mile run."

I thought, *Shit, after all I did for this fucking class to get it through the goddamn run, I can't fuck it up by not making it.*

I doubled my efforts and made sure I stayed in front of that damn truck and then suddenly I heard those breathtaking words, "QUICK TIME—MARCH!" I had made it…thank God!

I walked with my head down, trying to draw in breaths. I knew I'd gotten past that obstacle, with only one more to go, the Water Confidence Test.

At least that wouldn't involve any running.

Once we got back to the barracks the RI's loaded us up in deuce and a halves to take us out to Victory Pond where we would undergo the WCT. I guess they thought we needed to cool off with a little dip in the water. Uh huh.

When we arrived at Victory Pond, we sat in the bleachers facing the water. To our immediate front stood the apparatus that included a board about 40 feet long, and a foot wide, that had a three-block step that you had to step up and over and continue to the rope for the Ranger drop. The board and rope towered 40 feet above the water, stretching over three large poles. The RI's told us our task was to grab onto the rope, do an underhand crawl to the wooden Ranger Tab in the middle of the rope, touch the Tab, yell "RANGER!" and position ourselves for a 40-foot drop into the water.

The apparatus further back was the "Slide for Life," a long zip line into the water. The RI's informed us the task included manually climbing the tower 60 feet above the water, grabbing the T-bar, assuming an L-position, and sliding down the zip line towards the end that consisted of a square piece of wood covered by tires and inner tubes. The RI's warned us we needed to drop into the water before slamming into the tires and inner tubes at 30 miles an hour, which could be rather painful, maybe even deadly. The Ranger student had to drop or suffer painful injury. In a show of bravado and confidence, we were required to yell "RANGER!" as we dropped into the water, then swim to the side unassisted.

The speed and height of the drop would disorient the weaker swimmers, and expose them. The WCT would expose those who somehow got through or didn't take the Combat Water Survival Test, which was supposed to be a requirement for getting into Ranger School. Of course, I didn't take the CWST, but I was confident I could pass any swim test, even with my breathing issues. We didn't have to swim very far, just to the side of the pond. This wasn't about endurance, but about fear, and whether we could overcome our fear of water and heights in a less than comfortable setting.

Once the RI's explained the apparatus to us, they divided us into two groups, one to the Slide for Life, and the other to the board walk and rope drop. I lined up in the group for the Slide for Life, so I had an opportunity to watch the guys on the board walk and rope drop. That to me would be the harder of the two because of my fear of heights. I knew I wouldn't like dropping 40 feet into the water, and the whole running over the board and stepping up over the three-block barrier didn't thrill me either. When they had demonstrated the two apparatus, Gary Powell demonstrated the board walk and rope drop. He just ran down the board 40 feet above the water, leapt over the three blocks, did the rope crawl in record time, yelled "RANGER!" and dropped into the water like a walk in the park. Yeah, good for him. I was not happy and didn't want to admit to anyone that I was scared shitless of running across that board and dropping off the rope, but it had to be done, and dammit, I would do it.

Looking up at the two apparatus caused a flashback to an evening several weeks ago in my BOQ room.

❖   ❖   ❖

I was in the first week of jump school, and while watching TV, I heard a knock on my door. Three distinct knocks. I thought I knew who it was, and looked through the peephole. Yep, it was Harold "H.J." Mathis, a frat brother of mine who had attended an earlier IOBC class and gone on to Ranger School. In fact, he was still supposed to be in Ranger School. I opened the door with a curious expression on my face. He wasn't supposed to be here.

"Hey, H.J., what's up?"

"Hey Nupe, can I come in?" He asked in his deep voice. H.J. was former enlisted, had gone to Florida State, and pledged the Fraternity through the Honolulu Alumni Chapter. He stood a little shorter than me, darker skinned, balding, so he shaved his head, and always had a ready smile. He was a little older than me, but in good shape and really motivated to go to Ranger School.

"Oh yeah, sure, come in. I was just surprised to see you. I thought you were in Ranger School," I said as I opened the door wider for him to come into my BOQ room. He was dressed in a heavy black leather jacket, over a long-sleeved red-plaid shirt, jeans and brown "waffle stomper" boots.

He took off his jacket and sat down at the desk with a heavy sigh, while I took a seat on the bed, with the TV still on in the background. H.J. had this forlorn look on his face. He didn't look happy, and this was a guy who always had a ready smile.

"What's up?" I asked again.

"I'm out Nupe, I'm out." He said, with a little tremor in his voice.

"What happened?" I asked.

"You know man, I loved being in Ranger School. Did you know I was the motivational officer for my class?"

"No, I didn't know that. What's a motivational officer? What class?"

"Six dash eighty. The tac officer assigned me to keep the class motivated by any means necessary, so I made up chants, called cadences, and did whatever I could to keep the Ranger students motivated. Man, it was fucking cold out there and real tough to stay motivated all the time."

"Is that what happened? You got hypothermia?" *Shit*, I thought, *I was hypothermic in IOBC and it wasn't any fun.* And I already knew it was still cold in Georgia.

"No man, it was the Slide for Life that got me."

"The Slide for Life? Can't you swim?" I asked, knowing that I didn't take the CWST.

"Um, not really Nupe. The first sergeant in IOBC class let me slide on the swimming requirement and I didn't have to take the Combat Water Survival Test like everyone else." *That sounded familiar*, I thought.

"What happened?"

"You know you're like 70 feet in the air, and you have to slide down this cable on a T-bar at about 30 miles per hour and then drop into the water before hitting the tires at the end of the cable."

"Okay..." I prompted.

"So when it came time for me to drop, I dropped into that icy cold water at about 30 mph. Man…that water was so cold it took my breath away and I got disoriented and couldn't find my way to the surface. Damn Nupe, I almost drowned. They had to come get me out the water."

He was almost in tears. I felt bad for him.

"You're okay now?"

"Yeah, I'm okay, but I wanted you to know I didn't make it. But I know you'll make it. You're smart and serious about being Infantry and that's what it's going to take to make it through Ranger School."

I just looked at him and nodded, what could I say?

We sat there for a few moments absently watching TV, lost in our thoughts before H.J. spoke again.

"I've got my orders for Fort Hood, so I'll see you when you get there." He stood up and put his jacket back on. "Good luck in Ranger School Nupe, don't let anything stop you because they'll put all kinds of obstacles in your way to trip you up. But I know you'll make it."

"Thanks H.J., I'm sorry you didn't make it." I said as I got up and walked him to the door.

"Yeah, me too Nupe, me too." He shook my hand, opened the door, and then he left into the night.

Damn, if he didn't make it, was does that mean for me? I had a lot to think about after H.J. left. It was a long night.

⟨ ⟨ ⟨

Now I stood in front of those two apparatus. I'd come too far to falter now, especially when I knew other Black officers had failed to complete these two events, not just H.J. There were several other Black officers who had talked big, but didn't take the challenge of actually showing up for Ranger School. I had to give H.J. credit, at least he tried. But I couldn't fail…*no matter what.*

As I got closer to the steel tower, it seemed to loom far above me. The metal ladder, surrounded by bands of metal, appeared like a vertical silver tunnel, to keep the Ranger students from falling off the ladder.

When it was my turn, I grabbed that first rung and climbed as quickly as I could to the top. More difficult than I thought. I made it to the top, breathing hard. On the platform stood an RI, tasked to talk me through the device.

I looked around the wooden platform. I could see a lot of Fort Benning from up here. It extended farther into the air than it looked from down below.

The supporting metal pole rose another ten feet higher than the platform. The metal zip line extended down from the top of the pole, intersecting the platform at the edge, and continuing several hundred feet over the water to end at the tires. The tires looked a long way away.

A single metal rail surrounded the platform, designed to keep the Ranger student from falling off. Not too much comfort. The RI stood at the front edge of the platform, hooked into a stanchion to keep him from falling over the edge. He held the T-bar in his hand.

"What you waitin' for Ranger, get over here." He directed.

"Yes, sir." I said, and did a credible Airborne shuffle over to him, clinging to the rail. I would've preferred to crawl. I didn't like being up here. It must've shown on my face.

"You afraid of heights Ranger?" He grinned.

"No, sir!" I said, both of us knowing I lied.

"Ok," he grinned again, "sit right down here and grab onto the bar. When I say 'Go' you push yourself off in a good L-shaped position, just like jump school. Got it?"

"Yes, sir."

I sat down on the edge of the platform, reached up and grabbed the T-bar.

Once I was in position, the RI said, "Remember, when they say drop, you gotta drop or you'll slam into those tires. You don't want to do that. Got it?"

"Yes, sir"

"And make sure you yell 'Ranger' when you drop. Got it?"

"Yes, sir."

"Ok," he tapped me on the shoulder and yelled, "Go!"

I launched myself off the platform, put myself in the proper L-position, like jump school, and yelled "Ranger" all the way down. Within seconds I neared the bottom and the end rushed towards me as the RI on the shore yelled with his bullhorn, "Drop Ranger!"

I didn't think about it, I just dropped and hit the water at 30 mph. *Shit.*

The water was cold, but not the icy cold that H.J. experienced in February, when it was really cold. Once I hit the water, I stayed under to get my bearings, looked for my bubbles going upward and followed them up. I broke the water facing back towards the tower, got my bearings again, and swam to the shore.

I pulled myself out of the water. I had survived the Slide for Life. Now, the dreaded board walk and rope drop.

Similar to the Slide for Life, we were to climb up to a platform using a sturdy wooden ladder. Unlike the Slide for Life, no other support protected us as we climbed the 40 feet up the ladder.

We lined up in front of the Ranger drop as we came out the water. No chance to dry ourselves since we were about to go back into the water.

I watched as each of my classmates successfully negotiated the board and dropped from the rope. No hesitation from any of them. I hoped I looked as good when it came my turn.

When it was my turn, I didn't hesitate. The wet fatigues and water in my boots weighed me down, but I was determined to complete this event, no matter what. I climbed up the ladder. The forty-foot climb seemed interminable. At the top of the ladder I climbed through the rectangular hole in the platform and swung myself up onto the platform. An RI awaited me up there. He stood in the middle of the platform and signaled for me stay in place until it was my turn to go.

I watched as the student in front of me dropped from the rope with a loud "Ranger" and splashed into the water. He successfully swam to the side of the pond and climbed out without assistance.

The RI signaled me to walk to the end of the board. Finally, he said, unnecessarily, "Your turn Ranger. Go!" No further explanation needed.

Shit, here we go…

I moved to the end of the board and, unlike Gary, I didn't run, I walked forward with my eyes forward, and arms out for balance, to the three-block steps and had a clear view of the pond. At the three blocks, I dropped my arms, stepped up and over each of them very carefully. As I negotiated the rest of the board, I raised my arms out again and carefully walked to the end.

I really wanted to crawl, but I kept thinking, "*Courage is not the absence of fear, but overcoming one's fear.*"

That was my mantra during this ordeal. At the end of the board I had to look down to negotiate getting off the board and grab the rope to get into position to execute the underhand rope crawl. Not as easy as it sounds.

I dropped to my knees, grabbed the rope, and pulled myself to the rope. Once my feet reached the edge of the board where it met the rope, I swung my upper body underneath the rope, and then as my feet slid off the board, I hooked them on the rope by the ankles so that my body hung from the rope, upside down. I could now move along the rope, headfirst, towards the wooden Ranger Tab, using my hands to pull me, and my ankles to keep me anchored to the rope.

Once I got into position on the rope I easily crawled to the Ranger Tab and tapped it with my right hand. I disengaged my ankles first, one at a time, and carefully turned my hands to hang vertically from the rope, feet together, eyes forward. I yelled "Ranger" and waited on the command to drop. My eyes stared out to the front, not down at the water, while I waited.

After a moment, the RI on the shore with the bull horn yelled "Drop!"

I dropped and yelled "Ranger" again at the top of my lungs, kept my legs together, arms extended up, and hit the water. The drop to the water was both instantaneous and interminable. Once I hit the water, I immediately looked for the bubbles, and swam up to the surface, just like at the RGAFB pool and Fort Knox. I broke the surface facing the shore and easily swam to ladder. *That wasn't so bad*, I thought, *but I'm not doing that again…thank God!*

Everyone passed the water obstacles. They loaded us wet and happy into the trucks. One more step towards the Tab. We trucked back to our barracks and the RI's released us for our between-phase break. For a few hours we were on our own to eat and wash clothes. Once we got back, we packed our stuff and prepared for the several-hour bus ride to the Tennessee Valley Divide. To the mountains of Dahlonega, in north Georgia, at Camp Merrill, the Mountain Phase of Ranger School.

I had survived this far.

CHAPTER 31

"Dahlonega"

I was number one in the class coming out of Benning and apparently that was going to be a problem in Dahlonega. That was the word from Gary, who informed me of my ranking in the class based on my test scores, patrol grade, and peer evaluation. This time I nailed the peer evaluation—I had learned my lesson from Fort Knox and Riley. Gary pulled me into his office before we left Benning and let me know how I was doing.

"You're doing really well Ranger, you're number one in the class."

I just nodded, a glow of satisfaction in my brain.

"But that means you're going to be targeted by the RI's at Dahlonega. They don't like Black Ranger students and they will try everything to try to trip you up, so you need to be at your best the entire time. Especially if you're first in your class."

"Okay, got it. Thanks for the info. I'll do my best." *But,* I thought, *how could they really fuck with me as long as I performed the way I had in Benning?* I guess we'd have to see.

And with that in mind, I got on the bus with the rest of my platoon and tried to get some rest on the long bus ride to the Tennessee Valley Divide, the T-V-D.

The buses pulled up to our new area of torture, Camp Merrill. The air was cleaner up here, and the camp smaller. There was a small PX and medical clinic. Our new home was made up of squad-level metal and wooden structures we called "hooches." The camp was surrounded by magnificent Georgia pines that covered huge mountains that towered over the camp. The mountains looked insurmountable. I looked around in amazement. This was all new to me. This was going to be home for the next few weeks. I had made it to the second phase. Dahlonega.

We stood in formation as the busses drove away, and our new RI's gave us our hooch assignments. Not a Black face among them. Once they finished, we dragged our duffel bags to our assigned hooch, set up our bunks, and got ready for our orientation to the Mountain Phase of Ranger School.

Over the next two days the mountain RI's taught us various techniques in mountaineering techniques such as rappelling, two-party climbs using pitons, handholds, and ropes. We conducted two-party climbs up a 50-foot cliff with a belay man down below to ensure that if one of us let go of the rope or began to fall, then the job of the belay man was to pull on the rope connected to us to stop the fall.

They taught us how to use handholds offered by the natural crevasses in the rocks to climb; and how to pound in pitons and use them as a part of a climb. We became proficient in the myriad uses of the D-ring, not just in rappelling, but in all facets of mountaineering. The D-ring was a climber's best friend.

A final test of both our rappelling skills and our fear of heights would be going down the side of the 250-foot cliff of Yonah Mountain. It became more significant because it was done at night.

From every direction you could see Yonah towering above the Ranger Camp. A monolith worthy of proving the mettle of young Ranger students and our ability to withstand our fears of heights and the dark.

The RI's waited until we had finished our meal and dusk had fallen before loading us into the deuce and half's for our trip to the top of Yonah Mountain. We were dressed in our typical Ranger uniform, fatigues with the blouse worn outside the pants and sleeves down. We always wore our sleeves down to protect our arms from the sun, insects, and all the bushes, free-swinging limbs, and brambles that populated the forests and swamps of Georgia and Florida. This time we also wore our helmet liners to protect our heads during the long rappel down Yonah. Ranger students had died on Yonah, hence the helmet liners.

We took a circuitous route up and around the mountain, maybe to give us more of a feeling of ascension, and to heighten the experience. We drove for several minutes, and the anticipation grew with each passing minute. This would be the penultimate of rappelling, like what we would see in movies and on TV. Real Ranger shit.

As we arrived at the top, I could see a lighted area out the back of the truck, near the edge of the cliff. There were ten rappelling corrals with single lights next to each. Our trucks stopped well short of the lighted area, and we scrambled out into the low-light thrown off by the lanterns the RI's were using as illumination. Even with the lanterns it was pretty dark up there.

"Awright Rangers, line up in front of each station. We'll get you fitted with your rappelling seat, so you can take your trip down Yonah." One of the RI's said with a little chuckle.

The rappelling seat consisted of a ten-foot long, half-inch diameter piece of rope tied around the waist, and between your legs. Each of us lined up in front of one of the stations and awaited an RI to give us the rope so we could tie ourselves in.

"Here you go Ranger, tie yourself in." An RI threw me a rope to create my rappelling seat.

I caught the rope and began tying my seat. First around my waist, then between my legs, squat to pull the rope tight around my groin into a nice tight seat, so I could sit back in a good L-shape as I went down the mountain. The seat had to be tight, so the D-ring could be attached and the whole thing not fall apart during the rappel. Yeah, that would be unfortunate.

As each of us completed our seats, we raised our hands to signal we were ready for inspection.

"You ready Ranger?" An RI said as he walked up to me.

"Yes sir!" I replied.

"Let's check." The RI came up behind me and pulled the seat even tighter. "You got to make sure its tight Ranger. Until your nuts hurt. Do it again." He commanded.

Okay. This time I squatted even lower, and when I stood up I could feel the circulation to my testicles being cut off. Shades of torsion of the testes. Hell, I had been operated on for that very thing; but, if that's what he wanted that's what he got.

"Alright Ranger, I think you're ready." He said with a sadistic grin, and handed me my D-ring. "Snap it in. Make sure you have the opening up."

I snapped it in, and checked to make sure it was properly oriented, so it wouldn't release the rope on the way down. "Ready!" I said.

"Awright Ranger, take your place behind Station number 2."

I waddled over to Station 2 where another RI handed me a pair of leather gloves.

"Put these on Ranger."

The purpose of the gloves was to protect our hands from rope burn as the rope slid through our hands during the rappel. This was particularly significant given the length of this rappel.

At each station sat the anchor that would allow us to go over the side of the mountain. The anchor resembled the obstacles from the Run Dodge and Jump, but about four inches in diameter and driven into the rock at the edge of the cliff. The anchors stood about ten feet from the edge, which gave us plenty of space to walk back towards the edge before going over.

I watched the Ranger student in front of me get roped in. The RI took the rope near the anchor and looped it through the D-ring on the student's rappel seat. The student grasped the rope that lead from the anchor to his seat with his left hand, and grabbed the rope behind him and held it close to his back.

"Awright Ranger, start walking back towards the edge."

The student began shuffling back towards the edge, and when he got to the edge he began to lean back over the edge until he got into a L-shaped position. Once he was in position, he leapt off the edge into the darkness.

I stood there contemplating his fate until the RI at the anchor motioned me forward. The rope was taut as it bore the weight of my Ranger classmate.

"Ready Ranger?" He asked.

"Yes sir." I said.

"Okay, we need to wait until the rope goes slack, then we know your classmate made to the bottom."

"Yes sir."

As I watched, the rope became slack, and it was my turn.

"Okay Ranger, get in position in front of the anchor."

I moved in front of the anchor and he roped me in. I moved my hands into the proper position, and before he gave the commands I began to move towards the edge.

"Make sure you get in a good L-shaped position before going over the edge Ranger." He said as he followed me to the edge. Of course he was also roped in to the anchor as a safety precaution. His length of rope was longer, and he had a chain of D-rings connecting the rope and his rappel seat.

At the edge, I looked down and behind me. All a saw was darkness lightly illuminated by a mist. We were so high up there were clouds between me and the ground; and the darkness so black to make the ground invisible.

I inched my way backwards until I felt like I was going to fall, and used my abs to thrust my upper body forward to get that good L-shape position. Once there, I yelled, "On rappel!" and launched myself into the darkness.

Rappelling down the side of a mountain involved a series of smaller jumps. I propelled my self off the edge about 10 feet down and got my bearings. I let my eyes get adjusted to the darkness, so I could see the mountain on my way down. The cliff stared at me from four feet way. An unyielding monolithic behemoth waiting for me to make a mistake and go screaming down its side to my death. Well, that wasn't going to happen and I was going to disappoint the gods of Yonah that night.

I was in a good position and launched myself out again. This time closer to 20 feet. Each bound became longer and longer. I could see the bottom once I pierced the veil of the mist. There were lights down there and I could see faces turned upwards looking at me and the other Ranger students as we rappelled down Yonah. On each bound I felt my boots against the rock outcroppings of Yonah. Yeah, this was a rush that I didn't want to end, but as all good things it ended when I launched myself for the last time about 20 feet off the ground. Below me was another RI monitoring my progress. The bottom of the mountain was lit by another series of lanterns sitting on the ground. When my boots struck the ground, I released my rope and yelled, "Off rappel!" And backed away from the mountain. I had done it. I had conquered Yonah.

•   •   •

The other testable mountaineering skill was knot tying. The RI's put a special emphasis on tying several different types of knots and their purposes. They taught us how to build rope bridges from the most intricate to the simple one-rope bridge. In order to pass the knot test, you had to finish the knots within a certain period of time, and there could be no more than a 1-inch difference in the length of the two ends of the rope once tied. The ends of the rope were burnt to prevent fraying. My last experience with knots was as a Cub Scout, but I became so proficient in tying knots the RI's designated me as the student training assistant for the purpose of helping the other Ranger students pass the knot test. So, yeah, I knew my shit.

The rest of our training consisted of planning airborne and air assault operations in mountainous terrain, and patrol techniques in mountainous terrain. We also spent considerable time on terrain analysis and map reading, and took a refresher land nav course in mountainous terrain. We no longer did physical fitness training; we focused solely on performing our tasks and passing everything to move on to the next phase.

On the third day of training we went through a battery of tests to move forward to the patrolling phase of Camp Merrill. The rope bridge portion was a squad-level event which we passed with no problem. Then came the knot test.

The knot test consisted of Ranger students standing around a rope tied to a series of trees almost in the shape of a corral, where ropes hung for each student to execute the required knot—square knot, sheepshank, bowline, half hitch, two half hitches, round turn and two half hitches, clove hitch, slip knot, hitching tie, and running knot. I'd mastered all ten and maxed every practice test. I was very confident when my turn came to take the knot test. You had to pass at least eight to pass the test.

The white RI approached me as I stood by my knots on the corral. His name was Benson, and stood about six feet tall, was carrying a clipboard, and appeared to be chawing on something as he spoke.

"You ready, Ranger…?" He hesitated waiting for me to respond.

"Pittard, sir. Yes, I'm ready." I said as I turned towards my ropes. He made a notation on his clipboard.

"Alright, you may execute the knots," and then he named them in sequence. I had approximately five minutes to tie all the knots correctly.

Once I finished, I stood aside to let him inspect my work. He ambled over and looked half-heartedly at my knots.

"Ranger, three of your knots do not meet the minimum standard, you have failed the knot test," He pronounced in that irritating nasally twang they all seemed to affect up there, and made a notation on his clipboard.

What the fuck? Oh, hell no!

"You may retest this event whenever you feel you're ready. But if you fail again you will fail Ranger School." And with that he walked away.

Failed!? I screamed in my head, *Bullshit! I did not fail the fucking knot test. You fuckin' red necked sonofabitch! There were no knots that had more than a quarter inch difference on their ends much less a full inch! This is bullshit, bullshit, bullshit, bullshit…you damn right I'm gonna retest! I'm gonna retest right fuckin' now!*

That sonofabitch knew exactly who I was, and knew that he just knocked me out of the running for Honor Grad. You couldn't fail anything during Ranger School and be considered for Honor Grad. Wow! Gary was right, they were out to get me and they succeeded in the most insidious manner. Un-*fucking*-believable!

I immediately requested a retest, and it was granted. You couldn't fail the same test twice or you would be dropped from the course. I was not afraid of failing a second time regardless of who graded me. I took the test about an hour later, with the same RI, and of course I passed all ten knots. They looked almost the same as before, but the damage was done—I was no longer going to be an Honor Grad.

Damn.

❖　❖　❖

Later that day, the RI's gave me the honor of leading the first patrol from our platoon. Imagine that.

The patrol was a recon mission, to find an enemy encampment and report back what we found. I planned the mission, assigned the duties, and unlike other patrols, this one began in the latter part of the afternoon. Probably around 4 p.m., near quitting time for most of the people that worked at Camp Merrill, as we found out so dramatically.

Everything had gone according to plan as we formed up and began to move out of the assembly area. We crossed the line of departure on time and after we crossed the LD we moved into our staggered patrol formation in two teams. Unlike our previous patrols in Camp Darby or Rogers, our patrol route paralleled a main road from Camp Merrill to the town of Dahlonega, the same road used by civilian and military personnel leaving the post. My patrol was out in a field when some military vehicles came into sight. I signaled my patrol to get down because they could have been enemy patrols. No problem.

However, when several obviously civilian vehicles passed us I did not signal the patrol to get down. Apparently, some of those vehicles were driven by RI's and they communicated with Camp Merrill and informed them that they had seen my patrol in the field. Camp Merrill radioed my RI and let him know we'd been spotted by RI's on their way home, driving their civilian vehicles. The white RI informed me of this and gave me a NO GO on the spot. Now I was really fucked, and in danger of not even passing Ranger School. I had failed the knot test and now I had a No Go on my first patrol in the mountains. The RI relieved me and my assistant patrol leader took over, and completed the mission while I fell back as a part of the patrol. That was humiliating, which I'm sure was the point.

When we returned, there was nothing to say, we had to get ready for the next day.

❖　❖　❖

Gary came and found me while we planned for the next patrol, and took me off to the side out of earshot.

"How you holdin' up?" he asked.

"Ok I guess; but you called it, they were definitely out to get me." I replied.

"Yeah. When I heard about yesterday I told them that was bullshit. I've never heard of anyone given a no go for that reason and then relieved of their leadership. That was bullshit and I told them to back off." Gary was angry about what happened.

"What does that mean?" I asked hopefully.

"It means you'll get a fair evaluation on your next patrol. Your next patrol evaluators will be officers, so you'll get a fair shot."

"Okay." I smiled. *Hopefully not my former TAC from 7-80.*

"Oh yeah, and something else." He smiled back with a sly grin.

"What?"

"You're now the class S-4." His smile widened and I saw all his perfect white teeth. They were especially bright against his black skin.

I knew something was up. "What does that mean? What happened to the other guy?" I barely remembered the former S-4.

"He's gone. He was caught stealing and trying to sell the contraband that had been collected from the other students, so he's gone because of an honor violation."

"Why me?"

"I need someone I can trust, and who better than a Nupe?" He smiled again.

"Okay," I said. "It's on the Shield then."

"Yep." He said.

"Okay, what do I have to do?"

"When you're done with the mission planning come to the operations center and I'll get you with the RI in charge of logistics, okay?"

"Alright, I'll be there." I walked back to where they were still planning our next patrol.

✧   ✧   ✧

The Camp Merrill operations center was interesting. Not many Ranger students get the opportunity to see inside where they keep track of all the patrols, each student's progress, and the files on each student.

It was a one-story building made from logs. It reminded me of those log cabins pictured from the Civil War. The front door opened into the operations room abuzz with activity. Maps practically covered the largest wall of the operations center, depicting the terrain around Camp Merrill with patrol routes indicated with various colors. Ranger student names appeared on an adjacent wall, with patrols scheduled and evaluations next to each name. There were some missing spaces on the wall, presumably of students that were now gone.

RI's moved between the two areas making notations on the maps and by student's names. I could hear reports over Angry-77s, presumably from ongoing patrols, giving statuses and map positions. As reports came in, some RI's would make notations on the map. Others stood off to the side, conversing in low tones. I didn't see any Black RI's in the room. No surprise.

I didn't have much time to absorb all this before I heard in my ear, "Can I help you Ranger?" In that nasally twang I'd heard so much up here.

"Yes sir, I'm here to meet with the logistics RI?" That was a fancy way of saying supply sergeant.

"Oh yeah, okay, you're the new S-4. Hold on." He turned and looked around. "Hey Jim, the new S-4 is here." He called over to another RI who I'd observed earlier standing off to the side with his buddies.

"You Pittard?" The new RI asked as he wandered over from across the room. He was a white staff sergeant, about 5'8" tall and built like a fire plug. His cherubic face seemed to be almost like a little kid, kind of round with rosy cheeks.

His name tag said "Morris." *Like the Doors?* He reminded me of DS Youngblood. That couldn't be good.

"Yes sir." I stood a little straighter.

"Okay, follow me and I'll brief you on your duties." He turned towards the door and exited the operations center.

I followed him out of the operations center to an adjacent building. This one made of corrugated metal, like our hooches, except much larger. He opened the padlock on the door and we walked into an area that housed all kinds of supplies. Long metal counters stood in front of shelves that lined the walls stuffed with various items related to the class and its needs. C-ration boxes, boxes of LRRPs meals, replacement TA-50 equipment because of the frequency of loss or damage to Ranger student equipment covered the shelves. The inventory included D-rings, ropes, LBE, canteens, socks, belts, and some large plastic bags in the corner.

"You'll have the other key to this building while you're here."

"Really, why?"

"We need to have someone with immediate access in case I'm unavailable, and your tac officer trusts you. The last guy stole some stuff so he's gone."

Curiosity got the best of me. "What stuff?"

"See those bags over there?" He pointed at the large bags I had noticed earlier. "Those are the bags of collected contraband items like candy, gum, and other items that Ranger students are always trying to sneak in with or buy while they're here."

Yeah, we'd all been warned not to bring or buy certain items while in Ranger School, but Ranger students were always trying to get around the rules.

"That's a lot of stuff; all from my class?" I asked.

"Naw, that's probably stuff from the past few classes. We just keep it all together," he explained. He seemed to be an okay guy; not like DS Youngblood.

"What are my duties?"

"You're responsible for issuing equipment as necessary to your classmates, having them turn in old or damaged equipment, and sign for new equipment. You're also responsible for ensuring that the right amount of C-rats get issued for your classmates. You got that so far?"

I nodded.

He continued, "Make sure the squad leaders sign for the C-rats when you issue them. The squad leaders can distribute them to their squads. You need to make sure the squad leaders have a good count of their squad members. We can't have a surplus of C-rats in a squad because someone over counted. Lastly, you're responsible for the bags of contraband. We can't store it in here anymore, so, you'll have to store it in one of the unused hooches." As he went through his explanation he walked around the storage area, pointing out the various items and the hand receipt forms for the students to sign for the new equipment, and squad leaders to sign for the C-rats.

"I think I got it," I said, as I looked around the storage room. "But you'll be here during normal duty days?"

"Yeah, but you'll still be the guy issuing the equipment. I'll assist if necessary."

"Okay, and the bags?" I pointed at the three large bags.

"Get some of your Ranger buddies to help you move them to the new secure area. Here's the padlock for the hooch." He handed me a padlock and key. "Don't lose the key, or you'll have to pay for a new lock."

"Ok. Want me to move the bags now?"

"Yeah. Go get your crew and I'll wait here."

I ran from the supply room to my hooch and got my guys together. They were not happy about being detailed to help me with my new duties. I let them know we were moving the bags of candy and gum and I would have the only key. That seemed to perk them up. Beast, Richards, Dunn and Shorey came with me as we went back to the supply room.

Beast carried one of the bags, and the rest of us struggled with the other two. Once we got them to the unused hooch we dumped them on the cots to keep them off the floor in case of critters, and I locked up the hooch and put the key around my neck.

I don't know how the word got out, but I became the most popular guy in the class because I had the only key to the contraband. I had guys coming at me from all sides wanting to get me to give them some of the candy or gum. I turned down everybody, but I did hold a special place for my Ranger buddies. They would be able to share in my good fortune. Somehow, I knew these guys wouldn't rat on me and they didn't, and they reaped the rewards of being the squad members with the Class 8-80 S-4.

I mean there had to be some bennies associated with having to hand out supplies, and have people sign hand receipts. Yep, I put them all to work. I wasn't going to do all that shit by myself. But those guys could keep a secret and we were never caught with the contraband I took as our just due because of all this extra work. In fact, the RI's at Camp Merrill told me I was the best S-4 they'd seen. How ironic.

✧   ✧   ✧

My next turn as a patrol leader was a surprise. The first two times I had been the primary patrol leader involved in the planning and preparation of the patrol. Normally, the primary would take out the patrol and someone else would bring them back in, or in the case of my second patrol, I was relieved, and my assistant took over. On this occasion, I was a part of the planning because my squad and platoon mates discovered that I had a knack for planning patrols and writing up our ops orders, legibly using understandable language. Maybe my law school training. Anyway, I was always familiar with the plan and knew the objective and all the nuances of the plan. The patrol evaluators were two white officers, a captain who evaluated the patrol leader, and a lieutenant who evaluated the assistant patrol leader.

About halfway through this night patrol, the word came back for me to report up front from where I was acting as a regular rifleman in the patrol. When I got up there, the two evaluators sat with the patrol leader, an NCO from one of the Bats and the assistant patrol leader, Richards, an E from one of the Bats. As I came up they were looking at a map with red filters over their flashlights, to reduce the light signature at night. The red filters also had duct tape over them to reduce the signature even more to a slit of red light, emanating from the flashlight. They were also under a poncho to reduce the light signature even more.

As I got under the poncho with the other four, the white captain asked me, "Are you ready to take over as patrol leader?"

"Yes sir," I answered with some perplexity in my voice.

"You're taking over from Smith," he nodded towards the current patrol leader.

"Yes sir."

"Do you know the plan?"

"Yes sir."

"Do you know where we are?"

"Approximately sir, I'll have to look at a map to get myself oriented."

"Okay, you have five minutes to get oriented and briefed by Smith, then we head out. You got that Ranger?"

"Yes sir." I said. *Shit*, I thought, *now they're really trying to test me. What the fuck did I do to deserve this?*

I looked over at Smith and he didn't look happy. Yeah, I knew that feeling. I don't know what happened, but this patrol was mine now and I didn't plan to fuck this up. Over the next five minutes, Smith briefed me on the plan with both RI's listening in.

"This is where we are," he said and pointed to a place on the map. "And this is the objective." And pointed to an area circled in red on the map with the letters "OBJ."

"Yep, got it," I said. "We're conducting a raid on the enemy installation at the objective, destroy the installation, and kill anybody who's there, right?"

"You got it," he sighed. "The objective is still about three and half klicks away."

"Ok," I said. We'd traveled about one and half klicks already, so we still had a little ways to go.

He finished his briefing by making sure I understood the plan called for the patrol to be divided up into two sections, assault and support. I would lead the assault and my assistant patrol leader, Richards, would be in charge of the support section. Once we got to the RP, we were to get into position and then conduct the raid. After we completed the mission we were to withdraw back to the rally point, also called the RP, and then exfiltrate back to our lines.

After Smith's briefing, I said, "Okay, I'm up to speed."

"Then get it on the road Ranger," the RI said.

My first action after we came from under the poncho, and I regained my night vision, was to move to the front of the patrol to where the point man was kneeling. In almost each patrol, the formation was a staggered single file, with a point man out front guiding the patrol. Typically, the patrol leader was the third man in line—close enough to keep control of the point man, but not so close to be killed if the point man was taken out by a land mine or ambush.

The point man on this patrol was Cummings, a Black SSG, who was trying to get into one of the Bats. He was a dark-skinned, handsome, intelligent guy who could think on his feet, and didn't need a lot of guidance. I was happy he was point.

When I got up to his position, he was facing out away from the patrol, and I tapped him on the shoulder. "I'm the new patrol leader." I said.

"Pittard?" He said as he turned towards me.

"Yeah, you okay to continue point?"

"Yeah, I'm good. What's going on?" He asked.

"They relieved Smith and I'm taking over," I responded. Enough chit chat, time to go, the RI was watching. "What's the next major terrain feature?" I asked.

"There's a creek about half a klick from here in that shallow valley," He said.

"Okay, and then we turn north towards that ridge that borders the enemy installation on the west, correct?" I asked for confirmation to make sure we were on the same sheet of music.

"Yes, about three and half klicks from here," he correctly responded.

"Okay." I slapped him on the back. "Let's get them up and moving."

Cummings stood up, and gave the "get ready to move" signal with his hand, and the Rangers passed it back to the end of the patrol.

One of the unique items of the Ranger School uniform was the patrol cap. The cap, made from softer material than the regular fatigue hat, lay more squarely on one's head than the fatigue hat. In addition, the patrol cap, with its shorter bill, was more resistant to the tribulations one might face in the woods. On the back of each patrol cap were the "Ranger Eyes." Ranger Eyes consisted of two vertical rectangular pieces of luminescent tape, sewn on the back of each Ranger student's patrol cap. They allowed us to follow one another at night, even through dense foliage. Tonight was no exception. Up here in the TVD, there was a coolness in the air, and we kept our sleeves down for warmth and protection. The night sky was barely illuminated with a pale light from a thumbnail sliver of moon, showing through the cloud cover. On the ground, it was dark as hell.

There was so little light, we had to rely on our night vision and our intimate knowledge of the terrain to help us navigate. That's why it was so important to have a good point man to help navigate in such difficult, mountainous terrain, without the benefit of night vision goggles.

When I saw the patrol was up, I gave the signal to move out, and we started moving towards the creek down below.

I kept a silent count of how many meters we traveled over the mountainous terrain. That wasn't always easy, because as the contour lines on the map showed, we were going up and down many a hill or ridgeline as we conducted this patrol. Within 500 meters of where I took over, Cummings signaled the patrol to halt. At that point, everyone knelt and assumed a defensive posture facing outwards.

I moved up to his position to find out what was going on.

"Creek should be down there," he said. "Thought you would want to recon."

"Yep," I said. "Let me get Richards up here to hold down the fort until we get back." I sent a message along the patrol to have Richards come forward.

Within a few seconds, Richards knelt next to me. "What's up?"

"Cummings and I are going to recon the creek. Set up the support team over there to the south to overwatch us while we're down in the valley," I directed.

"Okay," Richards said. "Anything else?"

"Yeah, it's yours 'til I get back." And with that, Cummings and I began moving towards the bottom of the shallow valley, where the creek swirled on its southward journey.

Moving down the ridgeline towards the creek was not easy. We had to fight the steepness of the side of the ridge, the vines, overturned tree trunks, roots, and other vegetation strewn in our way, at night, while trying to be somewhat stealthy. We picked our way through all those obstacles as we got down to the bottom of the ridge. I could hear the trickling sound of water beyond the denser foliage that was sure to guard our approach to the creek. The RI captain was right behind us, watching everything I did.

As we approached the area where we thought the creek flowed, I let Cummings take the lead to find a way through the dense vegetation. He got down on his belly and crawled up to the denser foliage to make sure the creek was on the other side. I could barely see his Ranger eyes to keep track of his progress. Once he positioned himself and could observe the creek, he signaled me to move forward.

Like him, I crawled forward on my belly and joined him at the edge of the creek bank. Once I had the creek in sight, it looked wider than I had imagined from the map recon. It was big enough to be considered a stream, which may have required a different approach to crossing. Originally, the plan called for a fording of the creek because all indications had it only a few feet deep. However, this stream looked to be deeper than six feet, which would mean a swimmer crossing with a rope and the rest of us using the rope to cross. That would complicate matters and cause a delay in crossing.

"What do you think?" I asked Cummings. "Shallow enough to ford?" "Don't know," he said. "Better if I get down there and find out."

"Okay, be careful of the current," I said unnecessarily. We'd all heard the tales of how Ranger students had drowned in just this situation, because they hadn't anticipated the strength of the currents and got swept away and drowned. That had happened in Florida, crossing the bigger rivers we would eventually face, but it could also happen in this little stream, just like drowning in a bathtub with a few inches of water.

"Got it," Cummings responded, and began to carefully pick his spot to go into the water. He had a walking stick with him that he used to help "break bush" while on point. The sucker was about six feet long, so he used that from a prone position on the bank to probe the depth of the water.

He stuck it down like an oil dipstick trying to determine the level of the water. Once he pulled it back out, he felt the length of it to determine where the water began and ended.

He pointed to about halfway up the stick, and said, "Looks like about three feet, I think we can wade across."

"Okay, good. I'm going to go get the assault team to cross, then the support team. Stay here. You'll lead them after I bring them down."

"Okay," he said, and turned back towards the creek to continue to watch for any enemy activity before we crossed.

I made my way back up the ridge to where the rest of the patrol waited.

I informed Richards, "We can ford the creek, so I'm going to bring down the assault team, secure the far side, then have you bring down the support team. Keep overwatch until I give you the signal to come down."

"Will do," he said, and went to tell the support team.

I moved up to where the assault team waited and quickly briefed them on the plan to cross. It was basically the same plan discussed during the planning stage, but sometimes plans change once you're in the field. I wanted them to know of any differences in what we planned, versus what was actually on the ground.

Once they were briefed, we all moved down towards the creek. Once we reached Cummings, he and the assault team leader briefly conferred. They decided they would be the first to cross and establish positions on the other side while the rest of the team crossed. He and Cummings slipped into the water with their weapons held high, while me and the rest of the assault team covered their crossing from the near bank. Within a few minutes they were across, and quickly moved out 50 meters beyond the far bank to establish a defensive perimeter.

Once they were down, I signaled the next two to cross, and the assault team crossed in kind until everyone was safely across and in position on the far side. I then turned back to the ridge and gave Richards one flash with the filtered red light to have the support team make its way down the ridge to the creek and prepare to cross.

Once they were down with me, I crossed with one of the support team. Richards stayed back to command the support team and cover our crossing. As I slipped into that waist-high icy water, and held my rifle above my head, it reminded me of the film I saw of Ranger students lo those many years ago in the darkened classroom at Eastwood. This was my third patrol, but this one reminded me most of the movie. I felt a rush of adrenaline. I was really doing it, becoming an Army Ranger. Unbelievable.

I executed the rest of the plan flawlessly and received an "Honor Grad Go" from the white captain RI. He was very complimentary on my ability to handle adversity, particularly when I had to assume the mission in the middle of the patrol, and after he killed off Richards before the assault. He said he liked the way I made Cummings my assistant patrol leader, to keep the continuity of the patrol and to accomplish the mission. His comments felt good, and told me I knew what I was doing, and could do the job when given a fair chance to perform.

The rest of the time in Dahlonega was uneventful. I didn't have any more patrols because of the Honor Grad Go, so I concentrated on helping all my squad mates pass their patrols and performed my duties as S-4.

One of the challenges of being in Dahlonega was going up and down the damn mountains on patrol. That had to be one of most taxing things I had done in my life. Many times, particularly if I wasn't in a leadership role, I could just concentrate on putting one foot in front of the other as we went up and down the Tennessee Valley Divide. Sometimes I used my rifle as a crutch, to get up mountains where it seemed the ground was in my face because of the steepness of the gradient.

Many times, because I was so tired and hungry, I constantly thought of food. By that time, we ate two scant meals per day—usually a hot breakfast and LRRPs later in the day. Our operational tempo remained 20 hours a day, so we burned a lot of calories. Late at night, when I was really hungry, I imagined several types of snacks, like Oreos and Chips Ahoy, but my favorite was Fig Newtons, not my fiancé, Fig Newtons. Oh well, that's what happens when you're really hungry. Thank goodness for the contraband.

One of the traditions at Camp Merrill at Dahlonega, was leaving messages in the hooches. In each of the hooches there were messages left by previous classes and Ranger students. The messages typically told you their names, and class number. Some told you their school or their unit. I thought I would leave a unique message, not for myself, but for my brother, Dana. I knew, at some point, he would come through Ranger School, and I wanted to give him a motivational message. I got a black marker, and in the hooch where I stored all the contraband, left him a message.

It read, "**Drive on Ranger Pittard, USMA Class '81/ from Ranger Pittard, Class 8-80.**" I wrote it on two lines on the right-hand side of the hooch about halfway up from the floor; and about a third of the way along the side of the wall from the door.

I knew approximately when he might come through Ranger School, probably in late 1981 or early 1982, but of course I couldn't know which class number. Instead, I used his graduation year and the fact he was from West Point, the United States Military Academy, and my class number. Very few of my classmates knew I had put that message in there, since no one had access to that hooch but me. But those that did, thought it was pretty cool. It was almost like a time capsule for my brother and I hoped it might motivate him if he ever got down while up here in the mountains of northern Georgia.

I passed this phase of Ranger School, but I did not come out of it unscathed. But as I learned from the poem **Invictus**, *"my head was bloody, but unbowed."* I felt ready for the challenges of the last phase of Ranger School.

Florida here I come. Hooah!

CHAPTER 32

"Florida"

I'd never been to the state of Florida, and now would invade that state through the art of the vertical envelopment. In other words, we would make a mass tactical jump from a series of C-141s, at night, from Fort Benning. Alrighty then. This presented a new wrinkle in my experience as an airborne soldier. Well, that's what Rangers do, the hard shit.

After we returned to Benning from Dahlonega, we took our break between phases. The RI's allowed us to leave the Ranger training facility, get a regular meal, and wash our clothes. That's just about all the time you have to feel somewhat normal. Then it's back to work.

We got a decent night's sleep; then spent the better part of the day planning an airborne mass tactical operation involving the entire class, except the "dirty legs," the non-airborne qualified students. They were trucked into Florida. For those of us who were true "airborne" Rangers, our mission was an airborne infiltration behind enemy lines to invade the territory of the Escambian army, the mythical bad guys while we conducted operations in Florida. Camp Rudder is located at Auxiliary Field #6 at Eglin AFB in the panhandle of Florida near Panama City, Florida. Our airborne insertion introduced us to the Florida phase, better known as the "swamp" or "jungle" phase of Ranger School.

The drop zone, was a large white sandy area easily seen from the C-141 as we exited the aircraft. This was my ninth jump. We had an additional airborne operation in the mountains, which gave me more experience jumping with full equipment and weapons. Once we got off the drop zone we established defensive positions, before we moved out on our patrol which ended up at Camp Rudder. The Florida RI's assigned us four-man rooms in the barracks where we would be staying over the next few days while we underwent the training necessary for us to survive the next two weeks.

The next few days involved a whirlwind of training on skills that would be important during the Florida phase. The tactical portion of the Florida phase would be conducted through a 12-day patrol, an extremely long patrol punctuated by different missions each day and most nights. The RI's trained us on the Florida terrain including the many rivers and swamps, and crossing rivers using one-rope bridges. They trained us on indigenous reptiles, such as alligators, coral snakes, eastern diamondback rattlesnakes, water moccasins and copperhead snakes. That was fun being around all the reptiles in the Reptile House. I didn't have an unnatural fear of snakes like many people, probably from my experiences with snakes as a kid. Although when the RI's asked, I did not volunteer to hold the six-foot long poisonous snakes. I didn't have to prove my manhood that badly.

The RI's demonstrated how to track enemy combatants through the woods and swamps, including what signs to look for on the ground and on bushes and low-lying tree branches. In addition to tracking the enemy, the RI's taught us how to evade and escape from the enemy. The RI's took us through survival, escape, resistance and evasion (SERE) training, techniques we would use during the 12-day patrol and assembling and detonating explosive devices. RI's strapped us into Hueys and taught us "fast roping" techniques from hovering helicopters—helicopter rappelling from thirty to fifty feet from the ground. All exciting stuff!

Real Ranger shit.

Finally, as a part of our training on how to navigate the many rivers in and around Eglin AFB, the RI's put us through inflatable rubber boat training. Initially we trained on the white beaches of the Gulf of Mexico. We did exercises with the 8-man rubber boats to familiarize ourselves with the boat. Then we took the boats into the Gulf: learned to enter and exit the boat, and to get back in after the boat capsized, guide them back to the shore, and bring them aground on the beach.

The next phase of the rubber boat training involved putting the boats on a river and navigating the river using the techniques learned in the Gulf on how to row in unison and guide the boat. The squad designated me coxswain, in charge of our squad's boat, and I had to learn to guide the boat and keep the rowers in sync to maximize their efforts. We would use the rubber boats on at least one mission during the 12-day patrol.

And that was next.

✧　✧　✧

The first mission of many during this 12-day FTX, a night helicopter insertion and reconnaissance mission, took the better part of one day to plan. As we got our rucks to depart the barracks for the last time for the next two weeks, the RI's instructed us to leave a spare pair of jungle boots on our bunks. If we needed them, we could tell the RI's and they would retrieve the boots and bring them out to us. A good idea in concept, not so good in execution as I would find out.

The next several days were a montage of patrols, platoon-level missions, raids, another helicopter jump, a partisan link up, using the 8-man rubber boats in the Yellow River, recon patrols, stream crossing exercises, and digging defensive positions during the day in the hot and sandy wasteland around the swamps. The operational tempo was closer to 22 hours a day, and down to one meal a day.

We also had fun in the swamps. Conducting operations when you're suffering from sleep deprivation, and a lack of food was one thing, but to have to do it in the swamps added an additional level of excitement. We faced the challenge of traversing swampy areas up to our chests, and making our way through submerged wooded areas where the footing was treacherous, especially at night. On one occasion, when I plopped down to take a position, the ground wriggled under me as a snake escaped, probably as surprised as me. I didn't jump up and scream, but froze in place as it kept moving. I just exhaled as it slithered away and continued the mission. Charlie Mike.

I didn't know what a deer fly was until I got to Florida. A deer fly is an insect, kind of between a mosquito and a creature from hell. They were green and gold and had a proboscis that seemed to be half their body length and were relentless in their pursuit of human flesh. They seemed to be everywhere and threatened to drain all the blood from your emaciated body if you weren't careful.

We operated in the heat of the day with our jungle fatigue sleeves rolled down to protect us from these creatures and wore "bug juice" like cheap cologne. But to no avail. Those things would ride on your weapon just waiting for a chance to attack you and they would look at you with those beady, little insect eyes just hungrily awaiting the dinner bell to ring. Thank goodness I never ended up on the menu.

❖   ❖   ❖

Speaking of menu, about half way through the 12-day FTX we had our Survival Day, where we had to catch, kill, and eat our food for that day. We staggered into a large assembly area after a night patrol and road march. We road marched practically everywhere and with very little sleep and food, so staggered is probably the right term. As we entered the assembly area we passed fenced in areas filled with chickens and rabbits, blissfully unaware of the hungry expressions on our faces and intentions in our minds—FOOD!

As S-4, yes, I was still the class S-4; I ensured our one-meal-a-day rations reached us in a timely manner. The RI's positioned our meals in a secure location for us to pick up each day, or they trucked them to us in our defensive positions while we planned for the next mission. We could cook the C-rats and became very creative in making these C-rats more palatable. Yeah, there was nothing like "beanie weenies" or the ham and potatoes, and we loved to do creative cooking with the cheese, crackers, and other condiments we carried to flavor our meals. As a change, the class looked forward to the days when I issued LRRP meals, which had a different flavor and consistency.

On this day, we dropped our gear in our designated squad areas and formed up for our classes in survival. The RI's conducted these classes in outside classrooms with raw wooden benches and outlined by logs on the ground. Each hour we rotated from classroom to classroom. The RI's taught us how to kill small animals like rabbits by breaking their necks, and then draining the blood. They taught us how to kill and defeather chickens and drain the blood. They used live animals for those classes. I guess that was their dinner that day.

They also taught us how to catch or trap other small animals, using snares and other devices. This was all very interesting, but we wanted to get to the food part and eat. We had gotten hungrier after seeing the RI's kill the rabbits and chickens. This would be our best meal of the entire 12 days.

Once they released us from the survival class, the RI's informed each squad they were authorized one chicken and one rabbit to eat. The RI's also authorized a couple of large potatoes, carrots, and onions per squad. The RI's also told us that we could eat anything else we caught. In our squad, the squad leader gave me the assignment to capture and kill the rabbit. I guess someone thought I would be squeamish about killing the animal with my bare hands. Nope, that wasn't the case.

My attitude was, it's either him or us, and we were hungry. I had no qualms about sacrificing the rabbit for our meal. I entered the rabbit compound and looked around for a nice fat rabbit. I spotted a healthy-looking specimen and made my way over to it. The rabbit started to hop away, but it was not like the jack rabbits back home that could outrun a cheetah. This one was relatively slow, and it didn't take me long to grab it up with both hands. As I took it out of the compound, the rabbit kicked and struggled, but I held on to it until I got back to our squad assembly area, where the rest of the squad was firing up the stew pot.

We decided on a stew rather than roasting the rabbit and chicken, because we felt that would make the food last longer. The stew pot, an empty ammunition can, could hold all the necessary ingredients for our stew. The guy who caught the chicken told his story of chasing the chicken around the chicken enclosure until he finally caught it by the fence and killed it on the spot because of all the squawking and flapping. He had bitten the head off in true Ranger fashion. In my case, the rabbit had calmed down and was no longer struggling, maybe resigned to his fate.

One of my squad members said, "You going to make him a pet or we going to eat him?"

"Oh, we're going to eat him," I said.

I held the rabbit in my left hand with its neck exposed and hit him with a knife hand strike on the back of his neck where, we were taught, would break his neck, and watched as the blood started to run from its mouth and nose. It had stopped moving. Yeah, it was dead. I tossed the carcass to the designated skinner who was already working on the chicken, and I went in search of some water to wash my hands.

I found a creek not too far away from the assembly area and washed my hands. When I got back, the chicken had been cut up, the rabbit skinned and cut up, and both were in the pot boiling with the onions, carrots and potatoes. We seasoned the stew with pepper and salt from our C-rats and put in any other ingredients we thought might be tasty.

As we sat there waiting on the food to be ready, a grasshopper passed by and remembering my experience with fried grasshopper, I picked it up and threw it in the pot. About that time, a guy from another squad came by with a bull snake he had just killed and wanted to know if we wanted to use part of it for our pot. Oh, hell yeah! I gave him my Snake Sticker to skin the snake and cut it up. He cut it up in half and gave that to us. So, we put some snake in the pot. This was going to be interesting.

All of us had metal canteen cups and metal eating utensils, so when the stew was ready we dipped our canteen cups in to get our share. The stew took about an hour and a half to cook because of the toughness of the meat and the potatoes. The consistency of the stew wasn't what I remembered from home. It looked more like soup than stew, but that was okay, we were hungry. I got my canteen cup and made sure I got some chicken, rabbit, potatoes, carrots and onions. I wasn't sure if I got any snake, and couldn't see any remnants of the grasshopper, but I imagined it was all in there.

The flavor wasn't bad. It reminded me of a thin soup. We hadn't let it cook long enough. The meat was still a little tough, the potatoes not soft, and the carrots chewy. The fire we created, although made the water boil, and with the ammunition can closed acted as a pressure cooker, may still not have been hot enough. Or maybe we didn't let it cook long enough because we were hungry. Regardless, it was delicious!

We all ate too much, and almost immediately my stomach gurgled. Uh oh!

Yeah, I had to find somewhere private to rid myself of the food I had just eaten. Apparently, something didn't agree with my digestive system, and I had a case of the GI runs. Oh well, it was good while it lasted.

❖   ❖   ❖

Once I had eaten and dealt with my loose bowels, my duties as the S-4 kicked in and I was responsible for distributing three meals for each Ranger student, which would hold each of us over the next three days. Yeah, back to one meal per day for the next three days. Not much food, but that's what we were authorized for the next three days. I made the distribution after we had formed back up, before heading out on the next phase of the 12-day patrol. I put my three meals next to my ruck after having distributed the meals to my platoon and went to ensure the rest of the class got their meals. When I returned to my rucksack, which was on the end of the squad, my meals were gone. I could not believe it. Shit!

I looked over at the platoon next to mine and the closest squad was the all-Marine squad. They just looked over at me and laughed. I knew they had taken the meals, but I couldn't prove anything. Since I was the S-4, I knew there were no more meals available. I went to the RI's to see if there were any leftover meals after explaining my problem and they told me, as I already knew, I was shit out of luck. I think they got a kick out of my dilemma. *Fuck 'em.*

I also informed them of my need for my second pair of boots from my bunk back at Auxiliary Field #6. The white RI in charge said he would make sure they were brought out to me the next morning. My feet began to develop pain on the bottom and I thought it was a good time to use my second pair of brand new boots.

Over the next few days, until we got our next food drop, which I planned and executed, my Ranger buddies shared small portions of their C-rats with me. Mostly crackers, cheese, and peanut butter—shades of NMMI—but it kept me going, and as a side benefit, kept me stopped up. No more GI runs. Maybe this was their way of repaying me for the contraband I had given them. You never knew when a good deed would be returned.

Unfortunately, along with the lack of food, over the next few days my feet got worse. In each boot, a part of the sole of the boot had twisted loose, and it felt like a nail in the soles of my feet. The pain was in both feet. Each morning when the RI's came out to our assembly area, I requested my secondary boots from the departing RI's, and was always promised they would bring them out. That didn't happen, and I continued to move forward with the mission with these boots, even though they caused me a lot of pain with every step. I endured in silence and continued the mission. Charlie Mike.

The next important training event was our second exposure to SERE. We had been trained earlier in the concepts and taught basic evasion, resistance and escape techniques, and now we would use them. We had done the "survival" part of the training, and now we had a chance to do the rest at night.

The objective of the operation was to traverse a five-mile exercise area without getting caught. Unlike Fort Knox, troops would pursue us on the ground, in vehicles, and by helicopters with search lights—a whole array of obstacles to overcome. Not only did we have to make it past all the enemy troops looking for us, we actually had to navigate to the end point, and do it within a certain period of time or we would be disqualified and considered captured. They had set up a POW camp, and if we got captured we had to spend time in the camp as POW's and attempt to resist any interrogation, and possibly escape. I did not want to be caught and get subjected to that shit.

They paired each of us with a Ranger buddy. In my case, it was Beast. They assigned each team a number, gave us an opportunity to do a map reconnaissance, figure out the proper azimuth, and gave us a time limit to complete the course.

The RI's held us back until the time to leave. As we stood there, I told Beast our initial azimuth loud enough for the RI's to hear. Once when we were given the word, we took off in the given direction. We were dressed in our fatigues, with shirts out, patrol caps, black and green jungle boots, and faces and hands bathed in green and black camo. Once we got into the bush we would be hard to spot from the ground.

After about a half a click, out of site of the RI's at the start point, I stopped Beast and said, "Okay, we need to come up with a plan to keep from getting captured."

"Agreed. What do you suggest?" He asked.

For me, this was different from Fort Knox. We were in the final phase of Ranger School, and Bestian had proven himself to be quite capable in the field. I had no qualms about being paired up with him. I knew we could be successful evading the enemy forces.

"I did this once before, we need to avoid roads or any well-travelled areas or trails." I said.

"Okay, pretty obvious, what else?" He asked.

"We need to move in bursts, then stop to listen for sounds of the enemy," I continued.

"Okay, makes sense," Beast said.

"If we hear something, hit the ground immediately. Movement draws their attention," I continued. "I think we need to do something a little different."

"What's that?"

"They're going to expect us to move in the direction we left, right?"

"Yeah, so what?"

"And we know they're in radio communication with the RI's and enemy troops, right?"

"Yeah, get to the point, we're running out of time." Beast sounded exasperated.

"Let's double back and set off at a 90-degree azimuth, then circle around to our original direction." I suggested. I had been thinking of those damn jackrabbits at home, and how they had tried to outsmart us by doing that very thing.

Beast thought about it. "Okay, I like the idea. There isn't much cover out here, so we're gonna have to outsmart them. Let's do it."

"I got the azimuth already set, okay?"

He nodded his agreement, and we set out back towards the start point.

Our advantage was not being the only team out there, so the enemy's resources would be limited. We figured that if we could evade the initial attempt, we could be good for the rest of the course. We set out with our heads on a swivel and our ears on alert.

Once we got back near the start point, we set the new azimuth, and set out as fast as we could in that different direction.

Within a few minutes we heard the distinctive sounds of a helicopter approaching. Earlier we had discussed what to do if a helicopter approached with its searchlights. We decided we would find a depression in the ground and freeze.

"Hear that?" Beast asked.

"Yeah, shit, copters." I said. "Get down. Hide"

As soon as we saw the searchlights, we found low areas in the ground with plenty of brush and kept as still as possible. Overhead the "chukka chukka chukka" of the helicopter and the bright light of searchlight sought us out. Fortunately, the searchlight did not linger on us and continued on to its next potential victims.

"You okay?" Beast asked as we shook the dirt off while getting up.

"Yeah, I'm fine, let's keep moving. Keep an eye out for ground troops." I warned.

At that point, it was time to start circling around to our original azimuth. I set our next azimuth and we set off again.

In conjunction with the helicopters, were the ground troops and vehicles in radio communication with each other. Once the helicopter passed by, we got up and watched its progress across the course. At one point we saw it swoop down and capture some unlucky Ranger students in its splash of light and we could see vehicles moving towards that location.

"You see that?" Beast asked.

"Yeah, that could have been us." I breathed a sigh of relief.

"Let's keep moving." Beast said, and we continued on our way.

We had no other incidents of potential detection. We continued our techniques of evasion and made it to the end of the course in plenty of time. Unfortunately, not all our Ranger buddies were as fortunate. They regaled us with tales of their capture, detention, and interrogation at the hands of the evil Escambian army. The captured ones were eventually released and returned to our assembly area. I'm glad I didn't go through that. Whew!

❖   ❖   ❖

By this time our bodies and minds began to feel the effects of the 12-day patrol. We'd been out about nine days at this point and had been on the go almost continuously from day one. We were also getting pretty ripe. Even though we washed up every day, that still didn't hide the stench of being in the field for nine straight days without proper bathing. But you get used to the sharp odor of the unwashed.

Although my graded patrol was early on and I had received an Honor Grad Go, every patrol leader, on each patrol, each day, used me in a non-graded leadership capacity. In the platoon-sized patrols, the graded positions were the patrol leader, assistant patrol leader, and each squad leader, a total of five positions.

Each squad leader needed team leaders. For every mission, the squad leader designated me to perform as a team leader. No one else in our platoon was used as a team leader for every patrol. On one occasion, I overheard some of my classmates discussing me.

"What about Pittard as team leader?" One tasked as squad leader asked.

"Yeah, he's pretty good. You can rely on about 90 percent of what he says." Another said.

"Yeah, he's accurate damn near all of the time. If you want to pass, you need to make him one of your team leaders." A third said.

I had to smile to myself as I walked away; I'd come a long way since those days at Fort Knox and Fort Riley when my peers shunned me as being too young and too cocky. Now, my Ranger classmates coveted those same qualities.

In addition to performing as team leader, my classmates usually brought me in for the planning phase because of my knack for planning good ops and, in particular, writing good op orders. I either wrote or co-wrote all the op orders for my squad and platoon. Who knew good writing skills would be important in Ranger School? That good ole' law school training I guess. But my constant stints as a team leader really taxed me physically and mentally. Team leader positions were not graded but the team leaders had to know what was going on, had to stay awake to supervise their teams, and had to make the squad leader look good so he could get his Go on his patrol. Which meant I got no sleep and worked like a dog for the first nine days of the 12-day patrol. Something had to give.

While out on a night assault on Day 10, I finally "zombied-out." The sleep deprivation, lack of food, and the stress of being "on" for every mission, more so than anyone else in my platoon, finally took its toll.

We had stopped in a single line while waiting on the patrol leader to do his leader's recon of the objective. When we lay down, that was it for me, I "zombied" out. I had used all my reserves and had nothing left. When the platoon got up, my team and anyone behind us didn't move because they were waiting on my signal to get up. But I was out and didn't initially respond to any efforts to rouse me. When I finally got up, I looked behind me and saw the rest of the patrol get up with me. Damn, I'd almost fucked this thing up. The rest of night assault was a blur. I remember lights, and firing and moving, but I have no further memory of that mission. Somehow I made it to our assembly area, and the RI's informed the platoon that I was not to be used in a non-graded leadership position for the rest of the patrol. Apparently, they kept tabs on who was in the non-graded positions and noticed that I had been in a leadership position for every patrol up to that time. From then on, I was just a grunt and could relax a little bit for the rest of the patrol.

That next morning, Day 11, I again asked for my boots and was told by the departing white RI's that they would be sent out. We dug defensive positions in the sandy area while the patrol was being planned, and my boots did not appear with any RI's who came out to our area. Part of this mission was a ten-kilometer road march, more than six miles. I dreaded the road march because my feet started to feel like hamburger and stayed in constant, excruciating pain.

Imagine if you can, that each step felt like a nail sticking into your foot, and that is what my feet felt like during that six-mile road march. I kept my head down and literally gritted my teeth against the pain. In my mind I pictured myself in a hospital bed again, recovering from whatever damage was being done to my feet. I remembered the gruesome films from JROTC on trench foot, and watching how soldiers' feet were literally pulled apart because they failed to take care of them. I almost wanted to cry with that thought, but I kept my head down. I was not going to fail—I WAS NOT GOING TO STOP NO MATTER WHAT! That became my mantra. I had come too far and endured too much to fail now. So, I put one foot in front of the other for the longest six miles of my young life. This was worse than going up Agony or Misery at Knox. This *was* agony and misery. That ruck felt like it weighed a ton, and almost delirious with the pain in my feet, I made the 10K road march, one of the most difficult physical tasks I had ever accomplished. I didn't complain to my Ranger buddies, but they could clearly see I was in extreme pain. It was etched in my face, with sweat dripping from the effort, but no one could do anything about it, and I continued to endure.

We performed another night raid where we sent a snatch team into a fortified compound to rescue a prisoner. I was in the support team and overwatched the assault team and snatch team as they did their thing. The raid was successful and we moved five klicks back to our defensive positions for the night. Another fucking road march and I could barely feel my feet. That was even scarier than the earlier pain. When we got to our defensive positions I collapsed into my foxhole and passed out.

The next morning, Day 12, the last day of the patrol, Gary came out to see how we were doing, and stopped by my position. I had my boots off, looking at the bottom of my feet.

"How you holdin' up?" He asked.

"My feet feel like shit. I've been road marching in these same fuckin' boots for the past three days. I've been trying to get these damn RI's to bring me out my second pair of boots and they haven't done it." I said pointing to my feet.

He looked at the bottom of my feet and I thought he would blow a gasket.

"Who were the RI's?" He demanded.

"Smith, Davis and Brown," I told him. I had memorized those names, and burned their faces into my mind.

"Alright, I'm going to get to the bottom of this bullshit. Do you want me to take any action against those guys?" He asked.

"No, I just want my damn boots," I answered.

He immediately went back to Camp Rudder to get my boots and raise a little hell with the white RI's. Yeah, every RI I had talked with had been white. Although there had been Black RI's, the NCOICs had been all white, and they were the ones I had asked and had failed to produce my boots. Coincidence? Doubtful.

In the meantime, two medics showed up at our platoon area looking for me. One taller than the other, both white Spec4's.

"Who's Pittard?" The taller medic asked.

I heard them from my position, "Yeah, that's me," I said as I sat up in my foxhole.

They walked over to my position, "You need to come with us." The shorter one said.

"Why?"

"We've been ordered to give you immediate medical attention for your feet. Apparently, they're in pretty bad shape." The taller one said.

"Yeah, that's a no-shit statement," I responded. I began to slowly climb out of my foxhole.

They watched me as I got to my feet and saw how tenderly I stood up.

"Hurts pretty bad?" The shorter one said, almost unnecessarily.

"Yeah," I said. "It hurts like hell."

"Okay. Bring your ruck, I don't think you're coming back here." The taller one said.

"Okay," I said, and began to gather my rucksack.

"Alright, follow us." The taller one said.

You would have thought one of them would have volunteered to pick up and carry my ruck, knowing I was in extreme pain. No such luck. Grit your teeth and carry on Ranger.

I didn't say goodbye to my squad because I thought I might be returning before the end of the day. I just told them I was going to the first aid station for treatment on my feet.

At the first aid station there were a few other Ranger students getting treatment for various medical problems. The medics had me sit down and slip off my boots. Their first reaction to seeing my feet was the same, "Damn!"

The bottoms of my feet were covered with huge blisters.

"I've never seen blisters this large," the taller medic said.

That was a comfort. They had me sit back while they determined what to do. They also asked me to pull up my pants to see if I had sustained any water blisters on my knees from the extensive exposure and immersion in water over the past several days. Yep, they saw water blisters on both my knees. So now I had these huge, heart-stopping blisters on my feet and water blisters on my knees, I guess I was sort of fucked up. The phrase FUBAR came to mind, "fucked up beyond all recognition." *Damn.*

The lead medic decided to pop my foot blisters. He sterilized a needle-like instrument, took hold of my left foot and punctured the largest blister. The stream of fluid from that blister shot over his head because it had been under such pressure. Again he cursed, "damn," and concentrated on puncturing the rest of the blisters on that foot.

There were no more dramatic disgorgements of fluid on that foot, but it was still nasty stuff. He cleaned all the blisters, put some iodine-like ointment on them, and wrapped the blisters with gauze. He then turned to the other foot with some trepidation, expecting a repeat performance from the large blister waiting to be punctured. By this time, the rest of the Ranger students waiting to be treated, took some interest in my treatment. On the second occasion, the medic must have punctured the blister closer to the top of the foot because the fluid shot out over my head, over six feet through the air. Wow, that was gross! Yuck.

He then punctured and cleaned the rest of the blisters, put the ointment on them, and wrapped them in gauze.

The shorter medic, who had been treating the other Ranger students, commented, "I've never seen blisters that large before. How did you get them?"

"Let me show you." I showed them my boots and let them feel the protrusion in the bottom of each boot.

"Wow, that's pretty bad," the taller medic said. "Why didn't you request your second set of boots?"

"Yeah, I did all that but the RI's never brought my boots out." I grimaced and laughed. "I asked three different times over the past three days and the RI's never brought them out."

"That's pretty fucked up." The shorter medic said.

"Yep, I agree." I said.

The first medic went through the process of puncturing and cleaning the blisters on my knees. They were less dramatic than the foot blisters and did not require the same number of bandages.

"Okay, you're all fixed up, but I would recommend you stay off your feet for at least a day and let those blisters heal."

"Thanks, but I don't think I'm going to have much choice on that." I said.

A few minutes after I had been treated, Gary showed up with my second pair of boots. He wanted to speak to me in private, so I slipped on the new pair of boots without lacing them up and hobbled over to a nearby grove of trees. My goodness those boots felt good!

"I'm sorry you had to go through all that with your boots. The RI's will receive written reprimands for their negligence. Apparently, each of them thought someone else was going to do it instead of making sure it got done." He continued, "Because you received all honor grad go's and passed everything, and you were in so many non-graded leadership positions you've been 'Tabbed out.'"

"What does that mean?" I asked.

"You've qualified in everything and have earned the Tab. You're not required to complete the rest of the patrol because of your injuries and the fact they were caused by the negligence of the RI's. You're not required to complete the mission today since you weren't going to be graded. You're done."

Huh, okay, I was in! I was now an Airborne Ranger! But then I thought, *this was kind of fucked up. How were my Ranger buddies going to take this and what would they think? And what would the RI's think because they helped cause the problem?* I voiced these concerns to Gary.

"Don't worry about that. You had more leadership positions than anyone in this class, you were the S-4, you maxed just about everything. You've done more than anyone in this class to earn your Ranger Tab. I'll get someone else to do your S-4 duties for the rest of the day. You take it easy and I'll see you later today." With that, he patted me on the back, turned and strode off.

I hobbled back over to the first aid station. The first aid station consisted of an open-air tent and a foot locker where they kept their medical supplies, and a couple of portable desks and chairs to treat the patients. Outside the tent were logs to sit on and of course, plenty of grass. I grabbed a canvas chair and propped my feet up on a log as instructed by the medic. The other Ranger students, who had to remain behind because of injury, were curious about my conversation with Gary.

"What did Ayatollah Powellmeini want?" One of them asked.

Gary didn't tell me it was a secret, so I said, "He told me I was tabbed out."

"What's that mean?" another asked.

"I've completed all the requirements to earn the Tab, so there's nothing else left to do. I'm not going to be medically recycled, because I've done enough to earn the Tab."

They shook their heads at that—like they thought it wasn't fair or that I had received special consideration and a free pass to the Tab.

Well, *fuck them!* I thought. *I earned this shit. I'd already been medically recycled once before, and didn't want to go through that shit again. Except for one patrol I had all Honor Grad Go's; I maxed every test, twice, even though I'd been screwed on the knot test; I had more leadership positions than anyone in the class; had served as the class S-4; damn near wrote every op order for my squad and platoon; and now this bullshit with my feet. None of these white Ranger students had to put up with any of that bullshit, nor had they done as much during this class. Yeah, so fuck them,* I thought again, *I truly earned this shit.*

And yeah, I was just happy it looked like my dream of becoming an Airborne Ranger would become a reality, even if I had to crawl to graduation. I didn't care, I was going to wear the fuckin' black and gold Tab in a half moon shape.

Dammit, I had proven everyone wrong. I would be an Airborne Ranger!

CHAPTER 33

"The Tab"

My return to the barracks was ignominious to say the least. While the rest of the class road marched in from the last patrol, the medics trucked me in from the first aid station. The medics gave me instructions and enough supplies to treat my blisters, so I was good to go with my feet. My Ranger buddies sympathized with me as they saw me hobble in with my unlaced boots, because they knew of my ongoing battle with the RI's and my boots. I really didn't give a damn what the rest of the class thought. I knew what I'd endured to get to this point.

After we cleaned up, the RI's gave us an after-action report on the 12-day patrol and following that invited us to the All-Ranks club they had at Camp Rudder. I met Gary's beautiful wife Toni, just about as dark as he was, and very pretty in her colorful summer outfit. This was a nice experience, hanging out with the RI's and drinking a beer with your torturers. But the highlight of the day was mail call that evening. I got a bundle of mail from Karen that had piled up since Dahlonega. Apparently, she had been writing me almost every day and a lot of the mail had not caught up with me until now. I spent the rest of the night reading her letters and getting a real thrill from knowing that she would be there to pin the Tab on my left shoulder, on graduation day from Ranger School.

The trip out of Florida was not as dramatic as the earlier more eventful advent by parachute. They bussed us back to Benning on charter buses. We had lost almost 50 percent of the class over the eight weeks of Ranger School, and the rest of us felt like we had really accomplished something important in our lives.

When we arrived at the Ranger Department, we saw Ranger students just beginning their class, and still in City Week. Wow, they looked so…unused. Yeah, that would change. We piled into our barracks, different from the ones we occupied during City Week, without all the drama.

We spent the rest of the day out processing, taking the graduation picture, the exit interview with Gary, getting our final Ranger buzz cut, and going through the graduation rehearsal.

The commandant of the Ranger Department, no longer Sydnor, announced the Honor Grads and other awardees at the graduation rehearsal.

After rehearsal SSG Hunt pulled me off to the side and whispered in my ear, "You were ninth, just thought you'd want to know."

"Thank you," I said, surprised he'd say anything to me because during the entire course he hadn't said shit to me unless it was yelling at me or being critical. But that was expected, not this.

Huh, so I ended up ninth in the class. Not bad considering what I had gone through in Dahlonega. David Ware, a classmate of mine from IOBC, achieved the prestige of officer Honor Grad. I didn't begrudge him that honor. Dave had worked hard during Ranger School and had excelled in everything. I thought I was as good, but maybe not better than him, so I had no problem with him being named Honor Grad. Of course, the fact that I'd had artificial barriers placed in front of me by the racist bastards in Dahlonega, who took away any fair opportunity to compete for Honor Grad, did not sit well with me. Dave didn't have to deal with that shit since he was white. Other than that, I had no problem with him being Honor Grad.

After the graduation rehearsal and all the admin stuff was done, we attended a barbeque in our honor featuring T-bone steaks with beer. Damn, that was nice!

We had practiced the graduation exercises outdoors at the parade field. We practiced passing in review and the whole ceremony. Fortunately, we also practiced graduation inside one of the classrooms in case of inclement weather. As it turned out, that's exactly what happened. The next morning it threatened to rain right before the ceremony, so in an abundance of caution they moved the graduation inside.

On June 19, 1980, we lined up inside the largest available classroom to receive our "black and gold, in a half moon shape," Ranger Tabs. I craned my neck to try to catch a glimpse of Karen coming in to the ceremony, but as it began she had not yet arrived.

The graduation speaker began his forgettable speech and at that moment Karen walked in the door with Rena. I had arranged for Karen to spend the first night with the Boggs, and Rena had volunteered to bring her out to the Ranger compound for graduation. Karen was a sight for sore eyes! A true vision of loveliness!

Yeah, okay, I had it bad, and it had been a while since I'd seen her.

When it came time for loved ones or whomever to come up to pin the Tab on the graduate, Karen came up with a big smile on her face. I could tell she had taken great care with her makeup and her hair, yeah, she really looked good. I think I looked a lot less scrumptious, because I had lost 35 lbs. and was nothing but muscle and gristle. She pinned my Tab on my left shoulder and gave me a kiss and went back to her seat. Following the ceremony Rena came up to me to congratulate me and told me she had to leave, but looked forward to seeing us that evening for dinner. I thanked her for taking care of Karen and she left. I found out later that Karen's luggage had gone to Columbus, Ohio, instead of Columbus, Georgia, and she was actually wearing some of Rena's clothes to graduation. She wanted to make sure she didn't miss pinning on the Tab.

I turned to Karen, who had sustained me during the entire eleven weeks of Ranger School, and gave her a big kiss. I looked around for my Ranger buddies and introduced Karen to Beast, Ranger Ugly, Price, and some others who had stuck around. I introduced Karen to Gary, and he told her she should be proud of me for what I had gone through to get the Tab. Karen looked at me with a quizzical expression, and I told her I would explain later. Gary told us he looked forward to seeing us later that evening. He had brought Toni up from Florida and they wanted to get together at the O-club with me, Price and a few other new Rangers. I told him we would be there, and he left the classroom. Finally, we were able to leave. My stuff was already packed in my car. So after all the hoopla, it was finally time to go. I took a last look around the Ranger Department as I touched the newly pinned Tab on my shoulder and reflected on my experiences over the past three months and smiled. I was finally a United States Army Airborne Ranger.

I reflected on how my life had prepared me to finally wear the black and gold Tab. Growing up on various bases, playing Army as a kid, exploring in the woods, going on patrol, hunting and catching snakes, frogs, crawfish, lizards and other small animals; fishing, tracking animals in the woods, operating in the desert, swimming and jumping off the high dive as a kid; JROTC, drill team, Ft. Knox, Ft. Riley, NMMI, keeping in shape all those years; and my development as a leader. I also thought about all the guys who got in my way—the racist comments and bullying, as well as the Army guys who never thought I would amount to much in the Army or as an officer—all because of my race, age or size. Every time I was told I could not succeed that made me try even harder.

Yeah, well, fuck each and every dickhead that bullied me over the years. I was now a United States Army Ranger, and they could kiss my young black ass. I wish I could visit each and every one of those guys and kick their asses.

But I knew that would never happen, so I just reveled in the thought that I was now one of America's premier soldiers, despite the bullying, taunting, and low expectations of all those white motherfuckers along the way.

I refused to fail, and all that toughened me up and prepared me for the mental and physical rigors of Ranger School. I'm sure no one ever thought that I would ever become a U. S. Army Airborne Ranger. And that made it so much sweeter. Again, *fuck 'em!*

Two years later, to the day, Karen and I were married in a ceremony that included a saber guard and several groomsmen in dress blues. My brother Dana, one of my best men, had recently graduated Ranger School and had told everyone about reading the message on the wall of that hooch in Dahlonega and how it had helped to motivate him. Dana broke his wrist on a two-party climb in Dahlonega but hid that fact from the RI's. He completed the rest of Ranger School with a broken wrist. That was tough, but he did it, spurred on because he did not want to be medically recycled like me.

He and I were the only Ranger-qualified officers in the wedding; and I proudly wore my dress whites with a special black and gold metal Ranger Tab on my left front pocket flap. The fact that I wore the Tab continued to resonate throughout my career and the rest of my life.

And yeah, it had been well worth it.

EPILOGUE

The experience of Ranger School and earning the coveted Ranger Tab has held me in good stead my entire life. I can always say, whenever I'm in a tough situation, I've been through worse. Ranger School was worse—nothing in my experience was as physically taxing and mentally exhausting as Ranger School.

After graduation, I suffered from a lower grade form of PTSD, waking up in the middle of the night yelling "I'm awake," or "Get down," or "Move out," and other phrases from Ranger School. I would act out patrols in my sleep; and when jostled awake by Karen, I instinctively lashed out with aggressive defensive hand-to-hand strikes. Luckily, I never hurt her. My eating habits changed, and I ate every meal like it was my last, gobbling down my food as if we were about to resume the patrol, and had to consume my food before we continued the mission. I would also fall asleep at the drop of a hat, particularly while riding in any vehicle. As soon as a vehicle would start up, I would fall asleep—I'm sure a lingering response to having to grab a few winks of sleep whenever we could in Ranger School, particularly during travel periods in trucks. I can definitely understand a little of what guys go through, upon their return from real combat.

This sort of thing went on for several months. I never saw a shrink, because, back then, if you admitted to any kind of mental or psychological problems it could tank your career. So, I endured it in silence. Even with all that, as I've been told, "What doesn't kill you makes you stronger," and in this case that is true. I was stronger for my experience in Ranger School.

I never saw combat in my Army career. I was in the Army during Operations Urgent Fury, and Just Cause, but not in any of the units deployed to those combat theaters. As a young major, I sat at the Command & General Staff College at Fort Leavenworth, the school for rising Army leaders, when Iraq invaded Kuwait. I watched as my brother, Dana, distinguished himself fighting in the largest armored battle in military history during Desert Storm. For me, wrong place, wrong time, for combat in my military career.

I didn't serve in a Ranger battalion or an airborne unit. From the beginning of my career, the Army had me tracked and categorized as a mechanized infantry officer. The Army assigned me to either mechanized infantry units, light infantry units where officers had to be Ranger-qualified to be in leadership positions, or in the training base, at Fort Benning, training light infantry soldiers, mortar soldiers, anti-tank gunner infantry soldiers, or mech infantry soldiers.

During the time I commanded an Infantry training company at Fort Benning, my battalion commander, LTC Greg Wade, who eventually retired as a brigadier general, came up with an innovative way to end the training of the COHORT 10th Mountain Division battalion we were training. Earlier, LTC Wade had secured the opportunity to train an entire battalion from the 10th Mountain Division that was establishing a brigade at Fort Benning. This was a training concept probably not done since WWII or maybe Vietnam. We had the plum assignment to train an entire battalion that was recruited together, trained together, and would serve their first three years together in the 10th Mountain Division.

As a part of learning how to train "light fighters" from the 10th Mountain Division (Light), my drill sergeants and I had to attend the two-week Light Fighters leadership course conducted by the Ranger Department. It was a refresher course for me on rappelling, patrolling, survival skills, killing and gutting a deer or goat, going through the Combat Water Survival Test, and again out to Ranger Pond for another demonstration of Ranger skills. This time it was fun because I wore the Tab, and I got the respect I deserved from the RI's because I wore that little black and gold piece of cloth in a half-moon shape.

As a part of the innovative training we had the opportunity to train these "mountain" soldiers at the Ranger Camp at Dahlonega. The training would include advanced rappelling, knots, rope bridges, squad-level live fire courses, and an 18-mile "death march" with full mountain rucks through the mountains of North Georgia. All of the company commanders, save one, and the battalion commander were Ranger-qualified, so we were very familiar with Dahlonega.

My return to Dahlonega was also interesting. I had torn my left ACL in October playing football, but in true Ranger fashion and eschewing surgery, I rehabbed enough to make the trip and to participate in the 18-mile Death March. We even had a T-shirt to commemorate the event. The Death March occurred on my birthday, December 13, 1985. A great way to celebrate, because I was in my element. I relived the past by having that one hooch opened up, and yep, it was still there—my motivational message to my brother. That provided some level of amusement for my soldiers. And yeah, coming back to Dahlonega as a Ranger-qualified Infantry captain was satisfying. There was no doubt of the respect in the eyes of the RI's for those of us who wore the Tab and had returned to train our 10th Mountain soldiers in the mountains of North Georgia. I still didn't see any Black RI's. I guess some things never change.

✦　✦　✦

Since 2001, after the invasion of Afghanistan, most Americans have heard of Army Rangers, which historically has not always been the case. No matter where I was stationed, or where I went in uniform, I commanded instant respect when soldiers saw the Tab on my left shoulder. The Tab also bestowed a certain level of responsibility to live up to the ideals of being a Ranger at all times. And in that I know I was successful.

In the years since getting out of the Army, when I proudly display the Tab in my law office, along with my graduation photo from Ranger School, most of my clients know what it means—that I went through a lot of shit to earn that piece of cloth and in so doing joined a fraternity of soldiers and warriors that stands proud in its heritage and fighting skills. I'm proud to be a member of that dauntless, fabled fraternity.

And as you already know, ***Rangers Lead the Way!*** Hooah!

✦　✦　✦

ABOUT THE AUTHOR

Chris has been called a "Renaissance Man" for his many accomplishments and interests. A former U.S. Army Airborne Ranger Infantry officer, he has been repeatedly named a Texas Best Lawyer in Employment Law; a 1st Dan Black Belt in Tae Kwon Do; law school professor; former PBA bowler; avid chess player; and Life Member of Kappa Alpha Psi Fraternity, Inc.